APPLAUSE FIRST FOLIO EDITIONS

# The Tragedy of Richard the Third: with the Landing of Earle Richmond, and the Battel at Bosworth Field

BY

## William Shakespeare

PREPARED & ANNOTATED BY
NEIL FREEMAN

APPLAUSE
NEW YORK • LONDON

The Applause Shakespeare Library

Folio Texts

AN APPLAUSE ORIGINAL

# The Tragedy of Richard the Third: with the Landing of Earle Richmond, and the Battell at Bosworth Field

original concept devised by Neil Freeman

original research computer entry by Margaret McBride

original software programmes designed and developed by
James McBride and Terry Lim

Text layout designed and executed by Neil Freeman

Some elements of this text were privately published under the collective title of
*The Freeman–Nichols Folio Scripts 1991–96*

**Copyright ° 2000 by Folio Scripts, Vancouver, Canada**

ISBN: 1-55783-422-9

## Library of Congress Cataloging-in-Publication Data

Library of Congress Catalog Card Number: 00-103952

## British Library Cataloging-in-Publication Data

A catalogue record of this book is available from the British Library

### APPLAUSE BOOKS

| | |
|---|---|
| 1841 Broadway Suite 1100 | Combined Book Services Ltd. |
| New York, NY 10023 | Units I/K Paddock Wood Dist. Ctr. |
| Phone (212) 765-7880 | Paddock Wood, |
| Fax: (212) 765-7875 | Tonbridge Kent TN12 6UU |
| | Phone 0189 283-7171 |
| | ° Fax 0189 283-7272 |

Printed in Canada

# CONTENTS

# ACKNOWLEDGEMENTS

My grateful thanks to all who have helped in the growth and development of this work. Special thanks to Norman Welsh who first introduced me to the Folio Text, and to Tina Packer who (with Kristin Linklater and all the members of Shakespeare & Co.) allowed me to explore the texts on the rehearsal floor. To Jane Nichols for her enormous generosity in providing the funding which allowed the material to be computerised. To James and Margaret McBride and Terry Lim for their expertise, good humour and hard work. To the National Endowment for the Arts for their award of a Major Artist Fellowship and to York University for their award of the Joseph G. Green Fellowship. To actors, directors and dramaturgs at the Stratford Festival, Ontario; Toronto Free Theatre (that was); the Skylight Theatre, Toronto and Tamanhouse Theatre of Vancouver. To colleagues, friends and students at The University of British Columbia, Vancouver; York University, Toronto; Concordia University, Montreal; The National Theatre School of Canada in Montreal; Equity Showcase Theatre, Toronto; The Centre for Actors Study and Training (C.A.S.T.), Toronto; The National Voice Intensive at Simon Fraser University, Vancouver; Studio 58 of Langara College, Vancouver; Professional Workshops in the Arts, Vancouver; U.C.L.A., Los Angeles; Loyola Marymount, Los Angeles; San Jose State College, California; Long Beach State College, California; Brigham Young University, Utah, and Hawaii; Holy Cross College, Massachussetts; Guilford College, North Carolina. To Chairman John Wright and Associate Dean Don Paterson for their incredible personal support and encouragement. To Rachel Ditor and Tom Scholte for their timely research assistance. To Alan and Chris Baker, and Stephanie McWilliams for typographical advice. To Jay L. Halio, Hugh Richmond, and G.B. Shand for their critical input. To the overworked and underpaid proofreading teams of Ron Oten and Yuuattee Tanipersaud, Patrick Galligan and Leslie Barton, Janet Van De Graaff and Angela Dorhman (with input from Todd Sandomirsky, Bruce Alexander Pitkin, Catelyn Thornton and Michael Roberts). And above all to my wife Julie, for her patient encouragement, courteous advice, critical eye and long sufferance!

## SPECIAL ACKNOWLEDGEMENTS

Glenn Young and Paul Sugarman of Applause Books; Houghton Mifflin Company for permission to quote from the line numbering system developed for *The Riverside Shakespeare*: Evans, Gwynne Blakemore, Harry Levin, Anne Barton, Herschel Baker, Frank Kermode, Hallet D. Smith, and Marie Edel, editors, *The Riverside Shakespeare*. Copyright © 1974 by Houghton Mifflin Company.

# DEFINITIONS OF AND GUIDE TO PHOTOGRAPHIC COPIES OF THE EARLY TEXTS

(see Appendix A for a brief history of the First Folio, the Quartos,
and their uneasy relationship with modern texts)

## A QUARTO (Q)

A single text, so called because of the book size resulting from a particular method of printing. Eighteen of Shakespeare's plays were published in this format by different publishers at various dates between 1594–1622 prior to the appearance of the 1623 Folio. Of the eighteen quarto texts, scholars suggest that fourteen have value as source texts. An extremely useful collection of them is to be found in Michael J. B. Allen and Kenneth Muir, eds., *Shakespeare's Plays in Quarto* (Berkeley: University of California Press, 1981).

## THE FIRST FOLIO (F1)[1]

Thirty-six of Shakespeare's plays (excluding *Pericles* and *Two Noble Kinsmen,* in which he had a hand) appeared in one volume published in 1623. All books of this size were termed Folios, again because of the sheet size and printing method, hence this volume is referred to as the First Folio; two recent photographic editions of the work are:

Charlton Hinman, ed., *The Norton Facsimile (The First Folio of Shakespeare)* (1968; republished New York: W. W. Norton & Company, Inc., 1996).

Helge Kökeritz, ed., *Mr. William Shakespeare's Comedies, Histories & Tragedies* (New Haven: Yale University Press, 1954).

## THE SECOND FOLIO (F2)

Scholars suggest that the Second Folio, dated 1632 but perhaps not published until 1640, has little authority, especially since it created hundreds of new problematical readings of its own. Nevertheless, more than eight hundred modern text readings can be attributed to it. The most recent reproduction is D. S. Brewer, ed., *Mr.*

---

[1] For a full overview of the First Folio see the monumental two-volume work: Charlton Hinman, *The Printing and Proof Reading of the First Folio of Shakespeare* (2 volumes) (Oxford: Clarendon Press, 1963) and W. W. Greg, *The Editorial Problem in Shakespeare: a Survey of the Foundations of the Text,* 3rd. ed. (Oxford: Clarendon Press, 1954); for a brief summary, see the forty-six page publication from Peter W. M. Blayney, *The First Folio of Shakespeare* (Washington, DC: Folger Library Publications, 1991).

*William Shakespeare's Comedies, Histories & Tragedies, the Second Folio Reproduced in Facsimile* (Dover, NH: Boydell & Brewer Ltd., 1985).

The Third Folio (1664) and the Fourth Folio (1685) have even less authority, and are rarely consulted except in cases of extreme difficulty.

## THE THIRD FOLIO (F3)

The Third Folio, carefully proofed (though apparently not against the previous edition) takes great pains to correct anomalies in punctuation ending speeches and in expanding abbreviations. It also introduced seven new plays supposedly written by Shakespeare, only one of which, *Pericles*, has been established as such. The most recent reproduction is D. S. Brewer, ed., *Mr. William Shakespeare's Comedies, Histories & Tragedies, the Third Folio Reproduced in Facsimile* (Dover, NH: Boydell & Brewer Ltd., 1985).

## THE FOURTH FOLIO (F4)

Paradoxically, while the Fourth Folio was the most carefully edited of all, its concentration on grammatical clarity and ease of comprehension by its readers at the expense of faithful reproduction of F1 renders it the least useful for those interested in the setting down on paper of Elizabethan theatre texts. The most recent reproduction is D. S. Brewer, ed., *Mr. William Shakespeare's Comedies, Histories & Tragedies, the Fourth Folio Reproduced in Facsimile* (Dover, NH: Boydell & Brewer Ltd., 1985).

# WELCOME TO THESE SCRIPTS

These scripts are designed to do three things:

1. show the reader what the First Folio (often referred to as F1) set down on paper, rather than what modern editions think ought to have been set down
2. provide both reader and theatre practitioner an easy journey through some of the information the original readers might have garnered from F1 and other contemporary scripts which is still relevant today
3. provide a simple way for readers to see not only where modern texts alter the First Folio, and how, but also allow readers to explore both First Folio and modern versions of the disputed passage without having to turn to an Appendix or a different text

all this, hopefully without interfering with the action of the play.

What the First Folio sets on paper will be the basis for what you see. In the body of the play-text that follows, the words (including spellings and capitalisations), the punctuation (no matter how ungrammatical), the structure of the lines (including those moments of peculiar verse or unusual prose), the stage directions, the act and scene divisions, and (for the most part) the prefixes used for each character will be as set in the First Folio.

In addition, new, on page, visual symbols specially devised for these texts will help point out both the major stepping stones in the Elizabethan debate/rhetorical process contained in the plays (a fundamental part of understanding both the inner nature of each character as well as the emotional clashes between them), and where and how (and sometimes why) modern texts have altered the First Folio information. And, unlike any other script, opposite each page of text will be a blank page where readers can make their own notes and commentary.

However, there will be the rare occasion when these texts do not exactly follow the First Folio.

Sometimes F1's **words or phrases** are meaningless; for example, the lovely misprinting of 'which' in *Twelfth Night* as 'wh?ch', or in *Romeo and Juliet* the typesetting corruptions of 'speeh' for 'speech' and the running of the two words 'not away' as 'notaway'. If there are no alternative contemporary texts (a Quarto version of the play) or if no modification was made by any of the later Folios (The Second Folio of 1632, The Third Folio of 1664, or The Fourth Folio of 1685, termed F2, F3, and F4 respectively) then the F1 printing will be set as is, no matter how peculiar, and the modern correction footnoted. However, if a more appropriate alternative is available in a Quarto (often referred to as Q) or F2, F3, or F4, that 'correction' will be set directly into the text, replacing the F1 reading, and footnoted accordingly, as in the case of 'wh?ch', 'speeh', and 'notaway'.

The only time F1's **punctuation** will be altered is when the original setting is so blurred that an accurate deciphering of what F1 set cannot be determined. In such cases, alternative punctuation from F2–4 or Q will be set and a footnote will explain why.

The only time F1's **line structure** will not be followed is when at the end of a very long line, the final word or part of the word cannot fit onto the single line, nor be set as a new line in F1 because of the text that follows and is therefore set above or below the original line at the right hand side of the column. In such rare cases these texts will complete the line as a single line, and mark it with a ⁺ to show the change from F1. In all other cases, even when in prose F1 is forced to split the final word of a speech in half, and set only a few letters of it on a new line—for example in *Henry the Fifth*, Pistoll's name is split as 'Pi' on one line and 'stoll' (as the last part of the speech) on the next—these texts will show F1 exactly as set.

Some liberties have to be taken with the **prefixes** (the names used at the beginning of speeches to show the reader which character is now speaking), for Ff (all the Folios) and Qq (all the Quartos) are not always consistent. Sometimes slightly different abbreviations are used for the same character—in *The Tempest*, King Alonso is variously referred to as 'Al.', 'Alo.', 'Alon.', and 'Alonso'. Sometimes the same abbreviation is used for two different characters—in *A Midsummer Nights Dream* the characters Quince, the 'director' and author of the Mechanicals play, and Titania, Queen of the fairies, are given the same abbreviation 'Qu.'. While in this play common sense can distinguish what is intended, the confusions in *Julius Caesar* between Lucius and Lucullus, each referred to sometimes as 'Luc.', and in *The Comedy of Errors*, where the twin brothers Antipholus are both abbreviated to 'Antiph.', cannot be so easily sorted out. Thus, whereas F1 will show a variety of abbreviated prefixes, these texts will usually choose just one complete name per character and stay with it throughout.

However, there are certain cases where one full name will not suffice. Sometimes F1 will change the prefix for a single character from scene to scene, the change usually reflecting the character's new function or status. Thus in *The Comedy of Errors*, as a drinking companion of the local Antipholus, the goldsmith Angelo is referred to by his given name 'Ang.', but once business matters go awry he very quickly becomes a businessman, referred to as 'Gold'. Similar changes affect most of the characters in *A Midsummer Nights Dream*, and a complex example can be found in *Romeo and Juliet*. While modern texts give Juliet's mother the single prefix Lady Capulet throughout (incorrectly since neither she nor Capulet are named as aristocrats anywhere in the play) both Ff and Qq refer to her in a wonderful character-revealing multiplicity of ways—Mother, Capulet Wife, Lady, and Old Lady—a splendid gift for actress, director, designer, and reader alike.

Surprisingly, no modern text ever sets any of these variations. Believing such changes integral to the development of the characters so affected, these texts will. In such cases, each time the character's prefix changes the new prefix will be set, and a small notation alongside the prefix (either by reference to the old name, or by adding the symbol •) will remind the reader to whom it refers.

Also, some alterations will be made to F1's **stage directions,** not to the words themselves or when they occur, but to the way they are going to be presented visually. Scholars agree F1 contains two different types of stage direction: those that came in the original manuscript from which the Playhouse copy of the play was made, and a second set that were added in for theatrical clarification by the Playhouse. The scholars conjecture that the literary or manuscript directions, presumably from Shakespeare, mainly dealing with entries and key actions such as battles, are those that F1 sets centred on a separate line, while the additional Playhouse directions, usually dealing with offstage sounds, music, and exits, are those F1 sets alongside the spoken dialogue, usually flush against the right hand side of the column. In performance terms there seems to be a useful distinction between the two, though this is only a rule of thumb. The centred manuscript (Shakespearean?) directions tend to stop or change the action of the play, that is, the scene is affected by the action the direction demands, whereas the Playhouse directions (to the side of the text) serve to underscore what is already taking place. (If a word is needed to distinguish the two, the centred directions can be called 'action' directions, because they are events in and of themselves, while the side-set directions could be called 'supportive' or 'continuous' since they tend not to distract from the current onstage action.)

Since F1 seems to visually distinguish between the two types (setting them on different parts of the page) and there seems to be a logical theatrical differentiation as to both the source and function of each, it seems only appropriate that these scripts also mark the difference between them. Both Ff and Qq's side-set directions are often difficult to decipher while reading the text: sometimes they are set so close to the spoken text they get muddled up with it, despite the different typeface, and oftentimes have to be abbreviated to fit in. These are drawbacks shared by most modern texts. Thus these texts will distinguish them in a slightly different way (see p. xxvi below).

Finally, there will be two occasional alterations to Ff's **fonts.** F1 used **italics** for a large number of different purposes, sometimes creating confusion on the page. What these texts will keep as italics are letters, poems, songs, and the use of foreign languages. What they will not set in italics are real names, prefixes, and stage directions. Also at the top of each play, and sometimes at the beginning of a letter or poem, F1 would set a large wonderfully **decorative opening letter,** with the second letter of the word being capitalised, the style tying in with the borders that surrounded the opening and closing of each play. Since these texts will not be reproducing the decorative borders, the decorative letters won't be set either.

# MAKING FULL USE OF THESE TEXTS

## WHAT MODERN CHANGES WILL BE SHOWN

### WORDS AND PHRASES

Modern texts often tidy up F1's words and phrases. Real names, both of people and places, and foreign languages are often reworked for modern understanding; for example, the French town often set in F1 as 'Callice' is usually reset as 'Calais'. Modern texts 'correct' the occasional Elizabethan practice of setting a singular noun with plural verb (and vice versa), as well as the infrequent use of the past tense of a verb to describe a current situation. These texts will set the F1 reading, and footnote the modern corrections whenever they occur.

More problematical are the possibilities of choice, especially when a Q and F version of the same play show a different reading for the same line and either choice is valid—even more so when both versions are offered by different modern texts. Juliet's 'When I shall die,/Take him and cut him out in little starres' offered by Ff/Q1-3 being offset by Q4's 'When he shall die...' is a case in point. Again, these texts will set the F1 reading, and footnote the alternatives.

### LINE STRUCTURE CHANGES RELATED TO PROBLEMS OF 'CASTING-OFF'

The First Folio was usually prepared in blocks of twelve pages at a time. Six pairs of pages would be prepared, working both forward and backward simultaneously. Thus from the centre of any twelve-page block, pages six and seven were set first, then five and eight, then four and nine, then three and ten, then two and eleven, and finally one and twelve. This meant each compositor had to work out very carefully how much copy would fit not only each sheet, but also how much would be needed overall to reach the outer edges of pages one and twelve to match it to the previously set text, (prior to page one) or about to be set text (after page twelve). Naturally the calculations weren't always accurate. Sometimes there was too little text left for too great a space: in such cases, if the manuscript were set as it should have been, a great deal of empty paper would be left free, a condition often described as 'white' space. Sometimes too much text remained for too small a space, and if the manuscript were to be set according to its normal layout, every available inch would be taken up with type (and even then the text might not fit), a condition that could be described as 'crammed space'.

Essentially, this created a huge design problem, and most commentators suggest when it arose the printing house policy was to sacrifice textual accuracy to neatness of design. Thus, so the argument goes, in the case of white space, extra lines of type would have to be created where (presumably) none originally existed. *Hamlet* provides an excellent example with the Polonius speech 'Indeed that's out of the air' starting at line 78 of what most modern texts term Act Two Scene 2. Q2 sets the four-line speech as prose, and most modern texts follow suit. However, F1, faced with a potentially huge white space problem at the bottom of the right hand column of p. 261 in the Tragedy section, resets the speech as eleven lines of very irregular verse! In the case of crammed space, five lines of verse might suddenly become three lines of prose, or in one very severe case of overcrowding in *Henry The Fourth Part Two,* words, phrases, and even half lines of text might be omitted to reduce the text sufficiently.

When such cases occur, this text will set F1 as shown, and the modern texts' suggested alternatives will be footnoted and discussed.

## LINE STRUCTURE CHANGES NOT RELATED TO PROBLEMS OF 'CASTING-OFF'

In addition, modern texts regularly make changes to F1's line structure which are not related to 'white' or 'crammed' space, often to the detriment of both character and scene. Two major reasons are offered for the changes.

First, either (a few) prose lines suddenly appear in what essentially is a verse scene (or a few verse lines in a sea of prose) and the modern texts, feeling the scene should be standardised, restructure the offending lines accordingly. *The Tempest* is atrociously served this way[2], for where F1, the only source text, shows the conspirators Caliban, Stephano, and, very occasionally, Trinculo, speaking verse as well as prose even within the same speech (a sure sign of personal striving and inner disturbance) most modern texts readjust the lines to show only Caliban speaking verse (dignifying him more than he deserves) and Stephano and Trinculo only speaking prose (thus robbing them of their dangerous flights of fancy).

Second, some Ff verse lines appear so appallingly defective in terms of their rhythm and length that modern texts feel it necessary to make a few 'readjustments' of the lines around them to bring the offending lines back to a coherent, rhythmic whole. Many of the later plays are abominably served in this regard: in *Macbeth,* for example, over a hundred F1 passages involving more than 200 lines (90 percent of which were set by the usually reliable compositor A) have been altered by most modern texts. Most of these changes concentrate on regularising moments where a character is under tremendous upheaval and hardly likely to be speaking pure formal verse at that particular moment!

These changes come about through a mistaken application of modern grammat-

---

[2]   Commentators suggest the copy play used for setting F1, coming from Stratford as it did, and thus unsupervised by Shakespeare in the Playhouse preparation of the document, prepared by Ralph Crane, was at times defective, especially in distinguishing clearly between verse and prose: this is why most modern texts do not follow F1's choices in these dubious passages: readers are invited to explore *The Tempest* within this series, especially the footnotes, as a theatrical vindication of the original F1 setting

ical considerations to texts that were originally prepared not according to grammar but rhetoric. One of rhetoric's many strengths is that it can show not only when characters are in self-control but also when they are not. In a rhetorically set passage, the splutters of a person going through an emotional breakdown, as with Othello, can be shown almost verbatim, with peculiar punctuations, spellings, breaks, and all. If the same passage were to be set grammatically it would be very difficult to show the same degree of personal disintegration on the printed page.[3] F1's occasional weird shifts between verse and prose and back again, together with the moments of extreme linear breakdown, are the equivalents of human emotional breakdown, and once the anomalies of Elizabethan script preparation are accounted for,[4] the rhetorical breakdowns on F1's printed page are clear indications of a character's disintegration within the play. When modern texts tidy up such blemishes grammatically they unwittingly remove essential theatrical and/or character clues for reader and theatre person alike.

In these texts, F1's line structure will be set as is, and all such modern alterations (prose to verse, verse to prose, regularisation of originally unmetrical lines) will be shown. The small symbol ° will be added to show where modern texts suggest a line should end rather than where F1 shows it does. A thin vertical line will be set to the left alongside any text where the modern texts have converted F1's prose to verse, or vice versa. The more large-scale of these changes will be boxed for quicker reader recognition. Most of these changes will be footnoted in the text where they occur, and a comparison of the two different versions of the text and what each could signify theatrically will be offered. For examples of both, see p. xxiii below.

## THE SPECIAL PROBLEMS AFFECTING WHAT ARE KNOWN AS 'SHARED' OR 'SPLIT' VERSE LINES

### A definition, and their importance to the Shakespeare texts

Essentially, split lines are short lines of verse which, when placed together, form the equivalent of a full verse line. Most commentators suggest they are very useful in speeding the play along, for the second character (whose line attaches on to the end of the first short line) is expected to use the end of the first character's line as a

---

[3] For a full discussion of this, readers are directed to Neil Freeman, *Shakespeare's First Texts* (Vancouver: Folio Scripts, 1994).

[4] Readers are referred to an excellent chapter by Gary Taylor which analyses the whole background, conjectured and known, concerning the preparation of the first scripts. He points out the pitfalls of assuming the early texts as sole authority for all things Shakespearean: he examines the conjectured movement of the scripts from Shakespeare's pen to printed edition, and carefully examples the changes and alterations that could occur, (most notably at the hands of the manuscript copyists), as well as the interferences and revampings of the Playhouse, plus the effects of the first typesetters' personal habits and carelessness. Stanley Wells and Gary Taylor, *William Shakespeare: A Textual Companion* (Oxford: Clarendon Press, 1987), 1–68.

springboard and jump in with an immediate reply, enhancing the quickness of the debate. Thus in *Measure for Measure*, Act Two Scene 2, modern ll. 8–10, the Provost, trying to delay Claudio's execution, has asked Angelo whether Claudio has to die the following day: Angelo's questioning affirmation ends with a very pointed short line, followed immediately by a short line opening from the Provost.

| Angelo | Did I not tell thee yea? hadst thou not order?<br>Why do'st thou aske againe? |
| Provost | Lest I might be too rash:<br>Under your good correction, I have seene<br>When after execution... |

If the Provost replies immediately after, or just as, Angelo finishes, an explosive dramatic tension is created. Allowing a minor delay before reply, as many actors do, will reduce the impact of the moment, and create a hesitation where one probably does not exist.

## The occasional problem

So far so good. But the problems start when more than two short lines follow each other. If there are three short lines in succession, which should be joined, #1 and #2, or #2 and #3? Later in the same scene, Claudio's sister Isabella has, at the insistence of Claudio's friend Lucio, come to plead with Angelo for her brother's life. In Lucio's eyes she is giving up too easily, hence the following (modern ll. 45–49):

| Lucio | You are too cold: if you should need a pin,<br>You could not with more tame a tongue desire it:<br>To him, I say. |
| Isabella | Must he needs die? |
| Angelo | Maiden, no remedie? |

And here it seems fairly obvious Isabella and Angelo's lines should join together, thus allowing a wonderful dramatic pause following Lucio's urging before Isabella plucks up enough courage to try. Most modern texts set the lines accordingly, with Lucio's the short odd line out.

But what about the three lines contained in the exchange that follows almost straightaway?

| Isabella | But you might doe't & do the world no wrong<br>If so your heart were touch'd with that remorse,<br>As mine is to him? |
| Angelo | Hee's sentenc'd, tis too late. |
| Lucio | You are too cold. |
| Isabella | Too late? why no: I that doe speak a word |

> May call it againe: well, beleeve this
>                          (modern line numbering 53–56)

Does Angelo's 'Hee's sentenc'd...' spring off Isabella's line, leaving Isabella speechless and turning to go before Lucio urges her on again? Or does Angelo pause (to frame a reply?) before speaking, leaving Lucio to quickly jump in quietly giving Isabella no time to back off? Either choice is possible, and dramatically valid. And readers should be allowed to make their own choice, which automatically means each reader should able to see the possibility of such choices when they occur.

## The problem magnified by the way modern texts set split/shared lines

However, because of a peculiarity faced by the modern texts not shared by Ff/Qq, modern texts rarely show such possibilities to their readers but make the choice for them. The peculiarity comes about from a change in text layout initiated in the eighteenth century.

Ff/Qq always set short lines directly under one another, as shown in the examples above. In 1778 George Steevens, a highly respected editor, started to show split lines a new way, by advancing the second split line to just beyond where the first split line finishes, viz.

| | |
|---|---|
| Angelo | Did I not tell thee yea? hadst thou not order? |
| | Why do'st thou aske againe? |
| Provost |                               Lest I might be too rash: |
| | Under your good correction, I have seene |
| | When after execution... |

Since that date all editions of Shakespeare have followed this practice, which is fine as long as there are only two short lines, but when three follow each other, a choice has to be made. Thus the second Isabella/Angelo/Lucio sequence could be set as either

| | |
|---|---|
| Isabella | But you might doe't & do the world no wrong |
| | If so your heart were touch'd with that remorse, |
| | As mine is to him? |
| Angelo |                            Hee's sentenc'd, tis too late. |
| Lucio | You are too cold. |
| Isabella | Too late? why no: I that doe speak a word |
| | May call it againe: well, beleeve this... |

(the usual modern choice), or

| | |
|---|---|
| Isabella | But you might doe't & do the world no wrong |
| | If so your heart were touch'd with that remorse, |
| | As mine is to him? |

| | |
|---|---|
| Angelo | Hee's sentenc'd, tis too late. |
| Lucio | You are too cold. |
| Isabella | Too late? why no: I that doe speak a word |
| | May call it againe: well, beleeve this... |

This modern typesetting convention has robbed the reader of a very important moment of choice. Indeed, at the beginning of the twentieth century, Richard Flatter[5] suggested that what modern commentators consider to be split lines may not be split lines at all. He offers two other suggestions: pauses and hesitations could exist between each line, or the lines could in fact be spoken one on top of another, a very important consideration for the crowd responses to Anthony in the funeral scene of *Julius Caesar*. Either way, the universally adopted Steevens layout precludes the reader/theatre practitioner from even seeing such possibilities.

These texts will show the F1 layout as is, and will indicate via footnote when a choice is possible (in the case of three short lines, or more, in succession) and by the symbol } when the possibility of springboarding exists. Thus the Folio Texts would show the first Angelo/Provost example as:

| | |
|---|---|
| Angelo | Did I not tell thee yea? hadst thou not order? |
| | Why do'st thou aske againe? |
| Provost | Lest I might be too rash: } |
| | Under your good correction, I have seene |
| | When after execution... |

In nearly all cases the } shows where most modern texts insist on setting a shared split line. However, readers are cautioned that in many of the later plays, the single line so created is much longer than pentameter, and often very a-rhythmic. In such cases the lines could have great value as originally set (two separate short lines), especially when a key debate is in process (for example, *Measure for Measure, The Tragedie of Cymbeline, Othello,* and *The Winters Tale*).

## THE UNUSUAL SINGLE SPLIT LINE (PLEASE SEE 'A CAVEAT', P. XXXVIII)

So far the discussion has centred on short lines shared by two or more characters. Ff/Qq offer another complication rarely, if ever, accepted by most modern texts. Quite often, and not because of white space, a single character will be given two consecutive short lines within a single speech. *Romeo and Juliet* is chock full of this device: in the famous balcony scene (modern texts numbering 2.2.62–3) Juliet asks Romeo

How cam'st thou hither.

---

[5] Richard Flatter, *Shakespeare's Producing Hand* (London: Heinemann, 1948, reprint).

> Tell me, and wherefore?
> The Orchard walls are high, and hard to climbe

The first two lines (five syllables each) suggest a minute pause between them as Juliet hesitates before asking the all important second line (with its key second part 'and wherefore'). Since Qq rarely set such 'single split lines' most modern texts refuse to set any of them, but combine them:

> How cams't thou hither. Tell me and wherefore?

This basically F1 device is set by all the compositors and followed by all other Folios. This text will follow suit, highlighting them with the symbol → for quick recognition, viz.:

> How cam'st thou hither. →
> Tell me, and wherefore?
> The Orchard walls are high, and hard to climbe

## SENTENCE AND PUNCTUATION STRUCTURES

### A CHARACTER'S THOUGHTFUL & EMOTIONAL JOURNEY

A quick comparison between these texts and both the Ff/Qq's and the modern texts will reveal two key differences in the layout of the dialogue on the printed page — the bolding of major punctuation, and the single line dropping of text whenever a new sentence begins.

The underlying principle behind these texts is that since the handwritten documents from which they stem were originally intended for the actor and Playhouse, in addition to their poetical values, the Ff/Qq scripts represent a theatrical process. Even if the scripts are being read just for pleasure, at the back of the reader's mind should be the notion of characters on a stage and actors acting (and the word 'process' rather than 'practice' is deliberate, with process suggesting a progression, development, or journey).

The late Jean-Louis Barrault gave a wonderful definition of acting, and of this journey, suggesting an actor's job was to strive to remain in 'the ever-changing present'. If something happens onstage (an entry, an exit, a verbal acceptance or denial of what the actor's character has suggested), the 'present' has changed, and the character must readjust accordingly. Just as onstage, the actor should be prepared for the character to re-adjust, and in rehearsal should be examining how and why it does, so should the reader in the library, armchair, or classroom.

In many ways, the key to Shakespeare is discovering how each character's mind works; perceiving the emotions and intellects as they act and react helps the reader understand from where the poetical imagination and utterance stem.

Certain elements of each character's emotional and intellectual journey, and where it changes, are encoded into the sentence structure of Ff/Qq.

Elizabethan education prepared any schooled individual (via the 'petty school' and the private tutor) for the all important and essential daily rough and tumble of argument and debate. Children were trained not only how to frame an argument so as to win it hands down, but also how to make it entertaining so as to enthrall the neutral listener.

The overall training, known as 'rhetoric', essentially allowed intellect and emotion to exist side by side, encouraging the intellect to keep the emotion in check. The idea was not to deny the emotions, but ensure they didn't swamp the 'divinity' of reason, the only thing separating man from beast. While the initial training was mainly vocal, any written matter of the period automatically reflected the ebb and flow of debate. What was set on the printed page was not grammar, but a representation of the rhetorical process.

## DROPPING A LINE TO ILLUSTRATE F1'S SENTENCE STRUCTURE

Put at its simplest, in any document of the period, each sentence would represent a new intellectual and emotional stage of a rhetorical argument. When this stage of the argument was completed, a period would be set (occasionally a question mark or, much more rarely, an exclamation mark—both followed by a capital letter) signifying the end of that stage of the argument, and the beginning of the next.

Thus in the First Folio, the identification of each new sentence is an automatic (and for us, four hundred years later, a wonderful) aid to understanding how a character is reacting to and dealing with Barrault's ever-changing present.

To help the reader quickly spot the new steppingstone in an argument, and thus the point of transition, these texts highlight where one sentence ends and the new one begins by simply dropping a line whenever a new sentence starts. Thus the reader has a visual reminder that the character is making a transition to deal with a change in the current circumstances of the scene (or in the process of self-discovery in the case of soliloquies).

This device has several advantages. The reader can instantly see where the next step in the argument begins. The patterns so created on the page can quickly illuminate whenever a contrast between characters' thought patterns occurs. (Sometimes the sentences are short and precise, suggesting the character is moving quickly from one idea to the next. Sometimes the sentences are very long, suggesting the character is undergoing a very convoluted process. Sometimes the sentences contain nothing but facts, suggesting the character has no time to entertain; sometimes they are filled with high-flown imagery, perhaps suggesting the character is trying to mask a very weak argument with verbal flummery.) The patterns can also show when a character's style changes within itself, say from long and convoluted to short and precise, or vice versa. It can also immediately pinpoint when a character is in trouble and not arguing coherently or logically, something modern texts often alter out of grammatical necessity.

With patience, all this could be gleaned from the modern texts (in as far as they set the Ff sentence structure, which they often don't) and from a photostat of the First Folio, by paying special attention to where the periods are set. But there is one extra very special advantage to this new device of dropping a line: this has to do once more with the Elizabethan method of setting down spoken argument on paper, especially when the character speaking is not in the best of all possible worlds.

If an Elizabethan person/character is arguing well, neatly, cleanly, tidily, then a printed representation of that argument would also be clean, neat, and tidy—to modern eyes it would be grammatically acceptable. If the same character is emotionally upset, or incapable of making a clear and tidy argument, then the on-paper representation would be muddy and untidy—to modern eyes totally ungrammatical and often not acceptable. By slightly isolating each sentence these texts very quickly allow the reader to spot when a sentence's construction is not all that it should be, say in the middle of Viola's so-called ring speech in *Twelfth Night* (Act Two Scene 2), or Helena's declaration of love for Bertram in *All's Well That Ends Well* (Act One Scene 3), or the amazing opening to *As You Like It,* where Orlando's opening litany of complaint against his brother starts with a single sentence twenty lines long.

This is especially relevant when a surprising modern editorial practice is accounted for. Very often the Ff sentence structures are markedly altered by modern texts, especially when the Ff sentences do not seem 'grammatical'—thus Orlando's twenty-line monster is split into six separate, grammatically correct sentences by all modern texts. And then there is the case of Shylock in *The Merchant of Venice,* a Jewish man being goaded and tormented beyond belief by the very Christians who helped his daughter elope with a Christian, taking a large part of Shylock's fortune with her. A sentence comparison of the famous Act Three Scene 1 speech culminating in 'Hath not a Jew eyes?' is very instructive. All modern texts set the speech as between fifteen and seventeen sentences in length: whatever the pain, anger, and personal passion, the modern texts encourage dignity and self-control, a rational Shylock. But this is a Shylock completely foreign to both Q1 and Ff. Q1 show the same speech as only four sentences long, Ff five—a veritable onflow of intellect and passion all mixed together, all unstoppable for the longest period of time—a totally different being from that shown by the modern texts. What is more, this is a totally different Shylock from the one seen earlier in the Ff/Q1 version of the play, where, even in the extremes of discomfort with the old enemy Anthonio, his sentence structures are rhetorically balanced and still grammatical to modern eyes.

Here, with Shylock, there are at least three benefits to dropping the sentence: the unusualness of the speech is immediately spotted; the change in style between this and any of his previous speeches can be quickly seen; and, above all, the moment where the speech moves from a long unchecked outpouring to a quick series of brief, dangerously rational sentences can be quickly identified. And these advantages will be seen in such changed sentence circumstances in any play in any of these texts.

## THE HIGHLIGHTING OF THE MAJOR PUNCTUATION IN THESE TEXTS

A second key element of rhetoric encoded into the Ff/Qq texts clearly shows the characters' mind in action. The encoding lies in the remaining punctuation which, unlike much modern punctuation, serves a double function, one dealing with the formation of the thought, the other with the speaking of it.

Apart from the period, dealt with already, essentially there are two sets of punctuation to consider, minor and major, each with their own very specific functions.

Shakespearean characters reflect the mode of thinking of their time. Elizabethans were trained to constantly add to or modify thoughts. They added a thought to expand the one already made. They denied the first thought so as to set up alternatives. They elaborated a thought so as to clarify what has already been said. They suddenly moved into splendid puns or non-sequiturs (emotional, logical, or both) because they had been immediately stimulated by what they or others had just said. The **minor punctuation** (essentially the comma [,] the parenthesis or bracket [( )], and the dash) reflects all this.

In establishing thought processes for each character, minor punctuation shows every new nuance of thought: every tiny punctuation in this category helps establish the deftness and dance of each character's mind. In *As You Like It* (Act Three Scene 2, modern line numbering 400–402) the Ff setting of Rosalind's playing with her beloved Orlando has a wonderful coltish exuberance as she runs rings round his protestations of love:

> Love is meerely a madnesse, and I tel you,
> deserves as well a darke house,* and a whip,* as madmen do:

Her mind is adding extra thoughts as she goes: the Ff commas are as much part of her spirit and character as the words are—though most modern texts create a much more direct essayist, preaching what she already knows, by removing the two Ff commas marked *.[6]

A similar situation exists with Macbeth, facing Duncan whom he must kill if he is

---

[6]  Unfortunately, many modern texts eradicate the F and Q minor punctuation arguing the need for light (or infrequent) punctuation to preserve the speed of speech. This is not necessarily helpful, since what it removes is just a new thought marker, not an automatic indication to pause: too often the result is that what the first texts offer a character as a series of closely-worked out dancing thought-patterns (building one quick thought—as marked by a comma—on top of another) is turned into a series of much longer phrases: often, involved and reactive busy minds are artificially turned into (at best) eloquent ones, suddenly capable of perfect and lengthy rationality where the situation does not warrant such a reaction, or (at worst) vapid ones, speaking an almost preconceived essay of commentary or artificial sentimentality.

to become king (Act One Scene 4, modern line numbering 22–27). Ff show a Macbeth almost swamped with extra thoughts as he assures Duncan

> The service,* and the loyaltie I owe,
> In doing it,* payes it selfe.
> Your highnesse part,* is to receive our Duties,
> And our Duties are to your Throne,* and State,
> Children,* and Servants; which doe but what they should,*
> By doing every thing safe toward your Love
> And Honour.

The heavy use of minor punctuation—especially when compared with most modern texts which remove the commas marked *, leaving Macbeth with just six thoughts compared to Ff's twelve—clearly shows a man ill at ease and/or working too hard to say the right thing. Again the punctuation helps create an understanding of the character.

However, while the minor punctuation is extremely important in the discovery process of reading and/or rehearsal, paradoxically, it mustn't become too dominant. From the performance/speaking viewpoint, to pause at each comma would be tantamount to disaster. There would be an enormous dampening effect if reader/actor were to pause at every single piece of punctuation: the poetry would be destroyed and the event would become interminable.

In many ways, minor punctuation is the Victorian child of Shakespearean texts, it must be seen but not heard. (In speaking the text, the new thought the minor punctuation represents can be added without pausing: a change in timbre, rhythm, or pitch—in acting terms, occurring naturally with changes in intention—will do the trick.)

But once thoughts have been discovered, they have to be organised into some form of coherent whole. If the period shows the end of one world and the start of the new, and if the comma marks a series of small, ever-changing, ever-evolving thoughts within each world, occasionally there must be pause for reflection somewhere in the helter-skelter of tumbling new ideas. This is the **major punctuation's** strength; major punctuation consisting of the semicolon [;], and the colon [:].

Major punctuation marks the gathering together of a series of small thoughts within an overall idea before moving onto something new. If a room full of Rodin sculptures were analogous to an Elizabethan scene or act, each individual piece of sculpture would be a speech, the torso or back or each major limb a separate sentence. Each collective body part (a hand, the wrist, the forearm, the upper arm) would be a series of small thoughts bounded by major punctuation, each smaller item within that part (a finger, a fingernail, a knuckle) a single small thought separated by commas. In describing the sculpture to a friend one might move from the smaller details (the knuckle) to the larger (the hand) to another larger (the wrist) then another (the forearm) and so on to the whole limb. Unless the speaker is emotionally moved by the recollection, some pauses would be essential, certainly after finishing the whole description of the arm (the sentence), and probably after each major collective of the hand, the wrist, etc. (as marked by the major punctuation), but not after every small bit.

As a rule of thumb, and simply stated, the colon and semicolon mark both a thinking and a speaking pause. The vital difference between major and minor punctuation, whether in the silent reading of the text or the performing of it aloud, is you need not pause at the comma, bracket, or dash; you probably should at the colon, semicolon, and period.

**Why the Major Punctuation is Bolded in These Texts.**

In speaking the text or reading it, the minor punctuation indicates the need to key onto the new thought without necessarily requiring a pause. In so doing, the inherent rhythms of speech, scene, and play can clip along at the rate suggested by the Prologue in *Romeo and Juliet,* 'the two hours traffic of the stage', until a pause is absolutely necessary. Leave the commas alone, and the necessary pauses will make themselves known.

The 'major' punctuation then comes into its own, demanding double attention as both a thinking and speaking device. This is why it is bolded, to highlight it for the reader's easier access. The reader can still use all the punctuation when desired, working through the speech thought by thought, taking into account both major and minor punctuation as normal. Then, when needed, the bolding of the major punctuation will allow the reader easy access for marking where the speech, scene, or play needs to be broken down into its larger thinking/speaking (and even breathing) units without affecting its overall flow.

**The Blank Pages Within the Text**

In each text within this series, once readers reach the play itself they will find that with each pair of pages the dialogue is printed on the right-hand page only. The left-hand page has been deliberately left blank so that readers, actors, directors, stage managers, teachers, etc. have ample space for whatever notes and text emendations they may wish to add.

# PRACTICAL ON-PAGE HELP FOR THE READER

## THE VISUAL SYMBOLS HIGHLIGHTING MODERN ALTERATIONS

### THE BOX

This surrounds a passage where the modern texts have made whole-scale alterations to the Ff text. Each boxed section will be footnoted, and the changes analysed at the bottom of the page.

### THE FOOTNOTES

With many modern texts the footnotes are not easily accessible. Often no indication is given within the text itself where the problem/choice/correction exists. Readers are forced into a rather cumbersome four-step process. First, they have to search through the bottom of the page where the footnotes are crammed together, often in very small print, to find a line number where an alteration has been made. Then they must read the note to find out what has been altered. Then they must go back to the text and search the side of the page to find the corresponding line number. Having done all this, finally they can search the line to find the word or phrase that has been changed (sometimes complicated by the fact the word in question is set twice in different parts of the line).

These texts will provide a reference marker within the text itself, directly alongside the word or phrase that is in question. This guides the reader directly to the corresponding number in the footnote section of the bottom of each page, to the alteration under discussion—hopefully a much quicker and more immediate process.

In addition, since there are anywhere between 300 and 1,100 footnotes in any one of these texts, a tool is offered to help the reader find only those notes they require, when they require them. In the footnote section, prior to the number that matches the footnote marker in the text, a letter or combination of letters will be set as a code. The letter 'W', for example, shows that the accompanying footnote refers to word substitutions offered by modern texts; the letters 'SD' refer to an added or altered stage direction; the letters 'LS' show the footnote deals with a passage where the modern texts have completely altered the line-structure that F1 set. This enables readers to be selective when they want to examine only certain changes, for they can quickly skim through the body of footnotes until they find the code they want, perhaps those dealing with changes in prefixes (the code 'P') or when modern alterations have been swapping lines from verse to prose or vice versa (the code 'VP'). For full details of the codes, see pp. xxxiii–xxxv below.

Readers are urged to make full use of the footnotes in any of the Recommended Texts listed just before the start of the play. They are excellent in their areas of expertise. To attempt to rival or paraphrase them would be redundant. Thus the footnotes in these scripts will hardly ever deal with word meanings and derivations; social or political history; literary derivations and comparisons; or lengthy quotations from scholars or commentators. Such information is readily available in the *Oxford English Dictionary* and from the recommended modern texts.

Generally, the footnotes in these scripts will deal with matters theatrical and textual and will be confined to three major areas: noting where and how the modern texts alter F1's line structure; showing popular alternative word readings often selected by the modern texts (these scripts will keep the F1 reading unless otherwise noted); and showing the rare occasions where and how these scripts deviate from their source texts. When the modern texts offer alternative words and/or phrases to F2-4/Qq, the original spelling and punctuation will be used. Where appropriate, the footnotes will briefly refer to the excellent research of the scholars of the last three centuries, and to possible theatrical reasons for maintaining F1's structural 'irregularities'.

### THE SYMBOL °

This will be used to show where modern texts have altered F1's line structure, and will allow the reader to explore both the F1 setting and the modern alternative while examining the speech where it is set, in its proper context and rightful position within the play. For example, though F1 is usually the source text for *Henry the Fifth* and sets the dialogue for Pistoll in prose, most modern texts use the memorial Q version and change his lines to (at times extraordinarily peculiar) verse. These texts will set the speech as shown in F1, but add the ° to show the modern texts alterations, thus:

> Pistoll    Fortune is Bardolphs foe, and frownes on him:°
> for he hath stolne a Pax, and hanged must a be:° a damned
> death:° let Gallowes gape for Dogge, let Man goe free,°
> and let not Hempe his Wind-pipe suffocate:° but Exeter
> hath given the doome of death,° for Pax of little price.°
>
> Therefore goe speake,° the Duke will heare thy voyce;°
> and let not Bardolphs vitall thred bee cut° with edge of
> Penny-Cord, and vile reproach.°
>                            Speake Captaine for
> his Life, and I will thee requite.°
>                (*Henry V*, These Scripts, 2.1.450–459)

Read the speech utilising the ° to mark the end of a line, and the reader is exploring what the modern texts suggest should be the structure. Read the lines ignoring the ° and the reader is exploring what the F1 text really is. Thus both F1 and modern/Q versions can be read within the body of the text.

### THE VERTICAL LINE TO THE LEFT OF THE TEXT

This will be used to mark a passage where modern editors have altered F1's verse to prose or vice versa. Here is a passage in a predominantly prose scene from *Henry V*. Modern texts and F1 agree that Williams and Fluellen should be set in prose. However, the F1 setting for Henry could be in verse, though most modern texts set it in prose too. The thin vertical line to the left of the text is a quick reminder to the reader of disagreement between Ff and modern texts (the F1 setting will always be shown, and the disputed section will be footnoted accordingly).

| | | |
|---|---|---|
| King Henry | Twas I indeed thou promised'st to strike, | |
| | And thou hast given me most bitter termes. | |
| Fluellen | And please your Majestie, let his Neck answere | |
| | for it, if there is any Marshall Law in the World. | |
| King Henry | How canst thou make me satisfaction? | |
| Williams | All offences, my Lord, come from the heart: ne- | |
| | ver came any from mine, that might offend your Ma- | |
| | jestie. | (*Henry V,* These Scripts, 4.1.240–247) |

## THE SYMBOL } SET TO THE RIGHT OF TEXT, CONNECTING TWO SPEECHES

This will be used to remind readers of the presence of what most modern texts consider to be split or shared lines, and that therefore the second speech could springboard quickly off the first, thus increasing the speed of the dialogue and debate; for example:

| | |
|---|---|
| Angelo | Did I not tell thee yea? hadst thou not order? |
| | Why do'st thou aske againe? |
| Provost | Lest I might be too rash: |
| | Under your good correction, I have seene |
| | When after execution . . . |

Since there is no definitive way of determining whether Shakespeare wished the two short lines to be used as a shared or split line, or used as two separate short lines, the reader would do well to explore the moment twice. The first time the second speech could be 'springboarded' off the first as if it were a definite shared line; the second time round a tiny break could be inserted before speaking the second speech, as if a hesitation were deliberately intended. This way both possibilities of the text can be examined.

## THE SYMBOL → TO THE RIGHT OF THE TEXT, JOINING TWO SHORT LINES SPOKEN BY A SINGLE CHARACTER

This indicates that though Ff has set two short lines for a single character, perhaps hinting at a minute break between the two thoughts, most modern texts have set the two short lines as one longer one. Thus the first two lines of Juliet's

How cam'st thou hither. →

> Tell me, and wherefore?
> The Orchard walls are high, and hard to climbe

can be explored as one complete line (the interpretation of most modern texts), or, as F1 suggests, as two separate thoughts with a tiny hesitation between them. In most cases these lines will be footnoted, and possible reasons for the F1 interpretation explored.

### THE OCCASIONAL USE OF THE †

This marks where F1 has been forced, in a crowded line, to set the end of the line immediately above or below the first line, flush to the right hand column. These texts will set the original as one complete line—the only instance where these scripts do not faithfully reproduce F1's line structure.

### THE OCCASIONAL USE OF THE † TOGETHER WITH A FOOTNOTE (ALSO SEE P. XXXVII)

This marks where a presumed F1 compositorial mistake has led to a meaningless word being set (for example 'speeh' instead of 'speech') and, since there is a 'correct' form of the word offered by either F2–4 or Qq, the correct form of the word rather than the F1 error has been set. The footnote directs the reader to the original F1 setting reproduced at the bottom of the page.

### PATTERNED BRACKETS { } SURROUNDING A PREFIX OR PART OF A STAGE DIRECTION

These will be used on the infrequent occasions where a minor alteration or addition has been made to the original F1 setting.

### THE VARIED USE OF THE * AND ∞

This will change from text to text. Sometimes (as in *Hamlet*) an * will be used to show where, because of the 1606 Acte To Restraine The Abuses of Players, F1 had to alter Qq's 'God' to 'Heaven'. In other plays it may be used to show the substitution of the archaic 'a' for 'he' while in others the * and /or the ∞ may be used to denote a line from Qq or F2–4 which F1 omits.

### THE SYMBOL •

This is a reminder that a character with several prefixes has returned to one previously used in the play.

## THE VISUAL SYMBOLS HIGHLIGHTING KEY ITEMS WITHIN THE FIRST FOLIO

### THE DROPPING OF THE TEXT A SINGLE LINE

This indicates where one sentence ends, and a new one begins (see pp. xvii–xviii).

### THE BOLDING OF PUNCTUATION

This indicates the presence of the major punctuation (see pp. xviii–xxi).

### UNBRACKETED STAGE DIRECTIONS

These are the ones presumed to come from the manuscript copy closest to Shakespeare's own hand (F1 sets them centred, on a separate line). They usually have a direct effect on the scene, altering what has been taking place immediately prior to its setting (see p. ix).

### BRACKETED STAGE DIRECTIONS

These are the ones presumed to have been added by the Playhouse. (F1 sets them alongside the dialogue, flush to the right of the column.) They usually support, rather than alter, the onstage action (see p. ix).

(The visual difference in the two sets of directions can quickly point the reader to an unexpected aspect of an entry or exit. Occasionally an entry is set alongside the text, rather than on a separate line. This might suggest the character enters not wishing to draw attention to itself, for example, towards the end of *Macbeth,* the servant entering with the dreadful news of the moving Byrnane Wood. Again, F1 occasionally sets an exit on a separate line, perhaps stopping the onstage action altogether, as with the triumphal exit to a 'Gossips feast' at the end of *The Comedy of Errors* made by most of the reunited and/or business pacified characters, leaving the servant Dromio twins onstage to finish off the play. A footnote will be added when these unusual variations in F1's directions occur.)

As with all current texts, the final period of any bracketed or unbracketed stage direction will not be set.

## ACT, SCENE, AND LINE NUMBERING SPECIFIC TO THIS TEXT

Each of these scripts will show the act and scene division from F1. They will also indicate modern act and scene division, which often differs from Ff/Qq. Modern texts suggest that in many plays full scene division was not attempted until the eighteenth century, and act division in the early texts was sometimes haphazard at best. Thus many modern texts place the act division at a point other than that set in Ff/Qq, and nearly always break Ff/Qq text up into extra scenes. When modern texts add an act or scene division which is not shared by F1, the addition will be shown in brackets within the body of each individual play as it occurs. When Ff set a new Act or scene, for clarity these texts will start a fresh page, even though this is not Ff/Qq practice

### ON THE LEFT HAND SIDE OF EACH PAGE

Down the left of each page, line numbers are shown in increments of five. These refer to the lines in this text only. Where F1 prints a line containing two sentences, since these scripts set two separate lines, each line will be numbered independently.

## On The Top Right Of Each Page

These numbers represent the first and last lines set on the page, and so summarise the information set down the left hand side of the text.

## At The Bottom Right Of Each Page: using these scripts with other texts

At times a reader may want to compare these texts with either the original First Folio, or a reputable modern text, or both. Specially devised line numbers will make this a fairly easy proposition. These new reference numbers will be found at the bottom right of the page, just above the footnote section.

The information before the colon allows the reader to compare these texts against any photographic reproduction of the First Folio. The information after the colon allows the reader to compare these texts with a modern text, specifically the excellent *Riverside Shakespeare.*[7]

### Before the colon: any photostat of the First Folio

A capital letter plus a set of numbers will be shown followed by a lowercase letter. The numbers refer the reader to a particular page within the First Folio; the capital letter before the numbers specifies whether the reader should be looking at the right hand column (R) or left hand column (L) on that particular page; the lower case letter after the numbers indicates which compositor (mainly 'a' through 'e') set that particular column. An occasional asterisk alongside the reference tells the reader that though this is the page number as set in F1, it is in fact numbered out of sequence, and care is needed to ensure, say in *Cymbeline,* the appropriate one of two 'p. 389s' is being consulted.

Since the First Folio was printed in three separate sections (the first containing the Comedies, the second the Histories, and the third the Tragedies),[8] the pages and section in which each of these scripts is to be found will be mentioned in the introduction accompanying each play. The page number refers to that printed at the top of the reproduced Folio page, and not to the number that appears at the bottom of the page of the book which contains the reproduction.

Thus, from this series of texts, page one of *Measure for Measure* shows the ref-

---

[7]  Gwynne Blakemore Evans, Harry Levin, Anne Barton, Herschel Baker, Frank Kermode, Hallet D. Smith, and Marie Edel, eds., *The Riverside Shakespeare* (Copyright © 1974 by Houghton Mifflin Company). This work is chosen for its exemplary scholarship, editing principles, and footnotes.

[8]  The plays known as Romances were not printed as a separate section: *Cymbeline* was set with the Tragedies, *The Winter's Tale* and *The Tempest* were set within the Comedies, and though *Pericles* had been set in Q it did not appear in the compendium until F3. *Troilus and Cressida* was not assigned to any section, but was inserted between the Histories and the Tragedies with only 2 of its 28 pages numbered.

erence 'L61–c'. This tells the reader that the text was set by compositor 'c' and can be checked against the left hand column of p. 61 of the First Folio (*Measure For Measure* being set in the Comedy Section of F1).

Occasionally the first part of the reference seen at the bottom of the page will also be seen within the text, somewhere on the right hand side of the page. This shows the reader exactly where this column has ended and the new one begins.

(As any photostat of the First Folio clearly shows, there are often sixty-five lines or more per column, sometimes crowded very close together. The late Professor Charlton Hinman employed a brilliantly simple line-numbering system (known as TLN, short for Through Line Numbering System) whereby readers could quickly be directed to any particular line within any column on any page.

The current holders of the rights to the TLN withheld permission for the system to be used in conjunction with this series of Folio Texts.)

**After the colon: *The Riverside Shakespeare***

Numbers will be printed indicating the act, scene, and line numbers in *The Riverside Shakespeare,* which contain the information set on the particular page of this script. Again, using the first page of *Measure For Measure,* the reference 1.1.1–21 on page one of these scripts directs the reader to Act One Scene 1 of *The Riverside Shakespeare;* line one in *The Riverside Shakespeare* matches the first line in this text, while the last line of dialogue on page one of this text is to be found in line twenty-one of the *Riverside* version of the play.

# COMMON TYPESETTING PECULIARITIES
## OF THE FOLIO AND QUARTO TEXTS
### (And How These Texts Present Them)

There are a few (to modern eyes) unusual contemporary Elizabethan and early Jacobean printing practices which will be retained in these scripts.

## THE ABBREVIATIONS, 'S.', 'L.', 'D.', 'M.'

Ff and Qq use standard printing abbreviations when there is not enough space on a single line to fit in all the words. The most recognisable to modern eyes includes 'S.' for Saint; 'L.' for Lord; 'M.' for Mister (though this can also be short for 'Master', 'Monsieur', and on occasions even 'Mistress'); and 'D.' for Duke. These scripts will set F1 and footnote accordingly.

## 'Ÿ', 'W', AND ACCENTED FINAL VOWELS

Ff/Qq's two most commonly used abbreviations are not current today, viz.:
  ÿ, which is usually shorthand for either 'you'; 'thee'; 'thou'; 'thy'; 'thine'; or 'yours'
  w, usually with a ¨ above, shorthand for either 'which'; 'what'; 'when'; or 'where'.
Also, in other cases of line overcrowding, the last letter of a relatively unimportant word is omitted, and an accent placed over the preceding vowel as a marker, e.g. 'thä' for 'than'. For all such abbreviations these scripts will set F1 and footnote accordingly.

## THE SPECIAL CASE OF THE QUESTION AND EXCLAMATION MARKS ('?' AND '!')

### USAGE

Elizabethan use of these marks differs somewhat from modern practice. Ff/Qq rarely set an exclamation mark: instead the question mark was used either both as a question mark and as an exclamation point. Thus occasionally the question mark suggests some minor emphasis in the reading.

### SENTENCE COUNT

When either mark occurs in the middle of a speech, it can be followed by a capitalised or a lowercase word. When the word is lowercase (not capitalised) the sentence continues on without a break. The opposite is not always true: just because the following word is capitalised does not automatically signify the start of a new sentence, though more often than not it does.

Elizabethan rhetorical writing style allowed for words to be capitalised within a sentence, a practice continued by the F1 compositors. Several times in *The Winters Tale,* highly emotional speeches are set full of question marks followed by capitalised words. Each speech could be either one long sentence of ongoing passionate rush, or up to seven shorter sentences attempting to establish self-control.

The final choice belongs to the individual reader, and in cases where such alternatives arise, the passages will be boxed, footnoted, and the various possibilities discussed.

## THE ENDING OF SPEECHES WITH NO PUNCTUATION, OR PUNCTUATION OTHER THAN A PERIOD

Quite often F1–2 will not show punctuation at the end of a speech, or sometimes set a colon (:) or a comma (,) instead. Some commentators suggest the setting of anything other than a period was due to compositor carelessness, and that omission occurred either for the same reason, or because the text was so full it came flush to the right hand side of the column and there was no room left for the final punctuation to be set. Thus modern texts nearly always end a speech with the standard period (.), question mark (?), or exclamation mark (!), no matter what F1–2 have set.

However, omission doesn't always occur when a line is full, and F2, though making over sixteen hundred unauthorised typographical corrections of F1 (more than eight hundred of which are accepted by most modern texts), rarely replaces an offending comma or colon with a period, or adds missing periods—F3 is the first to make such alterations on a large scale basis. A few commentators, while acknowledging some of the omissions/mistakes are likely to be due to compositor or scribal error, suggest that ending the speech with anything other than a period (or not ending the speech at all) might indicate that the character with the speech immediately following is in fact interrupting this first speaker.

These texts will set F1, footnote accordingly, and sometimes discuss the possible effect of the missing or 'incorrect' punctuation.

## THE SUBSTITUTIONS OF 'i/I' FOR 'j/J' AND 'u' FOR 'v'

In both Ff/Qq words now spelled as 'Jove' or 'Joan' are often set as 'Iove' or 'Ioan'. To avoid confusion, these texts will set the modern version of the word. Similarly, words with 'v' in the middle are often set by Ff/Qq with a 'u'; thus the modern word 'avoid' becomes 'auoid'. Again, these texts will set the modern version of the word, without footnote acknowledgement.

## ALTERNATIVE SETTINGS OF A WORD WHERE DIFFERENT SPELLINGS MAINTAIN THE SAME MEANING

Ff/Qq occasionally set, what appears to modern eyes, an archaic spelling of a word for which there is a more common modern alternative, for example 'murther' for murder, 'burthen' for burden, 'moe' for more, 'vilde' for vile. Some modern texts set the Ff/Qq spelling, some modernise. These texts will set the F1 spelling throughout.

## ALTERNATIVE SETTINGS OF A WORD WHERE DIFFERENT SPELLINGS SUGGEST DIFFERENT MEANINGS

Far more complicated is the situation where, while an Elizabethan could substitute one word formation for another and still imply the same thing, to modern eyes the substituted word has a entirely different meaning to the one it has replaced. The following is by no means an exclusive list of the more common dual-spelling, dual-meaning words:

| | | |
|---|---|---|
| anticke–antique | mad–made | sprite–spirit |
| born–borne | metal–mettle | sun–sonne |
| hart–heart | mote–moth | travel–travaill |
| human–humane | pour–(powre)–power | through–thorough |
| lest–least | reverent–reverend | troth–truth |
| lose–loose | right–rite | whether–whither |

Some of these doubles offer a metrical problem too; for example 'sprite', a one syllable word, versus 'spirit'. A potential problem occurs in *A Midsummer Nights Dream*, where provided the modern texts set Q1's 'thorough', the scansion pattern of elegant magic can be established, whereas F1's more plebeian 'through' sets up a much more awkward and clumsy moment.

These texts will set the F1 reading, and footnote where the modern texts' substitution of a different word formation has the potential to alter the meaning (and sometimes scansion) of the line.

## 'THEN' AND 'THAN'

These two words, though their neutral vowels sound different to modern ears, were almost identical to Elizabethan speakers and readers, despite their different meanings. Ff and Qq make little distinction between them, setting them interchangeably. In these scripts the original printings will be used, and the modern reader should soon get used to substituting one for the other as necessary.

## 'I', AND 'AY'

Ff/Qq often print the personal pronoun 'I' and the word of agreement 'aye' simply as 'I'. Again, the modern reader should quickly get used to this and make the substitution whenever necessary. The reader should also be aware that very occasionally either word could be used and the phrase make perfect sense, even though different meanings would be implied.

## 'MY SELFE/HIM SELFE/HER SELFE' VERSUS 'MYSELF/HIMSELF/ HERSELF'

Generally Ff/Qq separate the two parts of the word, 'my selfe' while most modern texts set the single word 'myself'. The difference is vital, based on Elizabethan philosophy. Elizabethans regarded themselves as composed of two parts, the corporeal 'I', and the more spiritual part, the 'selfe'. Thus when an Elizabethan character refers to 'my selfe', he or she is often referring to what is to all intents and purposes a separate being, even if that being is a particular part of him- or herself. Thus soliloquies can be thought of as a debate between the 'I' and 'my selfe', and in such speeches, even though there may be only one character onstage, it's as if there were two distinct entities present.

These texts will show F1 as set.

# FOOTNOTE CODE
## (shown in two forms, the first alphabetical,
## the second grouping the codes by topic)

To help the reader focus on a particular topic or research aspect, a special code has been developed for these texts. Each footnote within the footnote section at the bottom of each page of text has a single letter or series of letters placed in front of it guiding readers to one specific topic; thus 'SPD' will direct readers to footnotes just dealing with songs, poems, and doggerel.

## ALPHABETICAL FOOTNOTE CODING

| | |
|---|---|
| A | asides |
| AB | abbreviation |
| ADD | a passage modern texts have added to their texts from F2–4/Qq |
| ALT | a passage (including act and scene division) that has been altered by modern texts without any Ff/Qq authority |
| COMP | a setting probably influenced by compositor interference |
| F | concerning disputed facts within the play |
| FL | foreign language |
| L | letter or letters |
| LS | alterations in line structure |
| M | Shakespeare's use of the scansion of magic (trochaic and seven syllables) |
| N | a name modern texts have changed or corrected for easier recognition |
| O | F1 words or phrases substituted for a Qq oath or blasphemy |
| OM | passage, line, or word modern texts omit or suggest omitting |
| P | change in prefix assigned to a character |
| PCT | alterations to F1's punctuation by modern and/or contemporary texts |
| Q | material rejected or markedly altered by Qq not usually set by modern texts |
| QO | oaths or blasphemies set in Qq not usually set by modern texts |
| SD | stage directions added or altered by modern texts |
| SP | a solo split line for a single character (see pp. xv–xvi above) |

| | |
|---|---|
| SPD | matters concerning songs, poems, or doggerel |
| ?ST | where, because of question marks within the passage, the final choice as to the number of sentences is left to the reader's discretion |
| STRUCT | a deliberate change from the F1 setting by these texts |
| UE | an unusual entrance (set to the side of the text) or exit (set on a separate line) |
| VP | F1's verse altered to prose or vice versa, or lines indistinguishable as either |
| W | F1's word or phrase altered by modern texts |
| WHO | (in a convoluted passage) who is speaking to whom |
| WS | F1 line structure altered because of casting off problems (see pp. x–xi above) |

## FOOTNOTE CODING BY TOPIC

### STAGE DIRECTIONS, ETC.

| | |
|---|---|
| A | asides |
| P | change in prefix assigned to a character |
| SD | stage directions added or altered by modern texts |
| UE | an unusual entrance (set to the side of the text) or exit (set on a separate line) |
| WHO | (in a convoluted passage) who is speaking to whom |

### LINE STRUCTURE AND PUNCTUATION, ETC.

| | |
|---|---|
| L | letter or letters |
| LS | alterations in line structure |
| M | Shakespeare's use of the scansion of magic (trochaic and seven syllables) |
| PCT | alterations to F1's punctuation by modern and/or contemporary texts |
| SPD | matters concerning songs, poems, or doggerel |
| ?ST | where, because of question marks within the passage, the final choice as to the number of sentences is left to the reader's discretion |
| SP | a solo split line for a single character ( see pp. xv–xvi above) |
| VP | F1's verse altered to prose or vice versa, or lines indistinguishable as either |

| WS | F1 line structure altered because of casting off problems (see pp. x–xi above) |
|---|---|

## Changes to Words and Phrases

| AB | abbreviation |
|---|---|
| F | concerning disputed facts within the play |
| FL | foreign language |
| N | a name modern texts have changed or corrected for easier recognition |
| O | F1 words or phrases substituted for a Qq oath or blasphemy |
| QO | oaths or blasphemies set in Qq not usually set by modern texts |
| W | F1's word or phrase altered by modern texts |

## Changes on a Larger Scale and Other Unauthorised Changes

| ADD | a passage modern texts have added to their texts from F2–4/Qq |
|---|---|
| ALT | a passage (including act and scene division) that has been altered by modern texts without any Ff/Qq authority |
| COMP | a setting probably influenced by compositor interference |
| OM | passage, line, or word modern texts omit or suggest omitting |
| Q | material rejected or markedly altered by Qq not usually set by modern texts |
| STRUCT | a deliberate change from the F1 setting by these texts |

## ONE MODERN CHANGE FREQUENTLY NOTED IN THESE TEXTS

### 'Minute' Changes to the Syllable Length of Ff lines

As noted above on pages xi–xii, modern texts frequently correct what commentators consider to be large scale metric deficiencies, often to the detriment of character and scene. There are many smaller changes made too, especially when lines are either longer or shorter than the norm of pentameter by 'only' one or two syllables. These changes are equally troublesome, for there is a highly practical theatrical rule of thumb guideline to such irregularities, viz.:

if lines are slightly **longer** than pentameter, then the characters so involved have too much information coursing through them to be contained within the 'norms' of proper verse, occasionally even to the point of losing self-control

if lines are slightly **shorter** than ten syllables, then either the information therein contained or the surrounding action is creating a momentary (almost need to breath) hesitation, sometimes suggesting a struggle to maintain self-control

These texts will note all such alterations, usually offering the different syllable counts per line as set both by F1 and by the altered modern texts, often with a brief suggestion as to how the original structural 'irregularity' might reflect onstage action.

# FINALLY, A BRIEF WORD ABOUT THE COMPOSITORS [9]

Concentrated research into the number of the compositors and their habits began in the 1950s and, for a while, it was thought five men set the First Folio, each assigned a letter, 'A' through 'E'.

'E' was known to be a seventeen-year-old apprentice whose occasional mishaps both in copying text and securing the type to the frame have led to more than a few dreadful lapses, notably in *Romeo and Juliet*, low in the left column on p. 76 of the Tragedies, where in sixteen F1 lines he commits seven purely typographical mistakes. Compositor 'B' set approximately half of F1, and has been accused of being cavalier both with copying text and not setting line ending punctuation when the line is flush to the column edge. He has also been accused of setting most of the so called 'solo' split lines, though a comparison of other compositors' habits suggests they did so too, especially the conglomerate once considered to be the work of a single compositor known as 'A'. It is now acknowledged that the work set by 'A' is probably the work of at least two and more likely five different men, bringing the total number of compositors having worked on F1 to nine ('A' times five, and 'B' through 'E').

It's important to recognise that the work of these men was sometimes flawed. Thus the footnotes in these texts will point the reader to as many examples as possible which current scholarship and research suggest are in error. These errors fall into two basic categories. The first is indisputable, that of pure typographical mistakes ('wh?ch' for 'which'): the second, frequently open to challenge, is failure to copy exactly the text (Qq or manuscript) which F1 has used as its source material.

As for the first, these texts place the symbol † before a footnote marker within the text (not in the footnote section), a combination used only to point to a purely typographical mistake. Thus in the error-riddled section of *Romeo and Juliet* quoted above, p. 109 of this script shows fourteen footnote markers, seven of them coupled with the symbol †. Singling out these typographical-only markers alerts the reader to compositor error, and that (usually) the 'correct' word or phrase has been set within the text. Thus the reader doesn't have to bother with the footnote below unless they have a morbid curiosity to find out what the error actually is. Also, by definition, the more † appearing in a passage, the worse set that passage is.

As to the second series of (sometimes challengeable) errors labelled poor copy work, the footnotes will alert the reader to the alternative Qq word or phrase usage preferred by most modern texts, often discussing the alternatives in detail, especially when there seems to be validity to the F1 setting.

---

[9] Readers are directed to the ground breaking work of Alice Walker, and also to the ongoing researches of Paul Werstine and Peter W. M. Blayney.

Given the fluid state of current research, more discoveries are bound to be published as to which compositor set which F1 column long after these texts go to print. Thus the current assignation of compositors at the bottom of each of these scripts' pages represents what is known at this moment, and will be open to reassessment as time goes by.

## A CAVEAT: THE COMPOSITORS AND 'SINGLE SPLIT LINES' (SEE PP. XV–XVI)

Many commentators suggest single split lines are not Shakespearean dramatic necessity, but compositorial invention to get out of a typesetting dilemma. Their argument is threefold:

first, as mentioned on pp. x–xi, because of 'white space' a small amount of text would have to be artificially expanded to fill a large volume of what would otherwise be empty space: therefore, even though the column width could easily accommodate regular verse lines, the line or lines would be split in two to fill an otherwise embarrassing gap

second, even though the source documents the compositors were using to set F1 showed material as a single line of verse, occasionally there was too much text for the F1 column to contain it as that one single line: hence the line had to be split in two

third, the device was essentially used by compositor B.

There is no doubt that sometimes single split lines did occur for typesetting reasons, but it should be noted that:

single split lines are frequently set well away from white space problems

often the 'too-much-text-for-the-F1-column-width' problem is solved by setting the last one or two words of the overly lengthy line either as a new line, or as an overflow or underflow just above the end of the existing line without resorting to the single split line

all compositors seem to employ the device, especially the conglomerate known as 'A' and compositor E.

As regards the following text, while at times readers will be alerted to the fact that typographical problems could have had an influence on the F1 setting, when single split lines occur their dramatic potential will be discussed, and readers are invited to explore and accept or reject the setting accordingly.

## INTRODUCTION TO THE TEXT OF
## *THE TRAGEDY OF RICHARD THE THIRD*
## *with the Landing of Earle Richmond,*
## *and the Battell at Bosworth Field* [1]

### pages 173 - 204 of the History Section [2]

All Act, Scene, and line numbers will refer to the
Applause text below unless otherwise stated.

Current research places the play between number four and eight in the canon. Its setting was nearly completed with one of its tandem plays, *Henry Six Part Three*, and was then
interrupted by seven other plays, the other tandem play *Henry the Eight*, and the Tragedies
*Coriolanus, Titus, Romeo & Juliet, Julius Cæsar, Macbeth* and *Hamlet*.

For composition, scholars have established a preliminary window of 1592 (because of
the largish cast size compared to later plays, a sign of pre-plague plays) to 1597, the year
Quarto 1 was published. Current theory, working back from publication to memorial text to
playing experience to the writing, suggests late 1592 - early 1593.

## SCHOLARS' ASSESSMENT

The number of early scripts and supposed manuscripts is daunting, the interlinking
occasionally a little tangled, and the choice of a final authoritative text at best uncertain.
There are (at least) two routes to trace, both stemming from Shakespeare's foul papers,[3] the
Q and F routes.

- Quarto 1 (Q1) of 1597: current research suggests a fascinating history of performance
  from a prompt-copy until an eventful summer tour of 1597 when the prompt-copy[4]
  was inadvertently left behind: hastily the whole company got together to rework
  the script (with the possible exception of the actors of Buckingham, the two Villains
  involved in the murder of Clarence and various Messengers) and it was this
  reworked text, with Shakespeare's input since he was presumably a member of the
  touring company, that was used for Q1.

---

[1] For a detailed examination, see Wells, Stanley and Taylor, Gary (eds.). *William Shakespeare: A Textual
Companion.* Oxford: Clarendon Press. 1987. pages 228 - 263. For a detailed analysis of the play's contents, see any of the Recommended Modern Texts.

[2] *Mr. William Shakespeare's Comedies, Histories, & Tragedies, 1623.*

[3] Shakespeare's first draft, with all the original crossings out and blots intact.

[4] A manuscript prepared by the Playhouse (copied from either fair or foul papers) with detailed information added necessary for staging a theatrical performance.

- Quarto 2 (Q2) of 1598, Quarto 3 (Q3) of 1602, and Quarto 4 (Q4) of 1605, based on their immediate predecessor, with no authorised or substantive emendations.
- Quarto 5 (Q5) of 1612, based on Q3 and Q4 with no authorised or substantive emendations.
- Quarto 6 (Q6) of 1622, based on Q5 with no authorised or substantive emendations.
- First Folio (F1) of 1623, which was based on a scribal transcript of the foul papers, as well as consultation with an annotated copy of Q3 and sometimes Q6. [5]

Thus the true source text is difficult to establish. While F1 is regarded by *A Textual Companion* as the control text (note, not sole authority) in the words of *The Arden Shakespeare Richard III* (see Recommended Texts below)

> There is every reason to think the manuscript [i.e. on which F1 was based] as authoritative, but pre-theatrical: the omission from it of the very stage-worthy 'clock' scene in Act Four Scene 2 [6] is enough to confirm that it must pre-date the revisions of the play as performed, and, as reported in Q . . .   (page 44)
>
> F's authority is much higher, as it is uncontaminated by a memorial link . . . However, every reading in which Q differs from F must be evaluated, since any such difference may originate with Shakespeare or perhaps have his sanction . . .   (page 50)

And *A Textual Companion* suggests what Qq cut 'consists of static poetic elaboration which slows up the dramatic pace . . .' (page 228) going on to state

> an editor must choose between a text which clearly represents Shakespeare's first intention and another which apparently represents an alteration made by the time the play was performed   (page 231)

Thus all modern editors take F for substance and Q1 for incidentals.

- WHO'S WHO ? AND WHO DOES WHAT? DIFFERENCES BETWEEN Q AND F

There can be enormous character confusion dependent upon whether Qq or F1 is treated as the source. For example, readers of modern texts trying to figure out the function of **Brakenbury** and the **Keeper**, the two characters most closely associated with duties in the Tower, will come to vastly different conclusions dependent upon which source their text follows. F1 suggests the Keeper accompanies Clarence (page 31), only to be relieved by Brakenbury; Qq set Brakenbury throughout. And, according to modern textual revisions, it is Brakenbury who bars the women access to the Princes in the Tower (page 92), not a new character, the Lieutenant, as set by Qq/F1. [7]

---

[5]   For details of the influence of Q3/Q6, see *A Textual Companion,* pages 229 - 230.

[6]   Q1's version of this scene is presented as an Appendix at the end of this play

[7]   Presumably modern editors have taken the F1 History column L 180 entry description (page 33 this text) 'Enter Brakenbury the Lieutenant' and applied it to this entry too.

The problem is even more magnified with **Catesby**, whose Qq presence sometimes assumes far greater importance than Ff. This is first noticed in the equivalent of F1's Act Three Scene 4 (page 75, footnote #1) when the Qq Catesby takes over from F1's Lovell and Ratcliffe in hurrying Hastings on to execution (page 78). Thus in Qq it is he who later brings in Hastings' head to shock the Maior of London (page 80). Again in the Qq equivalent of F1's Act Four Scene 3 (page 119) it is he and not Ratcliffe that brings in the news of Morton/Ely's flight. And in Richard's tent-pitching sequence, Qq bring in Catesby instead of F1's Earle of Surrey (page 127). In Qq, perhaps as compensation for Catesby usurping several of Ratcliffe's juicier F1 moments, Ratcliffe, not a Sheriffe, supervises Buckingham's execution (page 125).

There is disagreement between Qq and F1 as to **which Churchman** is initially supposed to welcome Edward and Elizabeth's eldest son, 'Yong Yorke', as the next rightful King (page 56). F1 sets the Archbishop of Yorke, Qq the Cardinall of Canterbury, whom both texts show as actually welcoming him in the next scene. While commentators claim the confusion stems from Holinshed [8] who virtually conflates the two historical characters, they are equally quick to point out Qq's setting avoids the necessity of another character and another costume. [9]

Finally, some modern readers may be puzzled in the short sequence between Hastings and a 'pursuivant' to find that character named Hastings too! This is a left-over from Qq, and explained more fully in footnote #4, page 71.

* **HISTORICAL ERROR**

Historically, the body of Henry VI was taken to Blackfriars, not White Friars as page 15, line 1. 2. 245 suggests: few modern texts correct F1.

## THE TEXT

was set by compositors A (22 columns) and B (42).

## F1'S STAGE MANAGEMENT OF THE PLAY

With such a sprawling, play dotted with many influential smaller characters, and with so many sources, it is not surprising that what most readers would regard as essential background information needed to clarify the action is often missing. When necessary this text will add detailed footnotes to clarify Qq/Ff ambiguities in the following areas.

---

[8]   Holinshed, Raphael. *Chronicles Of England, Scotland And Ireland.* 1587 (2nd. edition)

[9]   For further details see *The Arden Shakespeare King Richard III,* page 16, and *A Textual Companion,* page 237, footnote to line 2.4.0.1/1354.1.

## PREFIXES

The character **Stanley** is also known by his aristocratic title of Darby, sometimes spelled Derby. **Bishop Ely**, possessor of the 'good Strawberries' used as an excuse to have him absent during the condemnation of Hastings is also known as Lord Morton, one of many key people who flee to join Richmond. The Queene's relative first termed **Woodvile** in the dialogue (usually corrected to Woodville, and/or modernised to Woodvile) is also more commonly known as Rivers, F1's usual prefix for him.

The men who kill Clarence at Richard's behest are entitled '**Murtherers**' in both stage entries (pages 29 and 33 ) but referred to by prefix as unspecified 'Vil' (presumably shorthand for Villain[s] - which in itself raises interesting sociological questions, especially considering the social status of many Shakespearean characters committing murder) in the first scene. Thus either or both could be the character responding to Richard. In the second scene they are simply given numbers ('1' and '2') with no further description. For further details, see footnote #3 to page 29.

## THE VARIABLE RANGE OF STAGE DIRECTIONS

### • IMPLIED DIRECTIONS

As usual in an F1 (or Qq) play some directions need decoding from actions or dialogue within the text. This presented no problem to the original actors and prompt-book holder, for it was second nature for them to fill in many of the smaller details without extra annotation. Whatever minor moments did not make their way to the various publishing houses were not added by the publishers since, as often as not, they weren't really missing if the text in question was closely followed. Thus in many of the scenes, a reader can get by without such directions simply by paying careful attention to the action of the play as the dialogue unfolds. (However, when the action remains obscure, this text, as all others in this series, will add extra information via footnotes).

As example, the 'Coarse of Henrie the sixt' followed by Anne (page 7) must be open for her to refer to him being 'key-Cold', to address his injuries as 'these wounds', and for her to see 'dead Henries wounds,/Open their congeal'd mouthes' in his murderer's (Richard's) presence (page 9, lines 1. 2. 57-8).

### • Qq CAN FILL IN F1'S GAPS

With the prompt-copy background to Q1, it's not surprising that F1's occasionally dry descriptions can be expanded by the earlier text - as with the F1 description of 'Enter Richard in pompe' (page 96). Qq add the key point that Richard is 'Crowned', and after the first three lines of dialogue set the all important 'here he ascendeth the throne'. Where applicable, Q's directions will be added and annotated accordingly.

## ENTRIES AND EXITS

• ENTRIES ARE SOMETIMES INCOMPLETE . . .

. . . which is only to be expected in such a complex play. At the end of the confrontational wooing of Anne over the dead Henry VI, she suddenly orders Tressel and Barkley (two up-till-now-never-mentioned men) to leave with her (page 15, line 1. 2. 239). Presumably they are part of the entering mourning party, but only the generalised guards known as 'Halberds' were mentioned then.

Also, since Dorset and Hastings are included in the universal cursing of all the Yorkists and their supporters by the Lancastrian old Queene Margaret, they should be given entries, but are not. [10]

Similarly since the text makes reference to 'My neece Plantagenet/Led in the hand of her kind Aunt of Gloster' (lines 4. 1. 2-3) most modern texts add Clarence's daughter to the entry starting Act Quartus Scene Prima (page 92).

• SOMETIMES F1'S INFORMATION IS MISLEADING OR INCORRECT

In the entry to Act One Scene 3, Elizabeth should be described as the Queene, as she is in her subsequent prefixes, not the Queene Mother (page 18). The double naming of Woodville/Rivers causes problems at the top of Act Two (page 42) when the single character is given a double entry, one for each name. [11]

• UNUSUAL ENTRIES, OR TEXTUAL CROWDING ?

Most F1 entries are set centered on a line separate from the surrounding dialogue. Occasionally, as in this play, a few entries are set as exits (to the right of the text, on the same line as the dialogue that precedes it). If an overcrowded page (too much text for too little space) is not responsible for the setting, it is possible that these entries might signify either the entering character does not wish to draw attention to itself or where the reaction of those on-stage is equally important as the entry itself.

In this play the few self-effacing (side-set entries) are usually dismissed as being set on a crowded page, as with the 1. Murtherer (bottom Folio R 181, this text page 41), though in this case the underlying dramatic action could well support the idea that he might be sneaking up on his now reluctant colleague in the hopes (perhaps) of disposing of him as he has just done Clarence.

• EXIT PROBLEMS

The most complex problem surrounds the Ghosts blessing Richmond and cursing Richard (pages 132 - 4). Since Qq/F1 set no exits at all perhaps they wait on-stage, their presence growing more powerful until Richard awakes. Most modern texts set an exit once each sequence is finished.

---

[10]   For further details, see footnotes #1 page 18, and #5 page 19.

[11]   Qq solve the problem by omitting him from the entry completely.

Sometimes timing of exits is vague. Thus a niggling but theatrical problem concerns the Priest with Hastings (page 72) - no specific exit is set for him, just a general Exeunt for all at the end of the scene. Most modern texts remove him as Buckingham enters, but if he stays, as Hastings' comment 'when I met this holy man' seems to suggest, Buckingham's initial jibes will carry just that more sting.

And sometimes exits are non-existent, as with Clarence when leaving Richard (page 5). He should be accompanied by Brakenbury and the guards, whom F1 ignores.

### ASIDES & WHO-TO'S [12]

These can also be problematical, as with the Duchesse of Yorke's advice once Stanley delivers the bombshell that Richard is about to be crowned and demands that Anne be crowned with him as his Queene. It takes a careful analysis to realise who is being addressed in the following

> Go thou to Richmond, & good fortune guide thee,       (to Dorset)
> Go thou to Richard, and good Angels tend thee,        (to Anne)
> Go thou to Sanctuarie, and good thoughts possesse thee       (to
>                                    Elizabeth, and Clarence's daughter)
>                      (page 95, lines 4. 1. 99 - 101)

In comparison, part of Margaret's cursing of the Yorkists (pages 24 - 5, lines 1. 3. 202 and on) is much easier to decode. Though whether 'by Surfet dye your King' (page 24, line 1. 3. 204) is to all or just to King Edward's wife Elizabeth remains open, it takes but a brief moment from the ensuing dialogue to realise that Dorset is the 'Master Marquesse' who is 'malapert', and Richard is 'yonder dogge' whom Buckingham should avoid.

Sometimes the asides are not clearly seen since they happen so quickly, especially from Richard; witness his public 'Amen' to his mother, and the remainder of the speech to the audience (page 51, line 2. 2. 112 and on).

#### • A VERY RARE MOMENT

As also seen in *The third Part of Henry the Sixt,* there is a most unusual F1 only direction: here, a separate line side-set direction for Richard reads 'Speakes to himselfe' (page 28). Apart from these two plays, there are virtually no examples of Ff directions set to explain who is speaking to whom, let alone indicating such an action should be treated as an aside, as here.

---

[12]   Asides are lines spoken by one character either directly to the audience, or to a small sub-group within a larger group on-stage, and not meant to be heard by anyone else. 'Who-to's' are suggestions as to which particular on-stage character out of a larger-group is being addressed by a particular remark. These are usually modern text additions, for Q/F rarely set such indications.

## MODERN INTERVENTIONS

### HARDLY ANY VARIATIONS IN VERSE AND PROSE

With Spevack[13] finding 34 speeches in prose (based on the excellent modern edition, *The Riverside Shakespeare*[14] which he uses as his control text), such variations are rarely significant. However, as footnote #6 to page 34 discusses in detail, there is a possibility of verse for Clarence's Murtherers which would set a totally different quality to the opening of the scene.[15]

### TINY POCKETS OF METRICAL IRREGULARITY

There are however many moments where modern texts have made significant **line structure alterations**. A *Textual Companion* lists just over eighty-five Q and F passages involving over one hundred and fifty lines that needed to be altered for *The Oxford Shakespeares*.[16] Richard's naughty joke with Brakenbury, Clarence and the Guards about Mistris Shore

| | |
|---|---|
| Naught to do with Mistris Shore? | ( 7) |
| I tell thee Fellow, he that doth naught with her | (11) |
| (Excepting one) were best to do it secretly alone. | (14) |
| (page 4, lines 1. 1. 100 - 2) | |

has both gaps and increasing excesses resembling a locker room build akin to a boys' night out. Most modern text revisions

| | |
|---|---|
| Naught to do with Mistris Shore? I tell thee Fellow, | (12) |
| He that doth naught with her (excepting one) | (10) |
| Were best to do it secretly alone. | (10) |

put the only excess at the beginning, then quickly settle down to normality after. In a more serious moment, F1 allows Clarence a pause before blurting out an attempted joke to explain his arrest, a wonderful hint as to the turmoil underneath

[13] Spevack, M. *A Complete And Systematic Concordance To The Works Of Shakespeare.* (9 vols.) Hildesheim. Georg Holms. 1968 - 1980

[14] Gwynne Blakemore Evans, Harry Levin, Anne Barton, Herschel Baker, Frank Kermode, Hallet D. Smith, and Marie Edel, eds., *The Riverside Shakespeare* (Copyright © 1974 by Houghton Mifflin Company).

[15] Occasionally, passages set by modern texts as verse may have been prose in F1, and vice versa. The distinction is not mere pedantry: verse implies some harmony and grace in self-expression, prose brings a more prosaic, everyday quality to the dialogue. Theatrically it is usually well worthwhile to note when such F1 shifts from prose to verse (and vice versa) occur, the transition can suggest a change in attitude in or between the speakers so involved.

[16] Wells, Stanley and Taylor, Gary (eds.). *The Oxford Shakespeare, William Shakespeare, The Complete Works, Original Spelling Edition/Modern Spelling Edition.* Oxford: The Clarendon Press. 1986

| Richard | Brother, good day: What meanes this armed guard | (9-10) |
| | That waites upon your Grace? | *( 6) |
| Clarence | His Majesty tendring my persons safety, | (11) |
| | Hath appointed this Conduct, to convey me to th'Tower | (13-14) |

(page 2, lines 1. 1. 42 - 5)

and Qq is even wilder. Most modern texts insist on wiping out the asterisked pause, and set a calmer ending.

| Richard | Brother, good day: What meanes this armed guard | |
| | That waites upon your Grace? | |
| Clarence | His Majesty | (10) |
| | Tendring my persons safety, hath appointed | (11) |
| | This Conduct, to convey me to th'Tower | (10-11) |

In the appallingly deceitful moments before the death of Clarence is revealed to Royal household, Richard's overlengthy protestation of loyalty

Hold me a Foe: If I unwillingly, or in my rage,       (14)

(page 44, line 2. 1. 57)

is similarly markedly reduced by the modern practice of setting 'Hold me a foe:' as a separate line,

| Hold me a Foe: | (4) |
| If I unwillingly, or in my rage, | (10) |

thus creating a pause where an onrush originally was set by both Qq and F1.

    Similarly, Anne's awkward attempts at self-control in the onslaught of Richard's wooing, (page 10, lines 1. 2. 85 - 7), starting 'Fouler then heart can thinke thee' become much more regulated by modern text reworkings, as does Stanley's stumbling attempts to tell Richard the appalling news of Dorset's fleeing to the enemy Richmond (page 98, lines 4. 2. 54 - 6).

#### MOMENTS OF PERSONAL AWKWARDNESS

    F1's **single split lines** [17] can have an enormous impact, if allowed to stand.
It is probably white space [18] or lack of column width that creates the four sets of short lines within the final fourteen lines of the bottom of R 177 (page 22, lines 1. 3. 121 - 32 this text), though it marks the start to the amazing gloves-off spat between the Yorkists Richard and Elizabeth, joyfully overheard by the so far un-noticed Lancastrian Margaret. A similar situation exists with the Ghosts (L 202, pages 133 - 4, lines 5. 2. 180 - 218 this text), compounded by

---

[17]   These are two or more short verse lines, set for a <u>single</u> character, which if placed together would form a single full line of verse. These lines are rarely reproduced as set by any modern text : see the General Introduction, pages xv - xvi for further discussion.

[18]   The term used to describe the condition of a page with so little dialogue that there are large sections of empty space surrounding the text, leading modern commentators to suggest the compositors often restructured the original line sequence to create more lines than first set so as to occupy some of the blank space which would otherwise lie empty.

the suspect nature of a page based on Q3. But in most of the following cases white space is not a factor.

Anne is provided two split lines within three speeches as she challenges Richard's statements, starting with

> In thy foule throat thou Ly'st,                                    (6)
> Queene Margaret saw                                                (5)
>
> (page 10, lines 1. 2. 98 - 9)

and

> Do'st grant me Hedge-hogge,                                        (5)
> Then God graunt me too                                             (5)
>
> (page 11, lines 1. 2. 109 - 10)

suggesting a struggle to maintain self-control as she tries to get her points across.

There are similar moments, such as Edward discovering that, despite his orders to the contrary, his brother Clarence is dead (page 45, lines 2. 1. 83 - 4); Rivers' careful challenging of Buckingham's (and thus Richard's) decision that the supposed future King (the young Yorke) should be received with 'some little Traine' rather than the full panoply due to a new monarch (page 52, lines 2. 2. 126 - 7); the delicate unspoken moments in the first discussion between Richard and Tyrrel, leading to the death of the Princes in the Tower; the pause as Richard finally gets to the crux of his almost date-rape wooing of Elizabeth's absent daughter through her mother

> Then know,                                                         (2)
> That from my Soule, I love thy Daughter.                           (9)
>
> (page 112, lines 4. 3. 268 - 9)

## THE NATURE OF DEBATE

### • PUNCTUATION

With scholars suggesting F1 punctuation has little or no provenance, much minor tinkering has occurred, often reducing rhetorical triumphs or necessities to grammatical blandness. Thus early in the play, as Richard confides to the audience of his plot

> To set my Brother Clarence and the King
> In deadly hate, the one against the other:
> And if King Edward be as true and just,
> As I am Subtle, False, and Treacherous,
> This day should Clarence closely be mew'd up:*
> About a Prophesie, which sayes that G,
> Of Edwards heyres the murtherer shall be.
>
> (page 2, lines 1. 1. 34 - 40)

the asterisked F1 colon allows him to emphasise the mechanism he is going to use. Most modern texts set no punctuation, allowing the moment to slip by as part of the general plot.

There is also the usual changing of F1's non-demanding periods to question marks, and adding punctuation to the end of a speech, or changing punctuation other than a period at the end of a speech to a period, thus removing traces of one character interrupting another.[19] As example, F1 suggests Hastings is very foolish following his release from prison. As Richard, presumably seeking allies or at the very least attempting to disarm a potential foe, tries to impress upon Hastings how Richard himself has helped to bring about Hastings' release, he interrupts Richard with a vain glorious irrelevancy

{Richard}     For they that were your Enemies, are his,
              And have prevail'd as much on him, as you,*

Hastings      More pitty, that the Eagles should be mew'd,
              While Kites and Buzzards play at Liberty.

Richard       What newes abroad?                                    (4)
                  (pages 5 - 6, lines 1. 1. 134 - 8)

which would seem to upset Richard, judging by the short line that immediately follows, and Hastings' later fate.

**• SHARED SPLIT LINES** [20]

Spevack finds 65 of them, a larger number than in the three earlier History plays. They are often grouped around quick rapier-like debate exchanges in highly charged emotional situations. This applies especially to the moment Richard challenges Anne to kill him with his own sword (pages 14 - 15, lines 1. 2. 205 - 20). They are also used to great effect in the ferocious debate between Elizabeth and Richard over the fate of her daughter whom he wants to marry now that Anne is dead - notably the moment where she challenges him to find something he can swear by that he has not dis-honoured (page 117, lines 4. 3. 394 - 412).

**THE (SUPPOSED) LACK OF F1 OATHS**     (however, see Appendix B)

This is another play where thanks to the 1606 Acte to Restraine the Abuses of Players,[21] F1 has had to amend some of the Qq oaths and many references to God (the latter being usually reset as 'Heaven'). When oaths have been altered, this text will footnote the Q reading accordingly. However, to prevent a plethora of footnotes when F1's 'Heaven' is substituted, this text will set an asterisk before the word without further comment once the first usage has been noted. The asterisk will also be used to denote minor contrasts in word formations (notably prithee/prythee/prethee — see footnote #4 page 33) and expansions and contractions in word formations (e.g. 'on't' versus on it; see footnote #1 page 70) between Ff and Qq texts.

---

[19]   See Freeman, Neil H.M. *Shakespeare's First Texts*. Vancouver. 1994

[20]   Two or more short verse lines, set for two or more characters, which if combined would form a single full line of verse. See the General Introduction, pages xii - xv for further discussion.

[21]   An Act of Parliament to prevent unnecessary blasphemy, oaths, or questionable religious references from being printed. Any pre-1606 material being printed had to excise all such references before being given a license to reprint (hence the differences between many quarto and F1 versions of the same play).

**THE AMASSING OF TINY DETAILS POINTING TO RICHARD'S POSSIBLE DISINTEGRATION**

Among the constant variations offered by the alternate sources of Qq/F1, modern editors have (possibly unwittingly) created a far more rational Richard at the play's end than F1 shows. A series of cracks in word usage, line irregularities, prefix shifts and logic suggest a gradual disintegration starting with the bad news of Richmond's approach occasioning all the key defections from Richard, (page 119) to the end of the play. Few of the following seven points survive in any modern text.

- It starts on page 119 with lines 4. 3. 465 - 8, the sending of Catesby first to the Duke of Norfolke and then one line later also to Salisbury, (which most modern texts defuse by suggesting Ratcliffe should be told this, and changing the text accordingly), followed immediately by the rebuke 'Dull unmindful Villaine' (line 4. 3. 471).

- The second clue is a similar double command to Ratcliffe (see footnotes #5 and #6, to lines 5. 2. 87 and 5. 2. 92, page 129) which most modern texts solve by having Catesby perform one of the tasks.

- This is almost immediately followed by a series of irregular lines (5. 2. 108 - 12, page 130) as Richard orders everyone to leave, starting with 'Bid my Guard watch. Leave me.', which he immediately countermands by calling Ratcliffe back for further instructions.

- Fourth is the highly unusual series of short sentences he uses to express his nightmare, following the appearance of the Ghosts (pages 134 - 5, lines 5. 2. 223 - 246). [22]

- Fifth is the fact that once Ratcliffe comes to arm Richard as earlier ordered, the prefix moves from the troubled personality of Richard to that of his office, King (page 136, line 5. 2. 263).

- Sixth are the brief irregular lines as Richard insists on quiet for the striking of the clock, followed by a rushed on line as he suspects the sun will not be seen during the battle - a disadvantage perhaps (pages 138 - 9, lines 5. 2. 332 - 34).

- The final moment concerns the peculiar word choices Richard adopts in his tactical planning (pages 139 - 40, lines 5. 2. 353 - 58) - the dispersal of the troops known as 'Horse and Foot' followed within three lines by a similar dispersal under the terminology 'Foot and Horse'; the repetition of 'shall be' three times in four lines. Not only do commentators amend these moments, they also suggest five other word alterations, all designed to bring rationality to what F1 shows as a very confused man (see the footnotes concerning these verbal irregularities scattered throughout pages 139 - 41). [23]

---

[22] In a lecture/demonstration to theatre students at York University in Toronto the acclaimed English actor Sir Ian Richardson explored the possibility of Richard undergoing a schizophrenic fit, illustrating his point by identifying two distinct personalities during the first eleven lines of Folio History column R 202 (page 135, lines 5. 2. 229 - 246 this text).

[23] For further details, readers are referred to *A Textual Companion*, page 249, footnotes to lines 5.6.25/3340 - 5.6.29/3344

## FACTS

In *Casting Shakespeare's Plays* T.J. King [24] suggests there are 3,721 spoken F1 lines and that eleven actors can play sixteen principal and two minor roles. Six boys can play four principal female and three minor female roles. Eight men can play twenty-eight smaller speaking roles and seventeen mutes: one boy can play two small roles. [25]

The 'CATALOGUE' lists the play as *The Life & Death of Richard the Third*. One header sets *The Life and Death of Richard the Third*, the other *The Life and death of Richard the Third*. The title above the text is *The Tragedy of Richard the Third: with the Landing of Earle Richmond, and the Battell at Bosworth Field*. The pages are numbered correctly. There are two catch word variations, and four mistakes (R 175, R 176, R 184 and R 193).

F1's Act and Scene Division is accepted up to and including Act Three Scene 3:
• Act Three Scene 4 is then divided into four separate scenes.
• Act Four Scene 1 is set as is, Scene 2 is usually divided in two, with Scenes 3 and 4 becoming the modern texts' Scenes 4 and 5.
• Act Five Scene 1 is usually set as is.
• there is no consensus on the division of Act Five Scene 2, which modern texts separate into anywhere between four and six more Scenes.

Neil Freeman,
Vancouver, B.C.
Canada, 1999

---

[24] King, T.J. *Casting Shakespeare's Plays*. Cambridge. Cambridge University Press. 1992.
[25] Q1 is 302 spoken lines shorter.

*l*

## RECOMMENDED MODERN TEXTS WITH EXCELLENT SCHOLARLY FOOTNOTES AND RESEARCH

The footnotes in this text are concise, and concentrate either on matters theatrical or choices in word or line structure which distinguish most modern editions and this Folio based text. Items of literary, historical, and linguistic concern have been well researched and are readily available elsewhere. One of the best **research** works in recent years is

Wells, Stanley, and Gary Taylor, eds. *William Shakespeare: A Textual Companion*. Oxford: Clarendon Press, 1987.

In terms of modern **texts**, readers are urged to consult at least one of the following:

Evans, Gwynne Blakemore, Harry Levin, Anne Barton, Herschel Baker, Frank Kermode, Hallet D. Smith, and Marie Edel, eds. *The Riverside Shakespeare*. Copyright © 1974 by Houghton Mifflin Company.

Hammond, A. (ed.). *King Richard III*. The Arden Shakespeare. 1981

Works mentioned in the footnotes to the play-text include

Raphael Holinshed's *Chronicles*, republished & enlarged 1587.

# Dramatis Personæ *

* This Dramatis Personæ owes much to those of The Oxford Shakespeares

## The (Yorkist) Royal House Of England

DUTCHESSE OF YORKE, King Edward's Mother
KING EDWARD the IVth

| His Family | His Brothers |
|---|---|
| QUEENE Elizabeth, his wife | George, Duke of CLARENCE, |
| PRINCE EDWARD, his oldest son | Clarence's SON & DAUGHTER |
| Richard, the Duke of YORKE, his youngest son | RICHARD, Duke of Gloucester, later King Richard the Third |

### His Wife's Family

| | |
|---|---|
| her brother, Earle RIVERS | Marquesse of DORSET and Lord GREY, her sons |

## The Defeated House Of Lancaster

| The Dead | The Living |
|---|---|
| GHOST of King Henry the Sixth | MARGARET, Henry's Widdow |
| GHOST of Prince Edward, his son | Lady ANNE, Prince Henry's Widdow, later Richard's Wife |

### The Politically Cautious

The Lord Chamberlaine, Lord HASTINGS
his colleague, the Earle of Derby, Lord STANLEY
Stanley's son-in-law, Henry Earle of RICHMOND

| Supporters Of Richard | Supporters Of Richmond |
|---|---|
| Duke of BUCKINGHAM | Earle of OXFORD |
| Duke of NORFOLKE | Sir James BLUNT |
| his son, Earle of SURREY | Sir Walter HERBERT |
| Sir Richard RATCLIFFE | Sir William BRANDON |
| Sir William CATESBY | |

### Those Employed By Richard

| In The Death Of Clarence | In The Death Of The Princes |
|---|---|
| 1. VILLAINE | a PAGE |
| 2. VILLAINE | Sir James TYRREL |

### Others In The Court

| | |
|---|---|
| Sir Thomas VAUGHAN | Lord LOVEL |

### Others Involved In The Affairs Of State

| Sir Roberty BRAKENBURY | a CARDINALL |
|---|---|
| LIEUTENANT of the Tower of London | Bishop of ELY, also known as Morton |
| CHRISTOPHER, a Priest | another Priest |

### Other Commoners

| Lord MAIOR of London | CITIZENS of London |
|---|---|
| a SCRIVENER | Hastings, a PURSUIVANT |

Aldermen, Bishops, Messengers, Souldiers

**This Cast List has been specially prepared for this edition, and will not be found in the Facsimile**

# The Tragedy of Richard the Third:
## with the Landing of Earle Richmond, and the Battell at Bosworth Field

## Actus Primus. Scœna Prima

### ENTER RICHARD DUKE OF GLOSTER, SOLUS

Now[†] is the Winter of our Discontent,
Made glorious Summer by this Son of Yorke:
And all the clouds that lowr'd upon our house
In the deepe bosome of the Ocean buried.

5  Now are our browes bound with Victorious Wreathes,
Our bruised armes hung up for Monuments;
Our sterne Alarums [1] chang'd to merry Meetings;
Our dreadfull Marches, to delightfull Measures.

Grim-visag'd Warre, hath smooth'd his wrinkled Front:
10  And now, in stead of mounting Barbed Steeds,
To fright the Soules of fearfull Adversaries,
He capers nimbly in a Ladies Chamber,
To the lascivious pleasing of a Lute. [2]

But I, that am not shap'd for sportive trickes,
15  Nor made to court an amorous Looking-glasse:
I, that am Rudely stampt, and want loves Majesty,
To strut before a wonton ambling Nymph:
I, that am curtail'd of this faire Proportion,
Cheated of Feature by dissembling Nature,
20  Deform'd, un-finish'd, sent before my time
Into this breathing World, scarse halfe made up,
And that so lamely and unfashionable,
That dogges barke at me, as I halt by them. [3]

---

[W][1] Ff/Q2-6/most modern texts set 'Alarums' creating an eleven syllable line, one modern text sets Q1's 'alarmes'

[W][2] Ff/most modern texts = 'Lute', Qq = 'love'

[PCT][3] F1 sets a period, as if his self-description brings him to a complete halt: Q1/F2/most modern texts set a colon

1

Why I (in this weake piping time of Peace)
25    Have no delight to passe away the time,
Unlesse to see [1] my Shadow in the Sunne,
And descant on mine owne Deformity.

And therefore, since I cannot prove a Lover,
To entertaine these faire well spoken dayes,
30    I am determined to prove a Villaine,
And hate the idle pleasures of these dayes.

Plots have I laide, Inductions dangerous,
By drunken Prophesies, Libels, and Dreames,
To set my Brother Clarence and the King
35    In deadly hate, the one against the other :
And if King Edward be as true and just,
As I am Subtle, False, and Treacherous,
This day should Clarence closely be mew'd up : [2]
About a Prophesie, which sayes that G,
40    Of Edwards heyres the murtherer shall be.

Dive thoughts downe to my soule, here Clarence comes.

**ENTER CLARENCE, AND BRAKENBURY,[3] GUARDED**

Brother, good day : What meanes this armed guard    L 173 - b
That waites upon your Grace?

**Clarence**    His Majesty ° tendring my persons safety,
45    Hath appointed ° this Conduct, to convey me to th'Tower ° [4] [5]

**Richard**    Upon what cause?

**Clarence**    Because my name is George. [?]

**Richard**    Alacke my Lord, that fault is none of yours :
He should for that commit your Godfathers.
50    O [6] belike, his Majesty hath some intent,
That you should be new Christned in the Tower.

---

[W 1] Qq/most modern texts = 'spie', Ff = 'see'

[PCT 2] Ff set a colon, allowing Richard to highlight the introduction of the device that will bring Clarence down: Q1 sets a comma, while most modern texts set no punctuation

[PCT 3] F1 shows a mark, which F2 interprets as a comma

[LS 4] Ff set three irregular lines (6/11/13 or 14 syllables) suggesting whatever care with which Clarence begins his explanation is soon lost in the longer release: most modern texts set three almost regular lines (6 + 4/11/9 or 10) reversing Ff's pattern of release (Q1 adds 'His Majesty' to the second line as set by the modern texts, thus establishing a 6/15/9 or 10 syllable pattern, i.e. matching Ff's momentary hesitation before speaking, but exploding much more and much quicker)

[PCT 5] F1 sets no punctuation as if Richard interrupts him, F2/most modern texts set a period

[W 6] Qq/Ff create an eleven syllable line by setting 'O', which at least one metrically minded modern text omits

2

But what's the matter Clarence, may I know?

**Clarence**    Yea Richard, when I know: but [1] I protest
As yet I do not: But as I can learne,

55      He hearkens after Prophesies and Dreames,
And from the Crosse-row pluckes the letter G:
And sayes, a Wizard told him, that by G,
His issue disinherited should be.

And for my name of George begins with G,

60      It followes in his thought, that I am he.

These (as I learne) and such like toyes as these,
Hath [2] moov'd his Highnesse to commit me now.

**Richard**    Why this it is, when men are rul'd by Women:
'Tis not the King that sends you to the Tower,

65      My Lady Grey his Wife, Clarence 'tis shee,[3]
That tempts [4] him to this harsh Extremity.

Was it not shee, and that good man of Worship,
Anthony Woodevlle [5] her Brother there,
That made him send Lord Hastings to the Tower?

70      From whence this present day he is delivered?

We are not safe Clarence, we are not safe.

**Clarence**    By heaven, I thinke there is no man secure
But the Queenes Kindred, and night-walking Heralds,
That trudge betwixt the King, and Mistris Shore.

75      Heard you [6] not what an humble Suppliant
Lord Hastings was, for her [7] delivery?

**Richard**    Humbly complaining to her Deitie,
Got my Lord Chamberlaine his libertie.

Ile tell you what, I thinke it is our way,

80      If we will keepe in favour with the King,
To be her men, and weare her Livery.

---

W 1
  Qq/most modern texts = 'for', Ff = 'but'

W 2
  Qq/most modern texts = 'Have', Ff/at least one modern text = 'Hath'

PCT 3
  F1 sets a blur which appears to be a period, Q1/F2/most modern texts set a comma

W 4
  Q1/most modern texts = 'tempers', Q2,4-6/Ff = 'tempts': one commentator suggests either 'tempers to this extremity' or 'tempts to this harsh extremity'

N/P 5
  F1 = 'Woodevlle', F2 = 'Woodville', Qq/some modern texts = 'Woodvile', other modern texts = 'Woodeville': nearly all commentators point out this character is also known as 'Rivers', the prefix usually assigned him throughout the play

W 6
  Ff/some modern texts = 'you', Qq/some modern texts = 'ye'

W 7
  Qq/F4/most modern texts = 'for his', F1-3= 'for her': also, since Ff set a short line, most modern texts follow Qq and set before the comma 'was to her', rather than Ff's simple 'was'

3

The jealous ore-worne Widdow, and her selfe,
Since that our Brother dub'd them Gentlewomen,
Are mighty Gossips in our Monarchy.

| | | |
|---|---|---|
| 85 | **Brakenbury** | I beseech your Graces both to pardon me, |
| | | His Majesty hath straightly given in charge, |
| | | That no man shall have private Conference |
| | | (Of what degree soever) with your Brother. |

R 173 - b

| | | |
|---|---|---|
| | **Richard** | Even so, and please your Worship Brakenbury, |
| 90 | | You may partake of any thing we say: |
| | | We speake no Treason man ; We say the King |
| | | Is wise and vertuous, and his Noble Queene |
| | | Well strooke in yeares, faire, and not jealious. [1] |

| | | |
|---|---|---|
| 95 | | We say, that Shores Wife hath a pretty Foot, |
| | | A cherry Lip,[2] a bonny Eye, a passing pleasing tongue: |
| | | And that the Queenes Kindred [3] are made gentle Folkes. |

How say you sir? can you deny all this?

| | | |
|---|---|---|
| | **Brakenbury** | With this (my Lord) my selfe have nought to |
| | | doo. |

| | | |
|---|---|---|
| 100 | **Richard** | Naught to do with Mistris Shore? |
| | | I tell thee Fellow,° he that doth naught with her |
| | | (Excepting one) ° were best to [4] do it secretly alone. [5] |

| | | |
|---|---|---|
| | **Brakenbury** | What one, my Lord? |

| | | |
|---|---|---|
| | **Richard** | Her Husband Knave, would'st thou betray me? |

| | | |
|---|---|---|
| 105 | **Brakenbury** | I do beseech your Grace → [6] |
| | | To pardon me, and withall forbeare |
| | | Your Conference†[7] with the Noble Duke. |

---

R 173 - b / L 174 - b  :  1. 1. 81 - 104

W 1
   Qq/F3/most modern texts = 'jealous', F1-2 = 'jealious'
LS 2
   since Qq/Ff set a fourteen syllable line, at least one metrically minded modern text sets the phrase 'A cherry Lip"
   as a separate four syllable line, thus replacing the original on-rush with a pause
W 3
   Qq/Ff set an eleven syllable line, thus one modern text replaces their 'Kindred' with 'kin'
W 4
   Qq/some modern texts = 'he', Ff/other modern texts = 'to'
LS/W 5
   Ff set three irregular lines (7/11/14 syllables) suggesting Richard starts his off-colour remarks without much
   fuss and then builds to a powerful climax: some modern texts follow Qq (12/10/10), starting out large scale and
   finishing with control, others remove the words 'to do' from the first line and set that as regular pentameter too
SP 6
   Ff set two short lines (6/9) as if Brakenbury were finding his request awkward: most modern texts, presumably
   arguing that F1 had insufficient column width for the passage to be set as a single line, join both lines together
   as if Brakenbury loses control: (however, it should be pointed out that Q1 - adding the word 'forbeare' to the
   first line - set the passage at the bottom of an already crowded page, where there was insufficient space for it to
   be set any way other than jammed together)
W 7
   F2/most modern texts = 'Conference', F1 = 'Conferenee'

| | | |
|---|---|---|
| | Clarence | We know thy charge Brakenbury, and wil obey. |
| | Richard | We are the Queenes abjects, and must obey. |
| 110 | | Brother farewell, I will unto the King, |
| | | And whatsoe're [1] you will imploy me in, |
| | | Were it to call King Edwards Widdow, Sister, |
| | | I will performe it to infranchise you. |
| | | Meane time, this deepe disgrace in Brotherhood, |
| 115 | | Touches me deeper [2] then you can imagine. |
| | Clarence | I know it pleaseth neither of us well. |
| | Richard | Well, your imprisonment shall not be long, |
| | | I will deliver you, or else lye for you: [3] |
| | | Meane time, have patience. |
| 120 | Clarence | I must perforce: Farewell. |

**[Exit Clar.{ence}]** [4]

| | | |
|---|---|---|
| | Richard | Go treade the path that thou shalt ne're return: |
| | | Simple plaine Clarence, I do love thee so, |
| | | That I will shortly send thy Soule to Heaven, |
| | | If Heaven will take the present at our hands. |
| 125 | | But who comes heere? the new delivered Hastings? |

**ENTER LORD HASTINGS**

| | | |
|---|---|---|
| | Hastings | Good time of day unto my gracious Lord. |
| | Richard | As much unto my good Lord Chamberlaine: |
| | | Well are you welcome to this [5] open Ayre, |
| | | How hath your Lordship brook'd imprisonment? |
| 130 | Hastings | With patience (Noble Lord) as prisoners must: |
| | | But I shall live (my Lord) to give them thankes |
| | | That were the cause of my imprisonment. |
| | Richard | No doubt, no doubt, and so shall Clarence too, |
| | | For they that were your Enemies, are his, |
| 135 | | And have prevail'd as much on him, as you, [6] |

---

**W [1]** Qq/one modern text = 'whatsoever', an eleven syllable line: Ff/most modern texts = 'whatsoe're'

**W [2]** even though Qq/Ff's 'deeper' makes excellent sense, some modern texts set either 'nearer' or 'dearer'

**W [3]** Ff set an eleven syllable line, at least one modern text follows Qq and omits 'or', while one modern text omits 'else'

**SD [4]** most modern texts add Brakenbury and the guards to the exit

**W [5]** Qq/most modern texts = 'the', Ff = 'this'

**PCT [6]** F1 sets a comma, as if Hastings interrupts him: Q1/F2/most modern texts set a period

5

| | |
|---|---|
| **Hastings** | More pitty, that the Eagles should be mew'd, <br> Whiles [1] Kites and Buzards play [2] at liberty. |
| **Richard** | What newes abroad? |
| **Hastings** | No newes so bad abroad, as this at home: <br> The King is sickly, weake, and melancholly, <br> And his Physitians feare him mightily. |
| **Richard** | Now by S. John,[3] that Newes is bad indeed. |
| | O he hath kept an evill Diet long, <br> And over-much consum'd his Royall Person: <br> 'Tis very greevous to be thought upon. |
| | Where is he, in his bed? |
| **Hastings** | He is. |
| **Richard** | Go you before, and I will follow you. |

140

145

**[Exit Hastings]**

He cannot live I hope, and must not dye,
Till George be pack'd with post-horse [4] up to Heaven.          L 174 - b

150

Ile in to urge his hatred more to Clarence,
With Lyes well steel'd with weighty Arguments,
And if I faile not in my deepe intent,
Clarence hath not another day to live:
Which done, God take King Edward to his mercy,
And leave the world for me to bussle in.

155

For then, Ile marry Warwickes yongest daughter.

What though I kill'd her Husband, and her Father,
The readiest way to make the Wench amends,
Is to become her Husband, and her Father:
The which will I, not all so much for love,
As for another secret close intent,
By marrying her, which I must reach unto.

160

But yet I run before my horse to Market:
Clarence still breathes, Edward still lives and raignes,
When they are gone, then must I count my gaines.

165

**[Exit]**

L 174 - b / R 174 - b  :  1. 1. 132 - 162

[1] Qq/most modern texts = 'While', Ff = 'Whiles'

[2] Qq/most modern texts = 'prey', Ff = 'play'

[3] most modern texts expand F1's 'S.' to Qq's 'Saint': this is the only time this abbreviation will be footnoted: also, some name him 'John' as in Ff, others 'Paul' (the oath attributed habitually to Richard), as in Qq

[4] though Qq/Ff = 'post-horse', at least one modern text sets the gloss 'post haste'

# Scena Secunda

ENTER THE COARSE OF HENRIE THE SIXT WITH HALBERDS TO GUARD IT,
LADY ANNE BEING THE MOURNER [1]

**Anne**    Set downe, set downe your honourable load,
If Honor may be shrowded in a Herse;
Whil'st I a-while obsequiously lament
Th'untimely fall of Vertuous Lancaster.

5      Poore key-cold Figure of a holy King,
Pale Ashes of the House of Lancaster;
Thou bloodlesse Remnant of that Royall Blood,
Be it lawfull that I invocate thy Ghost,
To heare the Lamentations of poore Anne,
10     Wife to thy Edward, to thy slaughtred Sonne,
Stab'd by the selfesame hand that made these wounds.

Loe, in these windowes that let forth thy life,
I powre [2] the helplesse Balme of my poore eyes.

O cursed be the hand that made these holes:
15     Cursed [3] the Heart, that had the heart to do it:
[4]  Cursed † the Blood, that let this blood from hence:
More direfull hap betide that hated Wretch
That makes us wretched by the death of thee,
Then I can wish to Wolves, to Spiders, [5] Toades,
20     Or any creeping venom'd thing that lives.

If ever he have Childe, Abortive be it,
Prodigeous, and untimely brought to light,
Whose ugly and unnaturall Aspect
May fright the hopefull Mother at the view,
25     [6] And that be Heyre to his unhappinesse.

---

since a 'Gent.' opposes Richard (line 38, next page) most modern texts add one or more to the entry, while a
recent phenomenon has been to name at least two of them as Tressel and Barkley from Anne's naming of them,
line 239, page 15 below: also, since Anne both touches the body, and sees Henry's wounds 'bleed afresh' some
modern texts suggest the coffin is open

[2] Q1-5/Ff = 'powre', most modern texts = 'pour' from Q6's 'poure'

[3] Ff/most modern texts repeat 'Cursed' from the previous line: Qq set 'Curst be' both times (and omit the
following line)

[4] most modern texts set this Ff only line, though one text suggests placing it before 'Cursed the heart . . .': also,
F1 = 'Cnrsed', F2/most modern texts = 'Cursed'

[5] Qq/most modern texts = 'adders, spiders', Ff = 'Wolves, to Spiders'

LS [6] most modern texts set this Ff only line

If ever he have Wife, let her be made
More miserable by the death [1] of him,
Then I am made by my young Lord, and thee.

30

Come now towards Chertsey with your holy Lode,
Taken from Paules, to be interred there.

And still as you are weary of this [2] waight,
Rest you, whiles I lament King Henries Coarse.

### ENTER RICHARD DUKE OF GLOSTER

| | |
|---|---|
| **Richard** | Stay you that beare the Coarse, & set it down. |
| **Anne**<br>35 | What blacke Magitian conjures up this Fiend,<br>To stop devoted charitable deeds? |
| **Richard** | Villaines set downe the Coarse, or by S. Paul,<br>Ile make a Coarse of him that disobeyes. |

R 174 - b

| | |
|---|---|
| **Gentleman** [3] | My Lord stand backe, and let the Coffin passe. |
| **Richard**<br>40 | Unmanner'd Dogge,→ [4]<br>Stand'st thou when I commaund:<br>Advance thy Halbert higher then my brest,<br>Or by S. Paul Ile strike thee to my Foote,<br>And spurne upon thee Begger for thy boldnesse. |
| **Anne**<br>45 | What do you tremble? are you all affraid?<br>Alas, I blame you not, for you are Mortall,<br>And Mortall eyes cannot endure the Divell.<br><br>Avant thou dreadfull minister of Hell;<br>Thou had'st but power over his Mortall body,<br>His Soule thou canst not have: Therefore be gone. |
| 50   **Richard** | Sweet Saint, for Charity, be not so curst. |

---

W 1
    as commentators point out, when Anne quotes herself later line 81, page 94, she substitutes 'life' for what is
set here, 'death': nevertheless, most modern texts set Qq/Ff's 'death' as is
W 2
    Qq/most modern texts = 'the', Ff = 'this'

P 3
    though Qq/Ff set the prefix 'Gent.', because of Richard's next line, recent editorial practice assigns the line to a
'Halbedier', i.e. a soldier, not a coffin bearer or mourner
SP/WS 4
    in this, the left-hand column of page 175 in the History section of F1, Ff set three pairs of short lines which
most modern texts set as three single lines, arguing either white space or lack of column width was responsible
for the F1 setting, copied by F2-4: if the Ff setting (4/6 syllables) were to stand here, it might suggest Richard
quietly takes his time to start putting his challenger in his proper place: also, Qq/most modern texts = 'Stands',
Ff = 'Stand'st'

| | | |
|---|---|---|
| **Anne** | | Foule Divell,→ [1] |
| | | For Gods sake hence, and trouble us not, |
| | | For thou hast made the happy earth thy Hell: |
| | | Fill'd it with cursing cries, and deepe exclaimes: |
| 55 | | If thou delight to view thy heynous deeds, |
| | | Behold this patterne of thy Butcheries. |

Oh Gentlemen, see, see dead Henries wounds,
Open [2] their congeal'd mouthes, and bleed afresh.

Blush, blush, thou lumpe of fowle Deformitie:
60    For 'tis thy presence that exhales this blood
From cold and empty Veines where no blood dwels.

Thy Deeds [3] inhumane and unnaturall,
Provokes this Deluge most unnaturall.

O God! which this Blood mad'st, revenge his death:
65    O Earth! which this Blood drink'st, revenge his death.

Either Heav'n with Lightning strike thee murth'rer dead:
Or Earth gape open wide, and eate him quicke,
As thou dost [4] swallow up this good Kings blood,
Which his Hell-govern'd arme hath butchered.

70    **Richard**    Lady, you know no Rules of Charity,
Which renders good for bad, Blessings for Curses.

**Anne**    Villaine, thou know'st nor [5] law of God nor Man,
No Beast so fierce, but knowes some touch of pitty.

**Richard**    But I know none, and therefore am no Beast.

75    **Anne**    O wonderfull, when divels tell the truth! [6]

**Richard**    More wonderfull, when Angels are so angry:
Vouchsafe (divine perfection of a Woman)
Of these supposed Crimes, to give me leave
By circumstance, but to acquit my selfe.

---

SP [1]    the Ff two short lines (2 or 3/9 syllables) might suggest Anne is trying to maintain self-control: most modern
texts set Qq's longer out-burst as shown

W [2]    Ff/Qq = 'Open', at least one modern text sets 'Ope'

W [3]    Qq/most modern texts = 'deed', Ff = 'Deeds'

W [4]    Q1-5 = 'doest', Ff /most modern texts = 'dost', Q6 = 'didst'

W [5]    Qq/most modern texts = 'no', Ff = 'nor'

W [6]    Q2-6/Ff /most modern texts = 'truth', Q1/one modern text = 'troth'

| | | |
|---|---|---|
| 80 | **Anne** | Vouchsafe (defus'd infection of man [1] ) |
| | | Of these knowne evils, but to give me leave |
| | | By circumstance, to curse [2] thy cursed Selfe. |
| | **Richard** | Fairer then tongue can name thee, let me have |
| | | Some patient leysure to excuse my selfe. |
| 85 | **Anne** | Fouler then heart can thinke thee, |
| | | Thou can'st make ° no excuse currant, |
| | | But to hang thy selfe. ° [3] |
| | **Richard** | By such dispaire, I should accuse my selfe. |
| | **Anne** | And by dispairing shalt thou stand excused, |
| 90 | | For doing worthy Vengeance on thy selfe, |
| | | That did'st unworthy slaughter upon others. |
| | **Richard** | Say that I slew them not. |
| | **Anne** | Then say they were not slaine : |
| | | But dead they are, and divellish slave by thee. |
| 95 | **Richard** | I did not kill your Husband. |
| | **Anne** | Why then he is alive. |
| | **Richard** | Nay, he is dead, and slaine by Edwards hands. [4] |
| | **Anne** | In thy foule throat thou Ly'st,→ [5] |
| | | Queene Margaret saw |
| 100 | | Thy murd'rous Faulchion smoaking in his blood : |
| | | The which, thou once didd'st bend against her brest, |
| | | But that thy Brothers beate aside the point. |
| | **Richard** | I was provoked by her sland'rous [6] tongue, |
| | | That laid their guilt, upon my guiltlesse Shoulders. |

L 175 - b

---

L 175 - b / R 175 - b : 1. 2. 78 - 98

W [1]  Qq/F2/most modern texts = 'a man', F1 = 'man'

W [2]  Qq/Ff/most modern texts = 'to curse', at least one modern text = 't'accuse'

SP [3]  Ff set three short lines (7/8/5 syllables), perhaps suggesting Anne is taking great care in expressing her wish for Richard to kill himself: most modern texts follow Qq and set two pentameter lines as shown

W [4]  Qq/most modern texts = 'hand', Ff = 'hands'

SP [5]  if the Ff only two short lines (6/5 syllables) were to stand, it would allow Anne a moment to savour her triumph in defeating Richard in a point of witnessed fact: most modern texts, presumably arguing there was not enough column width in Ff to set a single line, follow Qq and join the two lines together

W [6]  Ff/most modern texts = 'sland'rous': Qq/at least one modern text = 'slanderous', thus demanding 'provoked', set earlier in the line, to be pronounced as two syllables and not three (if the preservation of metric values is of prime consideration )

| 105 | **Anne** | Thou was't provoked by thy bloody minde,<br>That never dream'st on ought but Butcheries:<br>Did'st thou not kill this King? |
| | **Richard** | I graunt ye. [1] |
| 110 | **Anne** | Do'st grant me Hedge-hogge,→ [2]<br>Then God graunt me too<br>Thou may'st be damned for that wicked deede,<br>O he was gentle, milde, and vertuous. |
| | **Richard** | The better for the King of heaven that hath him. |
| | **Anne** | He is in heaven, where thou shalt never come. |
| 115 | **Richard** | Let him thanke me, that holpe to send him thi-<br>ther:<br>For he was fitter for that place then earth. |
| | **Anne** | And thou unfit for any place, but hell. |
| | **Richard** | Yes one place else, if you will heare me name it. |
| 120 | **Anne** | Some dungeon. |
| | **Richard** | Your Bed-chamber. |
| | **Anne** | Ill rest betide the chamber where thou lyest. |
| | **Richard** | So will it Madam, till I lye with you. |
| | **Anne** | I hope so. |
| 125 | **Richard** | I know so.<br>But gentle Lady Anne,<br>To leave this keene encounter of our wittes,<br>And fall something into a slower method. |
| 130 | | Is not the causer of the timelesse deaths<br>Of these Plantagenets, Henrie and Edward,<br>As blamefull as the Executioner. |
| | **Anne** | Thou was't the cause, and most [3] accurst effect. |

W [1] Ff/some modern texts = 'I graunt ye', Q1-2/some modern texts = 'I grant yea.', one modern text = 'I grant ye, yea.'

SP [2] arguing there was insufficient F1 column width, most modern texts follow Qq and set these two short Ff lines (5/5 syllables) as one: if the Ff setting were to stand it might suggest Anne having to take a moment before her enormous request of asking God to damn Richard

W [3] in view of the phrasing of Richard's next response, one modern text replaces Qq/Ff's 'and most' with 'of that'

| | Richard | Your beauty was the cause of that effect: |
|---|---|---|
| | | Your beauty, that did haunt me in my sleepe, |
| 135 | | To undertake the death of all the world, |
| | | So I might live one houre in your sweet bosome. |
| | Anne | If I thought that, I tell thee Homicide, |
| | | These Nailes should rent ¹ that beauty from my Cheekes. |
| | Richard | These eyes could not endure ÿ ² beauties ³ wrack, |
| 140 | | You should not blemish it, if I stood by; |
| | | As all the world is cheared by the Sunne,⁴ |
| | | So I by that: It is my day, my life. |
| | Anne | Blacke night ore-shade thy day, & death thy life. |
| | Richard | Curse not thy selfe faire Creature,→ ⁵ |
| 145 | | Thou art both. |
| | Anne | I would I were, to be reveng'd on thee. |
| | Richard | It is a quarrell most unnaturall, |
| | | To be reveng'd on him that loveth†⁶ thee. ⁷ |
| | Anne | It is a quarrell just and reasonable, |
| 150 | | To be reveng'd on him that kill'd my Husband. |
| | Richard | He that bereft the ⁸ Lady of thy Husband, |
| | | Did it to helpe thee to a better Husband. |
| | Anne | His better doth not breath upon the earth. |
| | Richard | He lives, that loves thee better then he could. |
| 155 | Anne | Name him. |
| | Richard | Plantagenet. |
| | Anne | Why that was he. |
| | Richard | The selfesame name, but one of better Nature. |
| | Anne | Where is he? |

R 175 - b : 1. 2. 121 - 144

ʷ₁ Qq/most modern texts = 'rend', Ff = 'rent'

ᴬᴮ₂ F1-2 = 'ÿ', (printed as such because of lack of column width), F3/most modern texts = 'that'

ᴬᴮ₃ F1-2 = 'ÿ beauties', F3/most modern texts = 'that beauty's', Qq/one modern text = 'sweet beauties'

ʷ₄ Ff/Q3-6/most modern texts set variations of 'Sunne', Q1-2/at least one modern text = 'sonne'

ˢᴾ₅ since Richard is about to embark upon the startling move of wooing Lady Anne directly, Ff's two short lines(7/3 syllables), may suggest he is carefully preparing himself and his argument for this next enormous step: most modern texts follow Qq and set the two lines as one

ʷ₆ F1 = 'l oveth', F2/most modern texts = 'loveth'

ʷ₇ Ff/some modern texts = 'thee', Qq/some modern texts = 'you'

ʷ₈ Qq/F4/most modern texts = 'thee', F1-3= 'the'

12

| 160 | **Richard** | Heere: |
|---|---|---|

**[Spits at him]**

Why dost thou spit at me. [1]

| | **Anne** | Would it were mortall poyson, for thy sake. |
|---|---|---|
| | **Richard** | Never came poyson from so sweet a place. |
| | **Anne** | Never hung poyson on a fowler Toade. |
| 165 | | Out of my sight, thou dost infect mine eyes. |
| | **Richard** | Thine eyes (sweet Lady) have infected mine. |
| | **Anne** | Would they were Basiliskes, to strike thee dead. |
| | **Richard** | I would they were, that I might dye at once: |
| | | For now they kill me with a living death. |
| 170 | | Those eyes of thine, from mine have drawne salt Teares;  R 175 - b |
| | | Sham'd their Aspects with store of childish drops: |

> [2] These eyes, which never shed remorsefull teare,
> No, when my Father Yorke, and Edward wept,
> To heare the pittious moane that Rutland made
> When black-fac'd Clifford shooke his sword at him.
>
> Nor when thy warlike Father like a Childe,
> Told the sad storie of my Fathers death,
> And twenty times, made pause to sob and weepe:
> That all the standers by had wet their cheekes
> Like Trees bedash'd with raine.
>              In that sad time,
> My manly eyes did scorne an humble teare:
> And what these sorrowes could not thence exhale,
> Thy Beauty hath, and made them blinde with weeping.

| 175 | | |
|---|---|---|
| 180 | | |

I never sued to Friend, nor Enemy:
My Tongue could never learne sweet smoothing word.

But now thy Beauty is propos'd my Fee,
My proud heart sues, and prompts my tongue to speake.

**[She lookes scornfully at him]**

Teach not thy lip such Scorne; for it was made
For kissing Lady, not for such contempt.

---

PCT 1

  Qq/F1-2 set a period, suggesting Richard's question is non-demanding: F3/most modern texts set a question
mark

LS 2

  most modern texts set the following Ff only (bracketed) passage, though at least one modern text omits it

If thy revengefull heart cannot forgive,
Loe heere I lend thee this sharpe-pointed Sword,
Which if thou please to hide in this true brest,
And let the Soule forth that adoreth thee,
195    I lay it naked to the ¹ deadly stroke,
And humbly begge the death upon my knee,²

**[He layes his brest open, she offers at with his sword]** ³

Nay do not pause : For I did kill King Henrie,
But 'twas thy Beauty that provoked me.
Nay now dispatch : 'Twas I that stabb'd yong Edward,
200    But 'twas thy Heavenly face that set me on.

**[She fals the Sword]**

Take up the Sword againe, or take up me.

Anne       Arise Dissembler,⁴ though I wish thy death,
I will not be thy Executioner.

Richard    Then bid me kill my selfe, and I will do it.

205  Anne      ⁵ I have already.

Richard    That was in thy rage :
Speake it againe, and even with the word,
This hand, which for thy love, did kill thy Love,
Shall for thy love, kill a farre truer Love,
210      To both their deaths shalt thou be accessary.

Anne       I would I knew thy heart.

Richard    'Tis figur'd in my tongue.

Anne       I feare me, both are false.

Richard    Then never Man was ⁶ true.

215  Anne      Well, well, put up your Sword.

Richard    Say then my Peace is made.

---

▼₁ Q1-5/Ff/most modern texts = 'the', Q6 = 'thy'

ᴾᶜᵀ₂ F1 sets a comma, perhaps suggesting the action flows on from the statement: Q1/F2/most modern texts set a period

ˢᴰ₃ most modern texts suggest Richard kneels

ˢᴰ₄ of those texts suggesting Richard has knelt, most of them now suggest he rises

ᴸˢ₅ this marks the first of six pairs of short lines within the next seventeen F1 lines: some modern texts set them separately, as F1, allowing tiny hesitations within the debate, others combine them as six fast-paced single lines

▼₆ Q1-2/most modern texts = 'was man', Q3-6/Ff = 'Man was'

14

| | | |
|---|---|---|
| | **Anne** | That shalt thou know heereafter. |
| | **Richard** | But shall I live in hope. |
| | **Anne** | All men I hope live so. |
| 220 | | [1] Vouchsafe to weare this Ring. |
| | **Richard** | Looke how my Ring incompasseth thy Finger, |
| | | Even so thy Brest incloseth my poore heart : |
| | | Weare both of them, for both of them are thine. |
| | | And if thy poore devoted Servant may |
| 225 | | But beg one favour at thy gracious hand, |
| | | Thou dost confirme his happinesse for ever. |
| | **Anne** | What is it? |
| | **Richard** | That it may please you leave these sad designes, |
| | | To him that hath most [2] cause to be a Mourner, |
| 230 | | And presently repayre to Crosbie House : [3] |
| | | Where (after I have solemnly interr'd |
| | | At Chertsey Monast'ry this Noble King, |
| | | And wet his Grave with my Repentant Teares) |
| | | I will with all expedient duty see you, |
| 235 | | For divers unknowne Reasons, I beseech you, |
| | | Grant me this Boon. |
| | **Anne** | With all my heart, and much it joyes me too, |
| | | To see you are become so penitent. |
| | | Tressel and Barkley, go along with me. |
| 240 | **Richard** | Bid me farwell. |
| | **Anne** | 'Tis more then you deserve : |
| | | But since you teach me how to flatter you, |
| | | Imagine I have saide farewell already. |

L 176 - b

**[Exit two with Anne]**

∞ [4]

| | | |
|---|---|---|
| | **Gentleman** | Towards Chertsey, Noble Lord? |
| 245 | **Richard** | No :  to White Friars, [5] there attend my comming [6] |

---

L 176 - b / R 176 - b  :  1. 2. 198 - 226

P/ADD [1] most modern texts follow Qq and assign this line to Richard, and add one for Anne, viz. 'To take is not to give.'

W [2] Ff/most modern texts = 'most', Qq = 'more'

N/W [3] Ff = 'House', Qq = 'place', from which most modern texts set 'Place'

ADD / P [4] most modern texts add the following Qq line to Richard, 'Sirs take up the corse.', they also set the reply for a Servant (the prefix being 'Ser.'), not Ff's Gentleman

F [5] *Holinshed* states the body was taken to Blackfriars: nevertheless, most modern texts set Qq/Ff's 'White Friars'

PCT [6] F1-2 set no punctuation, as if the action flows on: Q1/F3/most modern texts set a period

**[Exit Coarse]** [1]

Was ever woman in this humour woo'd?

Was ever woman in this humour wonne?

Ile have her, but I will not keepe her long.

What?

250            I that kill'd her Husband, and his Father,
To take her in her hearts extreamest hate,
With curses in her mouth, Teares in her eyes,
The bleeding witnesse of my hatred by,
Having God, her Conscience, and these bars against me,
255     And I, no Friends to backe my suite withall,
But the plaine Divell, and dissembling lookes?

And yet to winne her?
                                        All the world to nothing.

Hah! [2]

260     Hath she forgot alreadie that brave Prince,
Edward, her Lord, whom I (some three monthes since)
Stab'd in my angry mood, at Tewkesbury?

A sweeter, and a lovelier Gentleman,
Fram'd in the prodigallity of Nature: [3]
265     Yong, Valiant, Wise, and (no doubt) right Royal,
The spacious World cannot againe affoord: [4]
And will she yet abase [5] her eyes on me,
That cropt the Golden prime of this sweet Prince,
And made her Widdow to a wofull Bed?

270     On me, whose All not equals Edwards Moytie?

On me, that halts, and am mishapen thus?

My Dukedome, to a Beggerly denier!

I do mistake my person all this while:
Upon my life she findes (although I cannot)
275     My selfe to be a marv'llous proper man.

---

SD [1] most modern texts add the Halberdiers and any remaining Gentlemen to the exit

LS [2] some modern texts follow Qq and add 'Ha!' to the end of the previous line, others follow Ff and set it as a one word, separate line

PCT [3] Q1/F1-3 set a rhetorical colon, highlighting the moment where Richard is about to list the virtues of Lady Anne's late husband: F4/most modern texts set a comma

PCT [4] again Q1/F1-2 set a rhetorical colon, this time highlighting Richard's understanding of Anne's apparent readiness to consider his proposal: F3/most modern texts set a comma

W [5] Qq/most modern texts = 'debase', Ff = 'abase'

Ile be at Charges for a Looking-glasse,
And entertaine a score or two of Taylors,
To study fashions to adorne my body:
Since I am crept in favour with my selfe,
I will maintaine it with some little cost.

But first Ile turne yon Fellow in his Grave,
And then returne lamenting to my Love.

Shine out faire Sunne, till I have bought a glasse,
That I may see my Shadow as I passe.

**[exit]**

# Scena Tertia

**ENTER THE QUEENE MOTHER,**[1] **LORD RIVERS, AND LORD GRAY**

| | | |
|---|---|---|
| Rivers | Have patience Madam, ther's no doubt his Majesty<br>Will soone recover his accustom'd health. | |
| Gray | In that you brooke it ill, it makes him worse,<br>Therefore for Gods sake entertaine good comfort,<br>And cheere his Grace with quicke and merry eyes | |
| Queene | If he were dead, what would betide on me? | R 176 - b |
| | [2] If he were dead, what would betide on me? | |
| Gray [3] | No other harme, but losse of such a Lord. | |
| Queene | The losse of such a Lord, includes all harmes. | |
| Gray | The Heavens have blest you with a goodly Son,<br>To be your Comforter, when he is gone. | |
| Queene | Ah! he is yong; and his minority<br>Is put unto the trust of Richard Glouster,<br>A man that loves not me, nor none of you. | |
| Rivers | Is it concluded he shall be Protector? | |
| Queene | It is determin'd, not concluded yet:<br>But so it must be, if the King miscarry. | |

(Line numbers in left margin: 5, 10, 15)

**ENTER BUCKINGHAM AND DERBY** [4]

---

R 176 - b / L 177 - b : 1. 3. 1 - 16

SD [1]
 as most commentators correctly point out, from the ensuing dialogue this is in fact Elizabeth, the Queene, not the Queene Mother: most modern texts, following Qq rephrase the direction accordingly: also, since Dorset is one of those listed and cursed by Margaret later in the scene, and Qq/Ff do not set him an entry, most modern texts have him enter now: also see footnote #5 re. Hastings, page 19

COMP/LS [2]
 commentators argue that F1's Compositor B's carelessness was the reason for exactly the same line being set at the bottom of page 176 and the top of page 177: Qq/F2-4/most modern texts cut the repetition

P [3]
 Qq/some modern texts assign this line to Rivers, Ff/other modern texts to Gray

N/P [4]
 despite Gray's subsequent line, there are two separate characters, Buckingham the first, Darby the second: historically, but after the time-span of the play is completed, this latter character will be known both as Stanley and the Earl of Derby: unfortunately, throughout the play the character is referred to as one or the other, rarely by both names at the same time: subsequent changes in name will be shown alongside the prefix, without further explanatory footnotes; readers should also note within text and stage directions the name is spelled both 'Darby' and 'Derby' - again, this is the only time the discrepancy will be footnoted

| Gray | Here comes the Lord [1] of Buckingham & Derby. |
|---|---|
| **Buckingham** | Good time of day unto your Royall Grace. |

20 **Derby**     God make your Majesty joyfull, as you have bin [2]

**Queene**     The Countesse Richmond, good my L. of Derby.
To your good prayer, will scarsely say, Amen.
Yet Derby, notwithstanding shee's your wife,
And loves not me, be you good Lord assur'd,
25 I hate not you for her proud arrogance.

**Derby**     I do beseech you, either not beleeve
The envious slanders of her false Accusers:
Or if she be accus'd on true report,
Beare with her weaknesse, which I thinke proceeds,
30 From wayward sicknesse, and no grounded malice.

**Queene** [3]     Saw you the King to day my Lord of Derby.

**Derby**     But now the Duke of Buckingham and I,
Are come from visiting his Majesty.

**Queene**     What [4] likelyhood of his amendment Lords.

35 **Buckingham**     Madam good hope, his Grace speaks chearfully.

**Queene**     God grant him health, did you confer with him?

**Buckingham**     I Madam, he desires to make attonement
Betweene the Duke of Glouster, and your Brothers,
And betweene them, and my Lord Chamberlaine,
40 And sent to warne them to his Royall presence.

**Queene**     Would all were well, but that will never be,
I feare our happinesse is at the height.

**ENTER RICHARD** [5]

**Richard**     They do me wrong, and I will not indure it,
Who is it that [6] complaines unto the King,

[1] Q1-2/most modern texts = 'come the Lords', F1 = 'comes the Lord'

[2] F1 sets no punctuation, as if the Queene interrupts him: Qq/F2/most modern texts set a period

[3] Ff/some modern texts assign this line to the Queene, others follow Qq and give it to Rivers; for further details see *The Arden Shakespeare King Richard III*, op. cit., page 153, footnote to line 30

[4] Ff/most modern texts = 'What', Q1-2/at least one modern text = 'With'

[5] later in the scene Margaret names and individually curses all her enemies, including Hastings for whom Qq/Ff set no entrance: most modern texts suggest he now enters with Richard

[6] Ff/most modern texts = 'is it', Qq/one modern text = 'are they', with the most modern texts setting 'complain' for Qq/Ff's 'complaines'

45                   That[†1] I (forsooth) am sterne, and love them not?

                  By holy Paul, they love his Grace but lightly,
                  That fill his eares with such dissentious Rumors.

                  Because I cannot flatter, and looke [2] faire,
                  Smile in mens faces, smooth, deceive, and cogge,
50                   Ducke with French nods, and Apish curtesie,
                  I must be held a rancorous Enemy.

                  Cannot a plaine man live, and thinke no harme,
                  But thus his simple truth must be abus'd,
                  With silken, slye, insinuating Jackes?

55    **Grey** [3]       To who [4] in all this presence speaks your Grace?

     **Richard**     To thee, that hast nor Honesty, nor Grace :
                  When have I injur'd thee?
                                 When done thee wrong?

                  Or thee? or thee? or any of your Faction?
60                   A plague upon you all.
                           His Royall Grace
                  (Whom God preserve better then you would wish)
                  Cannot be quiet scarse a breathing while,
                  But you must trouble him with lewd complaints.

65    **Queene**     Brother of Glouster, you mistake the matter :
                  The King on his owne Royall disposition,
                  (And not provok'd by any Sutor else)
                  Ayming (belike) at your interiour hatred,               L 177 - b
                  That in your outward action shewes it selfe
70                   Against my Children, Brothers, and my Selfe,
                  Makes him to send, that he may learne the ground.
                       ∞ [5]

     **Richard**     I cannot tell, the world is growne so bad,
                  That Wrens make prey, where Eagles dare not pearch.

                  Since everie Jacke[†6] became a Gentleman,
75                   There's many a gentle person made a Jacke.

---

[W1]   F1 = 'Thar', F2/most modern texts = 'That'

[W2]   Ff/most modern texts = 'looke', Qq = 'speake'

[P3]   Ff/most modern texts set the speech for Grey, Qq/some modern texts for Rivers

[W4]   Ff/most modern texts = 'who', Q1-5/one modern text = 'whom'

[ADD5]   most modern texts finish the speech with the Qq only line 'The ground of your ill will and remove it.'

[W6]   F1 = 'Jaeke', F2/Qq/most modern texts = 'Jacke'

| | |
|---|---|
| **Queene** | Come, come, we know your meaning Brother Gloster [†1] |
| | You envy my advancement, and my friends : |
| | God grant we never may have neede of you. |
| | |
| **Richard** | Meane time, God grants that I [2] have need of you. |
| 80 | Our Brother is imprison'd by your meanes, |
| | My selfe disgrac'd, and the Nobilitie |
| | Held in contempt, while great Promotions |
| | Are daily given to ennoble those |
| | That scarse some two dayes since were worth a Noble. |
| | |
| 85 **Queene** | By him that rais'd me to this carefull height, |
| | From that contented hap which I injoy'd, |
| | I never did incense his Majestie |
| | Against the Duke of Clarence, but have bin |
| | An earnest advocate to plead for him. |
| | |
| 90 | My Lord you do me shamefull injurie, |
| | Falsely to draw me in these vile suspects. |
| | |
| **Richard** | You may deny that you were not the meane |
| | Of my Lord Hastings late imprisonment. |
| | |
| **Rivers** | She may my Lord, for _____ |
| | |
| 95 **Richard** | She may Lord Rivers, why who knowes not so? |
| | She may do more sir then denying that : |
| | She may helpe you to many faire preferments, |
| | And then deny her ayding hand therein, |
| | And lay those Honors on your high desert. |
| 100 | What may she not, she may, I marry may she. |
| | |
| **Rivers** | What marry may she? |
| | |
| **Richard** | What marrie may she? |
| | Marrie with a King, |
| | A Batcheller, and a handsome stripling too, |
| 105 | I wis your Grandam had a worser match. |
| | |
| **Queene** | My Lord of Glouster, I have too long borne |
| | Your blunt upbraidings, and your bitter scoffes : |
| | By heaven, I will acquaint his Majestie |
| | Of those grosse taunts that oft I have endur'd. |

R 177 - b : 1. 3. 73 - 105

[PCT 1] F1 sets no punctuation, as if the Queene slips ungrammatically into elaborating her point: arguing lack of column width, most modern texts follow Qq and set a period: F2 sets a comma

[W 2] Qq/most modern texts = 'we', Ff = 'I'

110                I had rather be a Countrie servant maide
Then a great Queene, with this condition,
To be so baited, scorn'd, and stormed at,
Small joy have I in being Englands Queene.

**ENTER OLD QUEENE MARGARET** [1]

**Margaret**       And lesned be that small, God I beseech him,
115                Thy honor, state, and seate, is due to me.

**Richard**        What? threat you me with telling of the King?
                          $\infty$ [2]
I will avouch't in presence of the King:
I dare adventure to be sent to th'Towre.

'Tis time to speake,$\rightarrow$ [3]
120                My paines are quite forgot.

**Margaret**       Out Divell,$\rightarrow$
I do [4] remember them too well:
Thou killd'st my Husband Henrie in the Tower,
And Edward my poore son, at Tewkesburie.

125   **Richard**        Ere you were Queene,$\rightarrow$
I, or your Husband King:
I was a packe-horse in his great affaires:
A weeder out of his proud Adversaries,
A liberall rewarder of his Friends,
130                To royalize his blood, I spent mine owne. †[5]

**Margaret**       I and much better blood$\rightarrow$
Then his, or thine.                                R 177 - b

**Richard**        In all which time, you and your Husband Grey
Were factious, for the House of Lancaster;
135                And Rivers, so were you: Was not your Husband,
In Margarets Battaile, at Saint Albons, slaine?

---

**R 177 - b / L 178 - a : 1. 3. 106 - 129**

SD/A₁  most modern texts advance the entry to the beginning of the previous sentence, some adding that Margaret enters 'behind', Qq advances the entry one line: also, most modern texts suggest all her lines until she makes her presence known to (presumably) unaware squabbling royalty, line 167, next page, are spoken as asides

ASS/Q₂  most modern texts add the following Qq only line, 'Tell him and spare not, looke what I have said,', though, unlike Qq, which drop the next line but one, they maintain the rest of the speech

SP/WS₃  this is the first of four pairs of Ff only short lines (4/6; 3/11; 4/6; and 8/4 syllables), all set within the last fourteen lines at the bottom of page 177: arguing white space, most modern texts follow Qq and set them as four single lines: if any of the four Ff pairs were to be left as is, they might suggest the speaker taking care to maintain self-control despite the heat of the debate

W₄  Ff = 'do', most modern texts follow Qq and do not set the word

W₅  F1 = 'owue', F2/most modern texts = 'owne'

<table>
<tbody>
<tr><td></td><td></td><td>Let me put in your mindes, if you forget<br>What you have beene ere this, and what you are:<br>Withall, what I have beene, and what I am.</td></tr>
<tr><td>140</td><td>Margaret as<br>•**Queene Margaret** •[1]</td><td>A murth'rous Villaine, and so still thou art.</td></tr>
<tr><td></td><td>**Richard**</td><td>Poore Clarence did forsake his Father Warwicke,<br>I, and forswore himselfe (which Jesu pardon.)</td></tr>
<tr><td></td><td>**Queene Margaret**</td><td>Which God revenge.</td></tr>
<tr><td>145</td><td>**Richard**</td><td>To fight on Edwards partie, for the Crowne,<br>And for his meede, poore Lord, he is mewed up:<br>I would to God my heart were Flint, like Edwards,<br>Or Edwards soft and pittifull, like mine;<br>I am too childish foolish for this World.</td></tr>
<tr><td>150</td><td>**Queene Margaret**</td><td>High thee to Hell for shame, & leave this World<br>Thou Cacodemon, there thy Kingdome is.</td></tr>
<tr><td></td><td>**Rivers**</td><td>My Lord of Gloster: in those busie dayes,<br>Which here you urge, to prove us Enemies,<br>We follow'd then our Lord, our Soveraigne King,<br>So should we you, if you should be our King.</td></tr>
<tr><td>155</td><td>**Richard**</td><td>If I should be?<br>      I had rather be a Pedler:<br>Farre be it from my heart, the thought thereof.</td></tr>
<tr><td>160</td><td>**Queene**</td><td>As little joy (my Lord) as you suppose<br>You should enjoy, were you this Countries King,<br>As little joy you may suppose in me,<br>That I enjoy, being the Queene thereof.</td></tr>
<tr><td></td><td>**Queene Margaret**</td><td>A [2] little joy enjoyes the Queene thereof,<br>For I am shee, and altogether joylesse:<br>I can no longer hold me patient.</td></tr>
<tr><td>165</td><td>[3]</td><td>Heare me, you wrangling Pyrates, that fall out,<br>In sharing that which you have pill'd from me:<br>Which off [4] you trembles not, that lookes on me?</td></tr>
<tr><td></td><td></td><td>If not, that I am Queene, you bow like Subjects;<br>Yet that by you depos'd, you quake like Rebells.</td></tr>
<tr><td>170</td><td></td><td>Ah gentle Villaine, doe not turne away.</td></tr>
</tbody>
</table>

---

P[1] when 'Queene' is added to Margaret's prefix, it is always in conjunction with her given name: 'Queene' used on its own always refers to Elizabeth

W[2] Ff/Qq = 'A', one modern text sets 'Ay', while one gloss = 'And'

SD[3] most modern texts indicate that Margaret now makes her presence known, usually by coming forward

W[4] Qq/F2-4/most modern texts = 'of', F1 = 'off'

| | |
|---|---|
| **Richard** | Foule wrinckled Witch, what mak'st thou in my sight? [†] |
| **Queene Margaret** | But repetition of what thou hast marr'd,<br>That will I make, before I let thee goe. |

| | |
|---|---|
| **Richard** | [1] Wert thou not banished, on paine of death? |
| 175    **Queene Margaret** | I was : but I doe find more paine in banishment,<br>Then death can yeeld me here, by my abode. |

A Husband and a Sonne thou ow'st to me,
And thou a Kingdome ; all of you, allegeance :
This Sorrow that I have, by right is yours,
180    And all the Pleasures you usurpe, are mine.

**Richard**    The Curse my Noble Father layd on thee,
When thou didst Crown his Warlike Brows with Paper,
And with thy scornes drew'st Rivers from his eyes,
And then to dry them, gav'st the Duke a Clowt,
185    Steep'd in the faultlesse blood of prettie Rutland :
His Curses then, from bitternesse of Soule,
Denounc'd against thee, are all falne upon thee :
And God, not we, hath plagu'd thy bloody deed.

**Queene**    So just is God, to right the innocent.

190    **Hastings**    O, 'twas the foulest deed to slay that Babe,
And the most mercilesse, that ere [2] was heard of.

**Rivers**    Tyrants themselves wept when it was reported.

**Dorset**    No man but prophecied revenge for it.

**Buckingham**    Northumberland, then present, wept to see it.

195    **Queene Margaret**    What? were you snarling all before I came,
Ready to catch each other by the throat,
And turne you all your hatred now on me?

Did Yorkes dread Curse prevaile so much with Heaven,
That Henries death, my lovely Edwards death,      L 178 - a
200    Their Kingdomes losse, my wofull Banishment,
Should all but answer for that peevish Brat?

Can Curses pierce the Clouds, and enter Heaven?
Why then give way dull Clouds to my quick Curses.

Though not by Warre, by Surfet dye your King,
205    As ours by Murther, to make him a King.

---

L 178 - a / R 178 - a :   1. 3. 163 - 197

LS/OM [1]   while most modern texts set this Ff only sequence, at least one current modern text omits it

W [2]   Ff/most modern texts set an eleven syllable line including 'ere', Qq/at least one modern text = 'ever'

[1] Edward thy Sonne, that now is Prince of Wales,
For Edward our [2] Sonne, that was Prince of Wales,
Dye in his youth, by like untimely violence.

Thy selfe a Queene, for me that was a Queene,
210        Out-live thy glory, like my wretched selfe :
Long may'st thou live, to wayle thy Childrens death,
And see another, as I see thee now,
Deck'd in thy Rights, as thou art stall'd in mine.

Long dye thy happie dayes, before thy death,
215        And after many length'ned howres of griefe,
Dye neyther Mother, Wife, nor Englands Queene.

Rivers and Dorset, you were standers by,
And so wast thou, Lord Hastings, when my Sonne
Was stab'd with bloody Daggers : God, I pray him,
220        That none of you may live his naturall age,
But by some unlook'd accident cut off.

**Richard**        Have done thy Charme, ÿ [3] hateful wither'd Hagge.

**Queene Margaret**  And leave out thee? stay Dog, for ÿ shalt heare me.

If Heaven have any grievous plague in store,
225        Exceeding those that I can wish upon thee,
O let them keepe it, till thy sinnes be ripe,
And then hurle downe their indignation
On thee, the troubler of the poore Worlds peace.

The Worme of Conscience still begnaw thy Soule,
230        Thy Friends suspect for Traytors while thou liv'st, [4]
And take deepe Traytors for thy dearest Friends :
No sleepe close up that deadly Eye of thine,
Unlesse it be while some tormenting Dreame
Affrights thee with a Hell of ougly Devills.

235        Thou elvish mark'd, abortive rooting Hogge,
Thou that wast seal'd in thy Nativitie
The slave of Nature, and the Sonne of Hell :
Thou slander of thy heavie Mothers Wombe,
Thou loathed Issue of thy Fathers Loynes,
240        Thou Ragge of Honor, thou detested --

**Richard**        Margaret.

---

R 178 - a : 1. 3. 198 - 233

WHO [1] some modern texts suggest the next three sentences are spoken to the Queene

W [2] Qq/most modern texts = 'my', Ff = 'our'

AB [3] in this and the following line F1-2 = 'ÿ', (printed as such because of lack of column width), F3/most modern texts = 'thou'

W [4] Ff/most modern texts = 'liv'st'; at least one usually metrically minded modern text sets Qq's 'livest', even though this creates an eleven syllable line

| | | | |
|---|---|---|---|
| **Queene Margaret** | Richard. | **Richard** | Ha. |

**Queene Margaret** I call thee not.

**Richard** I cry thee mercie then : for I did thinke,
245 That thou hadst call'd me all these bitter names.

**Queene Margaret** Why so I did, but look'd for no reply,[1]
Oh let me make the Period to my Curse.

**Richard** 'Tis done by me, and ends in Margaret.

**Queene** Thus have you breath'd your Curse against your self.

250 **Queene Margaret** Poore painted Queen, vain flourish of my fortune,
Why strew'st thou Sugar on that Bottel'd Spider,
Whose deadly Web ensnareth thee about?

Foole, foole, thou whet'st a Knife to kill thy selfe :
The day will come, that thou shalt wish for me,
255 To helpe thee curse this poysonous Bunch-backt Toade.

**Hastings** False boding Woman, end thy frantick Curse,
Least to thy harme, thou move our patience.

**Queene Margaret** Foule shame upon you, you have all mov'd mine.

**Richard** Were you wel serv'd, you would be taught your duty.

260 **Queene Margaret** To serve me well, you all should do me duty,
Teach me to be your Queene, and you my Subjects :
O serve me well, and teach your selves that duty.

**Dorset** Dispute not with her, shee is lunaticke.

**Queene Margaret** Peace Master Marquesse, you are malapert,
265 Your fire-new stampe of Honor is scarce currant.     R 178 - a

O that your yong Nobility could judge
What 'twere to lose it, and be miserable.

They that stand high, have many blasts to shake them,
And if they fall, they dash themselves to peeces.

270 **Richard** Good counsaile marry, learne it, learne it Marquesse.

**Dorset** It touches you my Lord, as much as me.

**Richard** I, and much more : but I was borne so high :
Our ayerie buildeth in the Cedars top,
275 And dallies with the winde, and scornes the Sunne.

---

PCT 1
    F1 sets a blur which could be either a comma or a period: Qq set a comma, F2/most modern texts a period

| •Margaret• | And turnes the Sun to shade: alas, alas, |
| | Witnesse my Sonne, now in the shade of death, |
| | Whose bright out-shining beames, thy cloudy wrath |
| | Hath in eternall darknesse folded up. |
| 280 | Your ayery buildeth in our ayeries Nest: |
| | O God that seest it, do not suffer it, |
| | As it is [1] wonne with blood, lost be it so. |
| Buckingham [2] | Peace, peace for shame: If not, for Charity. |
| Margaret | Urge neither charity, nor shame to me: |
| 285 | Uncharitably with me have you dealt, |
| | And shamefully my hopes (by you) are butcher'd. |
| | My Charity is outrage, Life my shame, |
| | And in that shame, still live my sorrowes rage. |
| Buckingham | Have done, have done. |
| 290   Margaret | O Princely Buckingham, Ile kisse thy hand, |
| | In signe of League and amity with thee: |
| | Now faire befall thee, and thy Noble house: |
| | Thy Garments are not spotted with our blood: |
| | Nor thou within the compasse of my curse. |
| 295   Buckingham | Nor no one heere: for Curses never passe |
| | The lips of those that breath them in the ayre. |
| Margaret | I will not thinke but they ascend the sky, |
| | And there awake Gods gentle sleeping peace. |
| | O Buckingham, take heed of yonder dogge: |
| 300 | Looke when he fawnes, he bites; and when he bites, |
| | His venom tooth will rankle to the [3] death. |
| | Have not [4] to do with him, beware of him, |
| | Sinne, death, and hell have set their markes on him, |
| | And all their Ministers attend on him. |
| 305   Richard | What doth she say, my Lord of Buckingham. |

---

[1] Ff/most modern texts = 'is', Qq/one modern text = 'was'

[2] Ff/Qq assign this line to Buckingham: some commentators and at least one modern text give it to Richard: for more details see *The Arden Shakespeare King Richard III*, op. cit., page 166, footnote to line 173: those arguing against its conclusion (that the line should stay with Buckingham) suggest the 'charity' argument is one of Richard's favourite ploys

[3] Ff/Q2-5/most modern texts = 'rankle', Q1/one modern text set the intriguing 'rackle': also, Ff/most modern texts = 'to the', Qq = 'thee to'

[4] Qq/Ff/most modern texts = 'not', one modern gloss = 'naught'

| | |
|---|---|
| **Buckingham** | Nothing that I respect my gracious Lord. |
| **Margaret** | What dost thou scorne me→ [1]<br>For my gentle counsell?<br>And sooth the divell that I warne thee from. |
| 310 | O but remember this another day:<br>When he shall split thy very heart with sorrow:<br>And say (poore Margaret) was a Prophetesse:<br>Live each of you the subjects to his hate,<br>And he to yours, and all of you to Gods. |

**[Exit]**

| | |
|---|---|
| 315 | **Buckingham** [2] My haire doth stand an [3] end to heare her curses. |
| | **Rivers** And so doth mine, I muse why she's at libertie. |
| | **Richard** I cannot blame her, by Gods holy mother,<br>She hath had too much wrong, and I repent<br>My part thereof, that I have done to her. [4] |
| 320 | **{Margaret}** [5] I never did her any to my knowledge. |
| | **Richard** Yet you have all the vantage of her wrong:<br>I was too hot, to do somebody good,<br>That is too cold in thinking of it now:<br>Marry as for Clarence, he is well repayed: |
| 325 | He is frank'd up to fatting for his paines,<br>God pardon them, that are the cause thereof. |
| | **Rivers** A vertuous, and a Christian-like conclusion [6]<br>To pray for them that have done scath to us. |
| | **Richard** So do I ever, being well advis'd. |

**[Speakes to himselfe]** [7]

| | | |
|---|---|---|
| 330 | For had I curst now, I had curst my selfe. | L 179 - b |

---

L 179 - b  / 1. 3. 295 - 318

SP [1]  Ff set two short lines (5/6 syllables) whose pauses could serve to underscore Margaret's amazement that her warnings should be so ignored: most modern texts follow Qq and join the two lines together

P [2]  Qq/some modern texts assign the speech to Hastings, Ff/other modern texts give it to Buckingham

W [3]  Qq/most modern texts = 'on', Ff = 'an'

W [4]  though Qq omit the last two words, most modern texts follow Ff and set them as is

P [5]  Q1-5/most modern texts assign this speech to the Queene, Q6 to Hastings, F1-2 (incorrectly) to Margaret, F3 - 4 to Dorset

PCT [6]  F1 sets no punctuation, allowing Rivers to plunge on: Qq/F2/most modern texts set a more moderate comma

SD / A [7]  this is one of the most unusual stage directions in the whole of Ff: very rarely are any Ff directions set explaining who is speaking to whom, let alone indicating an aside, as here

**ENTER CATESBY**

| | |
|---|---|
| **Catesby** | Madam, his Majesty doth call for you, |
| | And for your Grace, and yours my gracious Lord. [1] |
| **Queene** | Catesby I come, Lords will you go with mee. |
| **Rivers** | We wait upon your Grace. |

**[Exeunt all but Gloster]**

335 **Richard**  I do the wrong, and first begin to brawle.

The secret Mischeefes that I set abroach,
I lay unto the greevous charge of others.

Clarence, who [2] I indeede have cast in darknesse,
I do beweepe to many simple Gulles,
340 Namely to Derby, Hastings, Buckingham,
And tell them 'tis the Queene, and her Allies,
That stirre the King against the Duke my Brother.

Now they beleeve it, and withall whet me
To be reveng'd on Rivers, Dorset, Grey.

345 But then I sigh, and with a peece of Scripture,
Tell them that God bids us do good for evill :
And thus I cloath my naked Villainie
With odde old ends, stolne forth of holy Writ,
And seeme a Saint, when most I play the devill.

**ENTER TWO MURTHERERS** [3]

350 But soft, heere come my Executioners,
How now my hardy stout resolved Mates,
Are you now going to dispatch this thing?

**Villaine{s}**  We are my Lord, and come to have the Warrant,
That we may be admitted where he is.

355 **Richard**  Well thought upon, I have it heare about me :

---

[W1] Q1-2 = 'noble Lo.', Q3-6 = 'noble Lord', Ff = 'gracious Lord': most modern texts set the gloss 'gracious lords'

[W2] Qq/most modern texts = 'whom', Ff = 'who'

[P/SD3] Qq direct an unspecified number of 'Executioners' to enter, and set the prefix 'Execu.' and 'Exec' - though in the following scene with Clarence the term 'murtherers' is used for the entry, and the numbers 1. and 2. are used as prefixes: Ff direct two 'Murtherers' to enter, but set the prefix 'Vil.', presumably for 'Villaine/s' - a rather nice touch compared to some of the Noble/Gentlemen murderers seen in other plays: also, in this scene Qq/Ff do not indicate which of the two or more characters speak when, though some modern texts take the safe route of assigning the first speech to one 'Murderer', the second to the other, and the final speech to 'both': readers are invited to assign the speeches to whomever as they see fit

When you have done, repayre to Crosby place;
But sirs be sodaine in the execution,
Withall obdurate, do not heare him pleade;
For Clarence is well spoken, and perhappes
360                    May move your hearts to pitty, if you marke him.

**Villaine{s}**     Tut, tut, my Lord, we will not stand to prate,
Talkers are no good dooers, be assur'd:
We go to use our hands, and not our tongues.

**Richard**       Your eyes drop Mill-stones, when Fooles eyes
365                fall Teares:
I like you Lads, about your businesse straight.

Go, go, dispatch.

**Villaine{s}**     We will my Noble Lord. [1]

R 179 - b  :  1. 3. 344 - 354

SD 1 most modern texts follow Qq and set an 'Exeunt' for all: Ff set no direction

# Scena Quarta

### ENTER CLARENCE AND KEEPER [1]

**Keeper**      Why lookes your Grace so heavily to day.

**Clarence**    O, I have past a miserable night,
So full of fearefull Dreames, of ugly sights,
That as I am a Christian faithfull man,
I would not spend another such a night
Though 'twere to buy a world of happy daies:
So full of dismall terror was the time.

**Keeper**      What was your dream my Lord, I pray you tel me [2]

**Clarence**    Me thoughts that I had broken from the Tower,
And was embark'd to crosse to Burgundy,
And in my company my Brother Glouster,
Who from my Cabin tempted me to walke,
Upon the Hatches:   There [3] we look'd toward England,
And cited up a thousand heavy times,
During the warres of Yorke and Lancaster
That had befalne us.
                        As we pac'd along
Upon the giddy footing of the Hatches,
Me thought that Glouster stumbled, and in falling
Strooke me (that thought [4] to stay him) over-boord,
Into the tumbling billowes of the maine.

O Lord, me thought what paine it was to drowne,
What dreadfull noise of water [5] in mine eares,
What sights of ugly death within mine eyes.

R 179 - b

---

R 179 - b / L 180 - b  :  1. 4. 1 - 23

SD/N/P 1
       some modern texts follow Ff and have a 'Keeper' accompany Clarence:  Qq/other modern texts name the
PCT 2  character as Brakenbury:  see footnote #5, page 33, and the specific Introduction to this play

W 3   F1 sets no punctuation, as if Clarence interrupts him:  F2/most modern texts set a period

W 4   Qq/most modern texts = 'thence', Ff = 'There'

W 5   Qq/Ff/most modern texts = 'thought', one modern gloss = 'sought'

      Q1-5/most modern texts = 'waters', Ff/Q6 = 'water':  also, Q1/most modern texts = 'my' in this and the next
line, Q2-5/Ff = 'mine'

| | | |
|---|---|---|
| 25 | | Me thoughts, I saw a thousand fearfull wrackes: |
| | | A [1] thousand men that Fishes gnaw'd upon: |
| | | Wedges of Gold, great Anchors, heapes of Pearle, |
| | | Inestimable Stones, unvalewed Jewels, |
| | [2] | All scattred in the bottome of the Sea, |
| 30 | | Some lay in dead-mens Sculles, and in the [3] holes |
| | | Where eyes did once inhabit, there were crept |
| | | (As 'twere in scorne of eyes) reflecting Gemmes, |
| | | That [4] woo'd the slimy bottome of the deepe, |
| | | And mock'd the dead bones that lay scattred by. |
| 35 | **Keeper** | Had you such leysure in the time of death |
| | | To gaze upon these secrets of the deepe? |
| | **Clarence** | Me thought I had, [5] and often did I strive |
| | | To yeeld the Ghost: but still the envious Flood |
| 40 | | Stop'd in my soule, and would not let it forth |
| | | To find the empty, vast, and wand'ring ayre: |
| | | But smother'd it within my panting bulke, |
| | | Who [6] almost burst, to belch it in the Sea. |
| | **Keeper** | Awak'd you not in this sore Agony? |
| | **Clarence** | No, no, my Dreame was lengthen'd after life. |
| 45 | | O then, began the Tempest to my Soule. |
| | | I past (me thought) the Melancholly Flood, |
| | | With that sowre Ferry-man which Poets write of, |
| | | Unto the Kingdome of perpetuall Night. |
| | | The first that there did greet my Stranger-soule, |
| 50 | | Was my great Father-in-Law, renowned Warwicke, |
| | | Who spake [7] alowd: What scourge for Perjurie, |
| | | Can this darke Monarchy affoord false Clarence? |
| | | And so he vanish'd. |
| | | Then came wand'ring by, |
| 55 | | A Shadow like an Angell, with bright hayre |
| | | Dabbel'd in blood, and he shriek'd out alowd |

[W] 1   Qq/most modern texts = 'Ten', Ff = 'A'

[LS] 2   most modern texts set this Ff only line as is

[W] 3   Ff/some modern texts = 'the', Qq/other modern texts = 'those'

[W] 4   Ff/most modern texts = 'That', Qq/one modern text = 'Which'

[LS] 5   most modern texts set the remainder of this Ff line and the first half of the next, even though Qq do not

[W] 6   Qq/most modern texts = 'Which', Ff/one modern text = 'Who'

[W] 7   Ff/most modern texts = 'spake', Qq/one modern text = 'cried'

|     |            |                                                          |
| --- | ---------- | -------------------------------------------------------- |
|     |            | Clarence is come, false, fleeting, perjur'd Clarence,    |
|     |            | That stabb'd me in the field by Tewkesbury:              |
|     |            | Seize on him Furies, take him unto Torment.              |
| 60  |            | With that (me thought) [1] a Legion of foule Fiends      |
|     |            | Inviron'd me, and howled in mine eares                   |
|     |            | Such hiddeous cries, that with the very Noise,           |
|     |            | I (trembling) wak'd, and for a season after,             |
|     |            | Could not beleeve, but that I was in Hell,               |
| 65  |            | Such terrible Impression made my Dreame.                 |
|     | **Keeper** | No marvell Lord, though it affrighted you,               |
|     |            | I am affraid (me thinkes) to heare you tell it.          |
|     | **Clarence** | Ah Keeper, Keeper, [2] I have done these things        |
|     |            | (That now give evidence against my Soule)                |
| 70  |            | For Edwards sake, and see how he requits mee.            |

> O God! if my deepe prayres cannot appease thee,
> But thou wilt be aveng'd on my misdeeds,
> Yet execute thy wrath in me alone:
> O spare my guiltlesse Wife, and my poore children. [3]

|     |            |                                                          |
| --- | ---------- | -------------------------------------------------------- |
| 75  |            | Keeper, I prythee [4] sit by me a-while,                 |
|     |            | My Soule is heavy, and I faine would sleepe.             |
|     | **Keeper** | I will my Lord, God give your Grace good rest.           |

**ENTER BRAKENBURY THE LIEUTENANT** [5]

|     |              |                                                        |             |
| --- | ------------ | ------------------------------------------------------ | ----------- |
|     | **Brakenbury** | Sorrow breakes Seasons, and reposing houres,         |             |
|     |              | Makes the Night Morning, and the Noon-tide night:      | L 180 - b   |
| 80  |              | Princes have but their Titles for their Glories,       |             |
|     |              | An outward Honor, for an inward Toyle,                  |             |
|     |              | And for unfelt Imaginations                            |             |
|     |              | They often feele a world of restlesse Cares:           |             |
|     |              | So that betweene their Titles, and low Name,           |             |
| 85  |              | There's nothing differs, but the outward fame.         |             |

**ENTER TWO MURTHERERS**

---

[W 1] Q1= 'me thoughts', which some modern texts set as 'methoughts'; Q2-5/Ff /some modern texts = 'me thought'

[W 2] most texts following Qq set 'O Brakenbury': Ff/other modern texts = 'Ah Keeper, Keeper'

[LS/OM 3] though most texts set this Ff only passage, at least one modern text omits it

[W 4] Ff set variations of 'prythee/prithee/prethee', some modern texts set 'pray thee' from Q1 (though discarding the rest of the line which differs from Ff): this is a standard pattern throughout the play, and any further occurrences will be marked with an asterisk without footnotes

[SD/OM 5] those modern editions basing their texts on Qq omit this stage direction, and continue the speech for Brakenbury who has been on-stage since the beginning of the scene

| | | |
|---|---|---|
| **1. Murtherer** | [1] | Ho, who's heere? |
| **Brakenbury** | | What would'st thou Fellow? |
| | | And how camm'st thou hither. |
| **2. Murtherer** | | I would speak with Clarence, and I came hi-ther on my Legges. |
| **Brakenbury** | | What so breefe? [2] |

| | |
|---|---|
| **1. Murtherer** | 'Tis better (Sir) then to be tedious: |
| | Let him see our Commission, and talke no more. |

**[Reads]**

95    **Brakenbury**    I am in this, commanded to deliver
The Noble Duke of Clarence to your hands.

I will not reason what is meant heereby,
Because I will be guiltlesse from [3] the meaning.

There lies the Duke asleepe, and there the Keyes.

100       Ile to the King, and signifie to him,
That thus I have resign'd to you my charge.

**[Exit]** [4]

**1. Murtherer**    You may sir, 'tis a point of wisedome: → [5]
Far you well.

**2. Murtherer**    [6] What, shall we [7] stab him as he sleepes.

---

LS [1]    most modern texts set this Ff only line, even though Qq's silent entry, and the replacing of Brakenbury's first Ff line with 'In Gods name what are you', has enormous theatrical impact

VP [2]    as set in Qq/Ff there is the possibility that these lines are in prose, as opposed to the verse of the scene to date: if this is prose, it beautifully counterpoints the next four speeches (up to and including the farewell before the Murtherers are left alone with the sleeping Clarence) which seem to be set as verse: some modern texts remove the contrast by setting the complete sequence in prose (with the exception of Brakenbury reading the commission)

W [3]    Ff/some modern texts = 'from', Qq/some modern texts = 'of'

SD [4]    this exit is for Brakenbury (and the Keeper, for those texts who brought him in at the beginning of the scene)

Q/SP [5]    Qq set a shorter prose line, usually ignored by most modern texts: Ff set two short (presumably verse) lines (9/3 syllables) perhaps suggesting either Brakenbury and the Keeper haven't quite left yet, - hence the need for the second line, or that the Murtherers are calling offstage to keep the mood of (strained?) courtesy alive until they are sure they won't be overheard: most modern texts join the two lines together, usually setting them as prose

VP [6]    since Q1 sets every new line within a single speech with a capital letter, it seems to set the whole passage between the two Murtherers in a form of verse, though the metric scheme is quite irregular throughout: most modern texts set the complete sequence as prose: Ff set a balance of the two, the verse possibly suggesting moments when the men are in a heightened form of awareness, and the prose a sinking back into the commonplace: to avoid a series of extra footnotes this text will set a vertical line to the left of the text where though it seems Ff set verse, most modern texts set prose, and encourage readers to explore the possible changes as and when they occur

W [7]    Q1-2/most modern texts = 'I', Q3-6/Ff = 'we'

34

| | | |
|---|---|---|
| 105 | **1. Murtherer** | No : hee'l say 'twas done cowardly, when he wakes [1] |
| | **2. Murtherer** | Why he shall never wake, untill the great Judgement day. |
| | **1. Murtherer** | Why then hee'l say, we stab'd him sleeping. |
| 110 | **2. Murtherer** | The urging of that word Judgement, hath bred a kinde of remorse in me. |
| | **1. Murtherer** | What? art thou affraid? |
| | **2. Murtherer** | Not to kill him, having a Warrant, But to be damn'd for killing him, from the which No Warrant can defend me. |
| 115 | **1. Murtherer** | [2] I thought thou had'st bin resolute. |
| | **2. Murtherer** | So I am, to let him live. |
| | **1. Murtherer** | Ile backe to the Duke of Glouster, and tell him so. |
| 120 | **2. Murtherer** | Nay, I *prythee stay a little : I hope this passionate humor of mine, will change, It was wont to hold me but while one tels twenty. |
| | **1. Murtherer** | How do'st thou feele thy selfe now? |
| | **2. Murtherer** | Some certaine dregges of conscience are yet within mee. |
| | **1. Murtherer** | Remember our Reward, when the deed's done. |
| 125 | **2. Murtherer** | Come,[3] he dies : I had forgot the Reward. |
| | **1. Murtherer** | Where's thy conscience now. |
| | **2. Murtherer** | O, in the Duke of Glousters purse. |
| | **1. Murtherer** | When hee opens his purse to give us our Reward, thy Conscience flyes out. |
| 130 | **2. Murtherer** | 'Tis no matter,[4] let it goe : There's few or none will entertaine it. |
| | **1. Murtherer** | What if it come to thee againe? |

---

PCT [1] F1 sets no punctuation, as if 2. Murtherer interrupts him: F2/most modern texts set a period

LS [2] most modern texts set this and the following Ff only speech

O [3] most modern texts set Qq's oath 'Zounds', which, because of the 1606 Acte to restraine the Abuses of Players, Ff was forced to reduce to 'Come'

LS [4] most modern texts set this Ff only phrase

| | |
|---|---|
| **2. Murtherer** | Ile not meddle with it, it makes a man a Coward: |
| | A man cannot steale, but it accuseth him: A man cannot |
| 135 | Sweare, but it Checkes him: A man cannot lye with his |
| | Neighbours Wife, but it detects him. |

'Tis a blushing
shamefac'd spirit, that mutinies in a mans bosome: It
filles a man full of Obstacles.

140                      It made me once restore a
Pursse of Gold that (by chance) I found: It beggars any
man that keepes it: It is turn'd out of Townes and Cit-
ties for a dangerous thing, and every man that means to
live well, endevours to trust to himselfe, and live with-
145  out it.                                    R 180 - b

| | |
|---|---|
| **1. Murtherer** | [1] 'Tis even now at my elbow, perswading me not to |
| | kill the Duke. |
| **2. Murtherer** | Take the divell in thy minde, and beleeve him not: |
| | He would insinuate with thee but to make thee sigh. |
| 150  **1. Murtherer** | I am strong fram'd, he cannot prevaile with me. |
| **2. Murtherer** | Spoke like a tall man, that respects thy reputation. |
| | Come, shall we fall to worke? |
| **1. Murtherer** | Take him on the Costard, with the hiltes of thy |
| | Sword, and then throw him into the Malmesey-Butte in |
| 155   | the next roome. |
| **2. Murtherer** | O excellent device; and make a sop of him. |
| **1. Murtherer** | [2] Soft, he wakes. |
| **2. Murtherer** | Strike. |
| **1. Murtherer** | No, wee'l reason with him. [3] |
| 160  **Clarence** | Where art thou Keeper? |
| | Give me a cup of wine. |
| **2. Murtherer** | You shall have Wine enough my Lord anon. |
| **Clarence** | In Gods name, what art thou? |

---

[O 1] most modern texts add the Qq oath 'Zounds', which Ff are forced to omit, see footnote #3, page 35

[VP 2] Qq/Ff/most modern texts now set the remainder of the scene in verse

[SD 3] Q3-6 set a stage direction for Clarence to awaken here, though the dialogue suggests he must be giving signs of waking at least two lines earlier

| | | |
|---|---|---|
| **1. Murtherer** [1] | A man, as you are. | |
| 165 | **Clarence** | But not as I am Royall. |
| | **1. Murtherer** | Nor you as we are, Loyall. |
| | **Clarence** | Thy voice is Thunder, but thy looks are humble. |
| | **1. Murtherer** | My voice is now the Kings, my lookes mine owne. |
| | **Clarence** | How darkly, and how deadly dost thou speake? |
| 170 | | Your eyes do menace me: why looke you pale? |
| | | Who sent you hither? |
| | | Wherefore do you come? |

| | |
|---|---|
| **2. Murtherer** [2] | To, to, to _____ |
| **Clarence** | To murther me? } |
| 175 **Both** | I, I. } |

| | |
|---|---|
| **Clarence** | You scarsely have the hearts to tell me so, |
| | And therefore cannot have the hearts to do it. |
| | Wherein my Friends have I offended you? |
| **1. Murtherer** | Offended us you have not, but the King. |
| 180 **Clarence** | I shall be reconcil'd to him againe. |
| **2. Murtherer** | Never my Lord, therefore prepare to dye. |
| **Clarence** | Are you drawne forth among a world of men |
| | To slay the innocent? |
| | What is my offence? |
| 185 | Where is the Evidence that doth accuse me? |
| | What lawfull Quest have given their Verdict up |
| | Unto the frowning Judge? |
| | Or who pronounc'd |
| | The bitter sentence of poore Clarence death, |
| 190 | Before I be convict by course of Law? |
| | To threaten me with death, is most unlawfull. |
| | I charge you, as you hope for any goodnesse,[3] |

[1] Qq/some modern texts assign this to 2. Murtherer, Ff/other modern texts to 1. Murtherer: for how the confusion arose see *The Arden Shakespeare King Richard III*, op. cit., pages 179 - 80, note to lines 150 - 1

[2] Qq set the prefix 'Am' which some modern texts set as 'Both', Ff/some modern texts assign the speech to 2. Murtherer

[3] Qq/most modern texts = 'to have redemption', Ff = 'for any goodnesse'

∞ [1]

That you depart, and lay no hands on me:
The deed you undertake is damnable.

195   **1. Murtherer**     What we will do, we do upon command.

    **2. Murtherer**     And he that hath commanded, is our King.

    **Clarence**        Erroneous Vassals,[2] the great King of Kings
Hath in the Table of his Law commanded
That thou shalt do no murther.

200                                      Will you then
Spurne at his Edict, and fulfill a Mans?

Take heed:   for he holds Vengeance in his hand,
To hurle upon their heads that breake his Law.

    **2. Murtherer**     And that same Vengeance doth he hurle on thee,
205                        For false Forswearing, and for murther too:
Thou did'st receive the Sacrament, to fight
In quarrell of the House of Lancaster.

    **1. Murtherer**     And like a Traitor to the name of God,
Did'st breake that Vow, and with thy treacherous blade,
210                        Unrip'st [3] the Bowels of thy Sov'raignes Sonne.

    **2. Murtherer**     Whom thou was't sworne to cherish and defend.

    **1. Murtherer**     How canst thou urge Gods dreadfull Law to us,
When thou hast broke it in such deere degree?

    **Clarence**        Alas! for whose sake did I that ill deede?
215                        For Edward, for my Brother, for his sake.

He sends you [4] not to murther me for this:         L 181 - b
For in that sinne, he is as deepe as I.

          [5] If God will be avenged for the deed,
O know you yet, he doth it publiquely,
220                        Take not the quarrell from his powrefull arme:
He needs no indirect, or lawlesse course,
To cut off those that have offended him.

---

ADD [1]
   most modern texts add the Qq only line 'By Christs deare bloud shed for our grievous sinnes'

W [2]
   Ff/most modern texts = 'Vassals', Qq = the singular 'Vassaile', which one modern text emends to 'Vassailes'

W [3]
   Qq/Ff /most modern texts = 'Unrip'st', which one modern text resets as 'Unrippedst', presumably for metric
reasons

W [4]
   Ff/most modern texts = 'you', Qq/one modern text = 'ye'

LS [5]
   most modern texts set this Ff only line

| | |
|---|---|
| **1. Murtherer** | Who made thee then a bloudy minister, |
| | When gallant springing brave Plantagenet, |
| 225 | That Princely Novice was strucke dead by thee? |
| | |
| **Clarence** | My Brothers love, the Divell, and my Rage. |
| | |
| **1. Murtherer** | Thy Brothers Love, our Duty, and thy Faults, |
| | Provoke us hither now, to slaughter thee. |
| | |
| **Clarence** | If you do love my Brother,[1] hate not me : |
| 230 | I am his Brother, and I love him well. |
| | If you are hyr'd for meed, go backe againe, |
| | And I will send you to my Brother Glouster : |
| | Who shall reward you better for my life, |
| | Then Edward will for tydings of my death. |
| | |
| 235   **2. Murtherer** | You are deceiv'd,→ [2] |
| | Your Brother Glouster hates you. |
| | |
| **Clarence** | Oh no, he loves me, and he holds me deere : |
| | Go you to him from me. |
| | } |
| **1. Murtherer** | I so we will. |
| | |
| 240   **Clarence** | Tell him, when that our Princely Father Yorke, |
| | Blest his three Sonnes with his victorious Arme, |
| | ∞[3] |
| | He little thought of this divided Friendship : |
| | Bid Glouster thinke on [4] this, and he will weepe,[5] |
| | |
| **1. Murtherer** | I Milstones, as he lessoned us to weepe. |
| | |
| 245   **Clarence** | O do not slander him, for he is kinde. |
| | |
| **1. Murtherer** | Right, as Snow in Harvest :   → [6] |
| | Come, you deceive your selfe, |
| | 'Tis he that sends us to destroy you heere. |
| | |
| **Clarence** | It cannot be, for he bewept my Fortune, |
| 250 | And hugg'd me in his armes, and swore with sobs, |
| | That he would labour my delivery. |

---

R 181 - b   :   1. 4. 220 - 246

[W 1] Q1-2/most modern texts = 'Oh if you love my brother', Ff = 'If you do love my Brother'

[SP 2] Ff set two short lines (4/7 syllables) suggesting the Murtherer takes great care to explain the political reality to Clarence:  most modern texts follow Qq and set the two lines as one

[ADD 3] most modern texts add the Qq only line 'And chargd us from his soule, to love each other'

[W 4] Q1-5/most modern texts = 'of', Q6/Ff = 'on'

[PCT 5] F1 sets blurred punctuation which could be a comma, perhaps suggesting 1. Murtherer interrupts Clarence: F2/most modern texts set a period

[SP 6] Ff set two short lines (6/6 syllables) allowing the Murtherer a pause (perhaps in surprise? for irony?): though some modern texts follow Qq and set the two lines as one, at least one text follows Ff

| | | |
|---|---|---|
| **1. Murtherer** | | Why so he doth, when he delivers you |
| | | From this earths thraldome, to the joyes of heaven. |
| **2. Murtherer** | | Make peace with God, for you must die my Lord. |
| 255 **Clarence** | [1] | Have you that holy feeling in your soules, |
| | | To counsaile me to make my peace with God, |
| | | And are you yet to your owne soules so blinde, |
| | | That you will warre with God, by murd'ring me. |
| | | O sirs consider, they [2] that set you on |
| 260 | | To do this deede, will hate you for the deede. |
| **2. Murtherer** | | What shall we do? |
| **Clarence** | | Relent, and save your soules: |

| | | |
|---|---|---|
| | [3] | Which of you, if you were a Princes Sonne, |
| | | Being pent from Liberty, as I am now, |
| 265 | | If two such murtherers as your selves came to you, |
| | | Would not intreat for life, as you would begge |
| | | Were you in my distresse. |

| | | |
|---|---|---|
| **1. Murtherer** | | Relent? no: 'Tis cowardly and womanish. |
| **Clarence** | | Not to relent, is beastly, savage, divellish: |
| 270 | [4] | My Friend, I spy some pitty in thy lookes: |
| | | O, if thine eye be not a Flatterer, |
| | | Come thou on my side, and intreate for mee, |
| | | A begging Prince, what begger pitties not. |
| **2. Murtherer** | [5] | Looke behind you, my Lord. |
| 275 **1. Murtherer** | | Take that, and that, if all this will not do, |

**[Stabs him]** [6]

Ile drowne you in the Malmesey-But within.

---

W [1]
  Qq use the singular ('thou' and 'thy soule') for the first four lines, as if Clarence were addressing just one of the men: most modern texts follow Ff and set the plural choices throughout

W [2]
  Ff /most modern texts = 'they', Qq = 'he'

LS / ALT [3]
  Qq do not set these five lines, and though Ff set them here as shown, some modern texts place them after the second line of Clarence's next speech, while one text sets them at the end of that speech: see *The Arden Shakespeare King Richard III*, op. cit., page 184, footnote to line 252, and *William Shakespeare: A Textual Companion*, page 236, footnote to lines 1.4.258 - 62/1021-5

WHO [4]
  some modern texts suggest this is addressed to 2. Murtherer

LS [5]
  most modern texts set this Ff only short line

SD [6]
  most modern texts suggest the stabbing start in the middle of the previous line, and add to the following direction that 1. Murtherer takes Clarence's body off-stage with him

**[Exit]**

| | |
|---|---|
| **2. Murtherer** | A bloody deed, and desperately dispatcht:<br>How faine (like Pilate) would I wash my hands<br>Of this most greevous murther. [1] |

**[Enter 1. Murtherer]** [2]

280    **1. Murtherer**    How now? what mean'st thou that thou help'st me not?

By Heaven [3] the Duke shall know how slacke you have beene.

R 181 - b

**2. Murtherer**

285

I would he knew that I had sav'd his brother,
Take thou the Fee, and tell him what I say,
For I repent me that the Duke is slaine.

**[Exit]**

**1. Murtherer**    So do not I: go Coward as thou art.

Well, Ile go hide the body in some hole,
Till that the Duke give order for his buriall:
290    And when I have my meede, I will away,
For this will out, and then I must not stay.

**[Exit]**

---

w[1]   Ff/most modern texts = 'greevous murther', Qq/one modern text = 'grievous guilty murder done'

UE[2]   this is an unusual entry, set to the side of the text (as if Playhouse entered) rather than the usual position, centred on a separate line: as such it might suggest 1 Murtherer doesn't wish to draw attention to his return (perhaps hoping to take 2 Murtherer by surprise) : however, the entry is set on an already crowded page, perhaps necessitating it being placed alongside the dialogue

w[3]   Q1-5/most modern texts = 'heaven's, Q6/Ff/one modern text = 'Heaven'

# Actus Secundus

**FLOURISH.**
**ENTER THE KING SICKE, THE QUEENE, LORD MARQUESSE**
**DORSET, RIVERS, HASTINGS, CATESBY,**
**BUCKINGHAM, WOODVILL** [1]

| | |
|---|---|
| **King** | Why so : now have I done a good daies work. |
| | You Peeres, continue this united League : |
| | I, every day expect an Embassage |
| | From my Redeemer, to redeeme me hence. |
| | And more to [2] peace my soule shall part to heaven, |
| | Since I have made my Friends at peace on earth. |
| | Dorset [3] and Rivers, take each others hand, |
| | Dissemble not your hatred, Sweare your love. |
| **Rivers** | By heaven, my soule is purg'd from grudging hate |
| | And with my hand I seale my true hearts Love. |
| **Hastings** | So thrive I, as I truly sweare the like. |
| **King** | Take heed you dally not before your King, |
| | Lest he that is the supreme King of Kings |
| | Confound your hidden falshood, and award |
| | Either of you to be the others end. |
| **Hastings** | So prosper I, as I sweare perfect love. |
| **Rivers** | And I, as I love Hastings with my heart, [4] |
| **King** | Madam, your selfe is not exempt from this : |
| | Nor you [5] Sonne Dorset, Buckingham nor you ; |
| | You have bene factious one against the other. |
| | Wife, love Lord Hastings, let him kisse your hand, |
| | And what you do, do it unfeignedly. |

Line numbers: 5, 10, 15, 20

L 182 - b  :  2. 1. 1 - 22

[1] as explained in footnote #5, page 3, Woodvill and Rivers are one and the same: hence most texts replace Woodvill with Grey

[2] Ff = 'more to', Qq = 'now in', most modern texts set the gloss 'more in'

[3] since Rivers and Hastings immediately speak of friendship in response to the King's command, most modern texts set Qq's text, 'Rivers and' rather than Ff's 'Dorset and Hastings', (with one modern text reversing the order)

[4] F1 sets a comma, suggesting the King interrupts her: F2/most modern texts set a period

[5] Ff/most modern texts = 'you', Qq/one modern text = 'your'

| | | |
|---|---|---|
| | **Queene** | There Hastings,[1] I will never more remember |
| | | Our former hatred, so thrive I, and mine. |
| 25 | **King** | Dorset, imbrace him: → [2] |
| | | Hastings, love Lord Marquesse. |
| | **Dorset** | This interchange of love, I heere protest |
| | | Upon my part, shall be inviolable. |
| | **Hastings** | And so sweare I. [3] |
| 30 | **King** | Now Princely Buckingham, seale ÿ [4] this league |
| | | With thy embracements to my wives Allies, |
| | | And make me happy in your unity. |
| | **Buckingham** | When ever Buckingham doth turne his hate |
| | | Upon your Grace, but [5] with all dutious love, |
| 35 | | Doth cherish you, and yours, God punish me |
| | | With hate in those where I expect most love, |
| | | When I have most need to imploy a Friend, |
| | | And most assured that he is a Friend, |
| | | Deepe, hollow, treacherous, and full of guile, |
| 40 | | Be he unto me: This do I begge of heaven, |
| | | When I am cold in love, to you, or yours. |

**[Embrace]**

| | | |
|---|---|---|
| | **King** | A pleasing Cordiall, Princely Buckingham |
| | | Is this thy Vow, unto my sickely heart: |
| | | There wanteth now our Brother Gloster heere, |
| 45 | | To make the blessed period of this peace. |
| | **Buckingham** | And in good time, |
| | | Heere comes Sir Richard Ratcliffe, and the Duke. | L 182 - b |

**ENTER RATCLIFFE, AND GLOSTER [6]**

---

SD 1  at least one modern text suggests the Queene offers Hastings her hand to be kissed

SP 2  this is the only set of reconciliations where Ff set two short lines (5/6 syllables), perhaps suggesting the reaction towards each other is not as apparently forgiving as some of the others, hence the need for the second line:

SD 3  most modern texts follow Qq and join the two lines as one

most modern texts suggest Dorset and Hastings now embrace

AB 4  F1= 'ÿ', (printed as such because of lack of column width), F2/most modern texts = 'thou'

W 5  Ff/most modern texts = 'Upon your Grace', Qq = 'On you and yours': also, whereas Qq/Ff = 'but', several modern texts = 'or'

SD 6  most modern texts follow Qq and set the entry before the previous speech

| | | |
|---|---|---|
| | **Richard** | Good morrow to my Soveraigne King & Queen<br>And Princely Peeres, a happy time of day. |
| 50 | **King** | Happy indeed, as we have spent the day:<br>Gloster,[1] we have done deeds of Charity,<br>Made peace†[2] of enmity, faire love of hate,<br>Betweene these swelling wrong incensed Peeres. |
| 55 | **Richard** | A blessed labour my most Soveraigne Lord:<br>Among this Princely heape, if any heere<br>By false intelligence, or wrong surmize |

Hold me a Foe : ° If I unwillingly,[3] or in my rage,° [4]

|    |    |    |
|---|---|---|
| | | Have ought committed that is hardly borne,<br>To [5] any in this presence, I desire |
| 60 | | To reconcile me to his Friendly peace:<br>'Tis death to me to be at enmitie :<br>I hate it, and desire all good mens love,<br>First Madam, I intreate true peace of you,<br>Which I will purchase with my dutious service. |
| 65 | | Of you my Noble Cosin Buckingham,<br>If ever any grudge were lodg'd betweene us. |
| | | Of you and you, Lord Rivers and of Dorset,[6]<br>That all without desert have frown'd on me :<br>[7] Of you Lord Woodvill, and Lord Scales of you, |
| 70 | | Dukes, Earles, Lords, Gentlemen, indeed of all. |
| | | I do not know that Englishman alive,<br>With whom my soule is any jot at oddes,<br>More then the Infant that is borne to night :<br>I thanke my God for my Humility. |
| 75 | **Queene** | A holy day shall this be kept heereafter :<br>I would to God all strifes were well compounded. |
| | | My Soveraigne Lord, I do beseech your Highnesse<br>To take our Brother Clarence to your Grace. |

---

R 182 - b  :  2. 1. 47 - 77

[W 1] Ff/most modern texts = 'Gloster', Qq/one modern text = 'Brother'

[W 2] F1 = 'peaee', F2/most modern texts = 'peace'

[W 3] Qq/most modern texts = 'unwittingly', Ff = 'unwillingly'

[LS 4] though Qq/Ff set a fourteen syllable line, suggesting a very effusive Richard, most modern texts split the line in two (4/10 syllables) as shown, creating a pause where none was originally shown

[W 5] Qq/most modern texts = 'By', Ff = 'To'

[W 6] Ff = 'Of you and you, Lord Rivers and of Dorset', Qq/most modern texts = 'Of you Lo: Rivers and Lord Gray of you', replacing 'Lo:' with 'Lord'

[OM 7] most modern texts omit this Ff only line, especially since it persists in identifying Rivers and Woodvill as two separate people, see footnotes #5, page 3, and #1, page 42

| | | |
|---|---|---|
| 80 | **Richard** | Why Madam, have I offred love for this,<br>To be so flowted in this Royall presence? |
| | | Who knowes not that the gentle Duke is dead?<br>You do him injurie to scorne his Coarse. |

**[They all start]**

| | | |
|---|---|---|
| | **King** [1] | Who knowes not he is dead? → [2]<br>Who knowes he is? |
| 85 | **Queene** | All-seeing heaven, what a world is this? |
| | **Buckingham** | Looke I so pale Lord Dorset, as the rest? |
| | **Dorset** | I my good Lord, and no man [3] in the presence,<br>But his red colour hath forsooke his cheekes. |
| 90 | **King** | Is Clarence dead?<br>               The Order was reverst. |
| | **Richard** | But he (poore man) by your first order dyed,<br>And that a winged Mercurie did beare:<br>Some tardie Cripple bare [4] the Countermand,<br>That came too lagge to see him buried. |
| 95 | | God grant, that some lesse Noble, and lesse Loyall,<br>Neerer in bloody thoughts, and [5] not in blood,<br>Deserve not worse then wretched Clarence did,<br>And yet go currant from Suspition. |

**ENTER EARLE OF DERBY**

| | | |
|---|---|---|
| | **Derby** | A boone my Soveraigne for my service done. |
| 100 | **King** | I *prethee peace, my soule is full of sorrow. |
| | **Derby** | I will not rise, unlesse your Highnes heare me. |
| | **King** | Then say at once, what is it thou requests. [6] |

---

[P] [1]
Ff set this response for the King, most modern texts follow Qq in assigning the line to Rivers, though the plot reasons advanced for so doing are not particularly strong, (see *The Arden Shakespeare King Richard III*, op. cit., page 191, footnote to line 82 which argues the 'tone' seems wrong for the character of the King)

[SP] [2]
at this crucial moment of (shocked?) response Ff set two short lines (6/4 syllables), allowing the moment full weight: most modern texts follow Qq and set the two lines as one

[W] [3]
Ff/most modern texts = 'no man', Qq/one modern text = 'no one'

[W] [4]
Qq/most modern texts = 'bore', Ff = 'bare'

[W] [5]
Qq/most modern texts = 'but', Ff = 'and'

[W] [6]
Qq/most modern texts = 'demaundst', Ff = 'requests'

| | |
|---|---|
| **Derby** | The forfeit (Soveraigne) of my servants life, |
| | Who slew to day a Riotous Gentleman, |
| 105 | Lately attendant on the Duke of Norfolke. |
| **King** | Have I a tongue to doome my Brothers death? |
| | And shall that tongue give pardon to a slave? |
| | My Brother kill'd [1] no man, his fault was Thought, |
| | And yet his punishment was bitter death. |
| 110 | Who sued to me for him? |

R 182 - b

Who (in my wrath)
Kneel'd and [2] my feet, and bid [3] me be advis'd?

Who spoke of Brother-hood? who spoke of love?

Who told me how the poore soule did forsake
115      The mighty Warwicke, and did fight for me?

Who told me in the field at Tewkesbury,
When Oxford had me downe, he rescued me :
And said deare Brother live, and be a King?

Who told me, when we both lay in the Field,
120      Frozen (almost) to death, how he did lap me
Even in his Garments, and did give himselfe
(All thin and naked) to the numbe cold night?

All this from my Remembrance, brutish wrath
Sinfully pluckt, and not a man of you
125      Had so much grace to put it in my minde.

But when your Carters, or your wayting Vassalls
Have done a drunken Slaughter, and defac'd
The precious Image of our deere Redeemer,
You straight are on your knees for Pardon, pardon,
130      And I (unjustly too) must grant it you.

But for my Brother, not a man would speake,
Nor I (ungracious) speake unto my selfe
For him poore Soule. The proudest of you all,
135      Have bin beholding to him in his life :
Yet none of you, would once[†4] begge for his life.

---

R 182 - b / L 183 - b   :   2. 1. 100 - 131

[w 1]   since four lines earlier Derby used the verb 'slew', some modern texts follow Qq and set 'slew' here: Ff/some modern texts = 'kill'd'

[w 2]   Qq/F2/most modern texts = 'at', F1= 'and'

[w 3]   Qq/some modern texts = 'bade', Ff/some modern texts = 'bid'

[w 4]   Qq/F2/most modern texts = 'once', F1 = 'onee'

O God!
        I feare thy justice will take hold
On me, and you ;  and mine, and yours for this.

140                  Come Hastings helpe me to my Closset.
Ah poore Clarence.

**[Exeunt some with K.{ing} & Queen]**

**Richard**          This is the fruits of rashnes :  Markt you not,
How that the guilty Kindred of the Queene
Look'd pale, when they did heare of Clarence death.

145                  O!  they did urge it still unto the King,
God will revenge it.
                  Come Lords will you go,
To comfort Edward with our company.

**Buckingham**     [1]  We wait upon your Grace.

**[exeunt]**

[1] most modern texts set this Ff only line

# Scena Secunda

### ENTER THE OLD DUTCHESSE OF YORKE, WITH THE TWO
### CHILDREN OF CLARENCE

| | |
|---|---|
| **Edward** [1] | Good Grandam [2] tell us, is our Father dead? |
| **Dutchesse** | No Boy. |
| **Daughter** | [3] Why do [4] weepe so oft? |
| | And beate your Brest? |
| 5 | And cry, O Clarence, my unhappy Sonne. |
| **Boy** | Why do you looke on us, and shake your head, |
| | And call us Orphans, Wretches, Castawayes, |
| | If that our Noble Father were alive? |
| **Dutchesse** | My pretty Cosins, you mistake me both, |
| 10 | I do lament the sicknesse of the King, |
| | As loath to lose him, not your Fathers death : |
| | It were lost sorrow to waile one that's lost. |
| **Boy** | Then you conclude, (my Grandam) he is dead : |
| | The King mine Unckle is too blame for it. [5] |
| 15 | God will revenge it, whom I will importune |
| | With earnest prayers, all to that effect. |
| **Daughter** | [6] And so will I. |
| **Dutchesse** | Peace children peace, the King doth love you wel. |
| | Incapeable, and shallow Innocents, |
| 20 | You cannot guesse who caus'd your Fathers death. |

---

[P 1] Ff assign him the prefix 'Edw' (Edward) for the first speech, and then 'Boy' thereafter

[W 2] Ff/most modern texts = 'Grandam' throughout, Qq/one modern text = 'Granam' throughout: this is the only time this variation will be footnoted

[ST 3] this speech could be set as anywhere between one and three sentences long

[W 4] Qq/F2/most modern texts set 'you', which F1 omits

[W 5] Ff/most modern texts = 'it', Qq/one modern text = 'this'

[LS 6] most modern texts set this Ff only line

| | | |
|---|---|---|
| **Boy** | Grandam we can:  for my good Unkle Gloster | L 183 - b |
| | Told me, the King provok'd to it by the Queene, | |
| | Devis'd impeachments to imprison him; | |
| | And when my Unckle told me so, he wept,†¹ | |
| 25 | And pittied me, and kindly kist my cheeke: | |
| | Bad me rely on him, as on my Father, | |
| | And he would love me deerely as a ² childe. | |

| | |
|---|---|
| **Dutchesse** | Ah!  that Deceit should steale such gentle shape,³ |
| | And with a vertuous Vizor ⁴ hide deepe vice, |
| 30 | He is my sonne, I, and therein my shame, |
| | Yet from my dugges, he drew not this deceit. |

| | |
|---|---|
| **Boy** | Thinke you my Unkle did dissemble Grandam? |
| **Dutchesse** | I Boy. |
| **Boy** | I cannot thinke it |
| 35 | Hearke, what noise is this? |

**ENTER THE QUEENE WITH HER HAIRE ABOUT HER EARS, RIVERS & DORSET AFTER HER ⁵**

| | |
|---|---|
| **Queene** | Ah!  who shall hinder me to waile and weepe? |
| | To chide my Fortune, and torment my Selfe. |
| | Ile joyne with blacke dispaire against my Soule, |
| | And to my selfe, become an enemie. |
| 40 **Dutchesse** | What meanes this Scene of rude impatience? |
| **Queene** | To make ⁶ an act of Tragicke violence. |
| | Edward my Lord, thy Sonne, our King is dead. |
| | Why grow the Branches, when the Roote is gone? |
| | Why wither not the leaves that want their sap? |
| 45 | If you will live, Lament:  if dye, be breefe, |
| | That our swift-winged Soules may catch the Kings, |
| | Or like obedient Subjects follow him, |
| | To his new Kingdome of nere-changing night. |

---

PCT ₁
    F1 sets a blur which could a period or a comma:  Q1/F2/most modern texts set a comma

W ₂
    Ff/most modern texts = 'a', Qq/one modern text = 'his'

W ₃
    Ff/most modern texts = 'shape', Qq/one modern text = 'shapes'

W ₄
    Ff/most modern texts = 'Vizor', Qq/one modern text = 'visard'

SD / ALT ₅
    some modern texts follow Qq and omit Rivers and Dorset from the entry, thus forcing two cuts later in the scene, the first of twelve lines, the second of nineteen, see footnotes #4 on page 51 and #5 page 52

W ₆
    Qq/Ff = 'make', one interesting gloss = 'marke'

| | | |
|---|---|---|
| **Dutchesse** | 50 | Ah so much interest have $^1$ in thy sorrow, |
| | | As I had Title in thy Noble Husband: |
| | | I have bewept a worthy Husbands death, |
| | | And liv'd with looking on his Images: |
| | | But now two Mirrors of his Princely semblance, |
| | | Are crack'd in pieces, by malignant death, |
| | 55 | And I for comfort, have but one false Glasse, |
| | | That greeves me, when I see my shame in him. |

Thou art a Widdow:  yet thou art a Mother,
And hast the comfort of thy Children left,
But death hath snatch'd my Husband from mine Armes,
60  And pluckt two Crutches from my feeble hands,
Clarence, and Edward.
                          O, what cause have I,
(Thine being but a moity of my moane)
To over-go thy woes, and drowne thy cries.

65 **Boy**  Ah Aunt!  you wept not for our Fathers death:
How can we ayde you with our Kindred teares?

**Daughter**  Our fatherlesse distresse was left unmoan'd,
Your widdow-dolour, likewise be unwept.

**Queene**  Give me no helpe in Lamentation,
70  I am not barren to bring forth complaints:
All Springs reduce their currents to mine eyes,
That I being govern'd by the waterie Moone,
May send forth plenteous teares to drowne the World.
Ah, for my Husband, for my deere Lord Edward.

75 **Children**  Ah for our Father, for our deere Lord Clarence.

**Dutchesse**  Alas for both, both mine Edward and Clarence.

**Queene**  What stay had I but Edward, and hee's gone?

**Children**  What stay had we but Clarence?  and he's gone.

**Dutchesse**  What stayes had I, but they?  and they are gone.

80 **Queene**  Was never widdow had so deere a losse.

**Children**  Were never Orphans had so deere a losse.

**Dutchesse**  Was never Mother had so deere a losse.
Alas!  I am the Mother of these Greefes,
Their woes are parcell'd, mine is generall.

---

R 183 - b  :  2. 2. 47 - 81

$^{w}1$  Qq/F2/most modern texts = 'I', which F1 omits

R 183 - b

| | |
|---|---|
| 85 | She for an Edward weepes, and so do I :<br>I for a Clarence weepes,[1] so doth not shee :<br>These Babes for Clarence weepe,[2] so do not they. |
| | Alas! you three, on me threefold distrest :<br>Power[3] all your teares, I am your sorrowes Nurse, |
| 90 | And I will pamper it with Lamentation. |

**Dorset** [4] Comfort deere Mother, God is much displeas'd,
That you take with unthankfulnesse his doing.

In common wordly things, 'tis call'd ungratefull,
With dull unwillingnesse to repay[5] a debt,
95 Which with a bounteous hand was kindly lent :
Much more to be thus opposite with heaven,
For it requires the Royall debt it lent you.

**Rivers** Madam, bethinke you like a carefull Mother
Of the young Prince your sonne : send straight for him,
100 Let him be Crown'd, in him your comfort lives.

Drowne desperate sorrow in dead Edwards grave,
And plant your joyes in living Edwards Throne.

**ENTER RICHARD, BUCKINGHAM, DERBIE, HA-
STINGS, AND RATCLIFFE**

**Richard** Sister have comfort, all of us have cause
To waile the dimming of our shining Starre :
105 But none can helpe our harmes by wayling them.

Madam, my Mother, I do cry you mercie,
I did not see your Grace
[6] Humbly on my knee,
I crave your Blessing.

110 **Dutchesse** God blesse thee, and put meeknes in thy breast,
Love Charity, Obedience, and true Dutie.

**Richard** Amen,[7] and make me die a good old man,
That is the butt-end of a Mothers blessing ;
I marvell that her Grace did leave it out.

---

R 183 - b / L 184 - b : 2. 2. 82 - 111

[1] Qq//F2/most modern texts = 'weepe', F1 = 'weepes'
[2] most modern texts add a Qq only split line, 'and so doe I,/I for an Edward weepe,'
[3] Qq/F3/most modern texts = 'Poure', F1= 'Power', F2 = 'Powre'
[4] most modern texts set these next two Ff only speeches (see footnote #5, page 49)
[5] since Ff set an eleven syllable line, metrically minded modern texts replace Ff's 'repay' with 'pay'
[6] most modern texts indicate that Richard kneels
[7] most modern texts suggest Richard now rises and that the rest of his speech is spoken as an aside

| | | |
|---|---|---|
| 115 | **Buckingham** | You clowdy-Princes, & hart-sorowing-Peeres, |
| | | That beare this heavie mutuall loade of Moane, |
| | | Now cheere each other, in each others Love: |
| | | Though we have spent our Harvest of this King, |
| | | We are to reape the Harvest of his Sonne. |
| 120 | | The broken rancour of your high-swolne hates,[1] |
| | | But lately splinter'd,[2] knit, and joyn'd together, |
| | | Must gently be preserv'd, cherisht.[3]   and kept: |
| | | Me seemeth good, that with some little Traine, |
| | | Forthwith from Ludlow, the young Prince be fet[4] |
| 125 | | Hither to London, to be crown'd our King. |
| | **Rivers** | [5] Why with some little Traine,→[6] |
| | | My Lord of Buckingham? |
| | **Buckingham** | Marrie my Lord, least by a multitude, |
| | | The new-heal'd wound of Malice should breake out, |
| 130 | | Which would be so much the more dangerous, |
| | | By how much the estate is greene, and yet ungovern'd. |
| | | Where every Horse beares his commanding Reine, |
| | | And may direct his course as please himselfe, |
| | | As well the feare of harme, as harme apparant, |
| 135 | | In my opinion, ought to be prevented. |
| | **Richard** | I hope the King made peace with all of us, |
| | | And the compact is firme, and true in me. |
| | **Rivers** | And so in me, and so (I thinke) in all.[7] |
| | | Yet since it is but greene, it should be put |
| 140 | | To no apparant likely-hood of breach, |
| | | Which haply by much company might be urg'd: |
| | | Therefore I say with Noble Buckingham, |
| | | That it is meete so few should fetch the Prince. |
| | **Hastings** | And so say I. |

---

L 184 - b  :  2. 2. 112 - 140

W [1]  Ff/most modern texts = 'hates', Qq/one modern text = 'hate'

W [2]  though Qq/Ff set variations of 'splinter'd', most modern texts set the directly contrasting image, 'splinted'

PCT [3]  F1 shows blurred punctuation here, most reminiscent of a period: F2/most modern texts set a comma

W [4]  though Qq set the more recogniseable 'fetcht', some modern texts set Ff's 'fet'

LS [5]  most modern texts set this and the following four Ff only speeches (see footnote #5, page 49 above)

SP [6]  arguing that this Ff only speech was set as two short lines (6/6 syllables) through lack of column width, most modern texts set the two lines as one: if the Ff setting were to stand it might suggest Rivers is taking great care to question one of the most powerful politicians in the play

PCT [7]  in this Ff only passage F1 sets a blur which could be a period or comma, which F2 sets as a comma: most modern texts set a period

| | | |
|---|---|---|
| 145 | **Richard** | Then be it so, and go we to determine |
| | | Who they shall be that strait shall poste to London. [1] |
| | | |
| | | Madam, and you my Sister, will you go |
| | | To give your censures in this businesse. [2] |

**[Exeunt]**                                          L 184 - b

**[Manet Buckingham, and Richard]**

| | | |
|---|---|---|
| | **Buckingham** | My Lord, who ever journies to the Prince, |
| 150 | | For God [3] sake let not us two stay at home: |
| | | For by the way, Ile sort occasion, |
| | | As Index to the story we late talk'd of, |
| | | To part the Queenes proud Kindred from the Prince. |
| | | |
| | **Richard** | My other selfe, my Counsailes Consistory, |
| 155 | | My Oracle, My Prophet, my deere Cosin, |
| | | I, as a childe, will go by thy direction, |
| | | Toward [4] London then, for wee'l not stay behinde. |

**[Exeunt]**

---

L 184 - b / R 184 - b  :  2. 2. 141 - 154

N/W [1]   both here and in twelve lines time most modern texts set Qq's 'Ludlow' rather Ff's 'London': some modern texts uncharitably blame compositor B's 'careless misreading' for the error, when, as the editors of *William Shakespeare: A Textual Companion*, op. cit., page 237, footnote to line 2.3.112/1295, point out the mistake more likely 'derives from the fact that Richard was historically in the north at the time of Edward's death, and it may be related to the apparent confusion about whether Act Two Scene 4 takes place in London or York'

W [2]   Ff/most modern texts = 'businesse', Qq/one modern text = 'waighty busines'

W [3]   Qq/F2/most modern texts = 'Gods', F1 = 'God'

W [4]   Ff/most modern texts = 'Toward', Qq/one modern text = 'Towards'

# Scena Tertia

**ENTER ONE CITIZEN AT ONE DOORE, AND ANOTHER AT
THE OTHER**

| | | |
|---|---|---|
| **1. Citizen** | | Good morrow Neighbour, whether away so fast? |
| **2. Citizen** | | I promise you, I scarsely know my selfe: Heare you the newes abroad? |
| 5 **1. Citizen** | | Yes, that the King is dead. |
| **2. Citizen** | | Ill newes byrlady, seldome comes the better: I feare,[1] I feare, 'twill prove a giddy world. |

**ENTER ANOTHER CITIZEN**

| | | |
|---|---|---|
| **3. Citizen** | | Neighbours, God speed. |
| **1. Citizen** | [2] | Give you good morrow sir. |
| 10 **3. Citizen** | | Doth the newes hold of good king Edwards death? |
| **2. Citizen** | | I sir, it is too true, God helpe the while. |
| **3. Citizen** | | Then Masters looke to see a troublous world. |
| **1. Citizen** | | No, no, by Gods good grace, his Son shall reigne. |
| **3. Citizen** | | Woe to that Land that's govern'd by a Childe. |
| 15 **2. Citizen** | | In him there is a hope of Government, Which in his nonage, counsell under him, And in his full and ripened yeares, himselfe No doubt shall then, and till then governe well. |
| **1. Citizen** 20 | | So stood the State, when Henry the sixt[3] Was crown'd in Paris, but at nine months old. |

[1] F1 = 'Ifeare', F2/most modern texts = 'I feare'

[2] most modern texts set this Ff only line

[3] Qq = 'Harry the sixt', F1-2 = 'Henry the sixt', F3/most modern texts = 'Henry the Sixth'

| | |
|---|---|
| **3. Citizen** | Stood the State so? |
| | No, no, good friends, God wot |
| | For then this Land was famously enrich'd |
| | With politike grave Counsell ; then the King |
| 25 | Had vertuous Unkles to protect his Grace. |
| **1. Citizen** | Why so hath this, both by his Father and Mother. |
| **3. Citizen** | Better it were they all came by his Father : |
| | Or by his Father there were none at all : |
| | For emulation, who shall now be neerest, |
| 30 | Will touch us all too neere, if God prevent not. |
| | O full of danger is the Duke of Glouster, |
| | And the Queenes Sons, and Brothers, haught and proud : |
| | And were they to be rul'd, and not to rule, |
| | This sickly Land, might solace as before. |
| 35 **1. Citizen** | Come, come, we feare the worst : all will be well. |
| **3. Citizen** | When Clouds are seen, wisemen put on their clokes ; |
| | When great leaves fall, then Winter is at hand ; |
| | When the Sun sets, who doth not looke for night ? |
| | Untimely stormes, makes [1] men expect a Dearth : |
| 40 | All may be well ; but if God sort it so, |
| | 'Tis more then we deserve, or I expect. |
| **2. Citizen** | Truly, the hearts of men are full of feare : |
| | You cannot reason (almost) with a man, |
| | That lookes not heavily, and full of dread. |
| 45 **3. Citizen** | Before the dayes of Change, still is it so, |
| | By a divine instinct, mens mindes mistrust |
| | Pursuing [2] danger : as by proofe we see |
| | The Water swell before a boyst'rous storme : |
| | But leave it all to God. |
| 50 | Whither away ? |
| **2. Citizen** | Marry we were sent for to the Justices. |
| **3. Citizen** | And so was I : Ile beare you company. |

R 184 - b

**[Exeunt]**

---

R 184 - b / L 185 - b : 2. 3. 18 - 47

[1] Ff/most modern texts = 'makes', Qq/one modern text = 'make'

[2] Q1-2/most modern texts = 'Ensuing', Q3/Ff = 'Pursuing', (even though F1's catchword on the bottom of page R 184 is Qq's 'Ensuing', the word set at the top of page L 185 is 'Pursuing')

# Scena Quarta

ENTER ARCH-BISHOP,[1] YONG YORKE, THE QUEENE,
AND THE DUTCHESSE [2]

| | | |
|---|---|---|
| **Archbishop** | [3] | Last night I heard they lay at Stony Stratford, |
| | | And at Northampton they do rest to night: |
| | | To morrow, or next day, they will be heere. |

| | |
|---|---|
| **Dutchesse** | I long with all my heart to see the Prince: |
| | I hope he is much growne since last I saw him. |

| | |
|---|---|
| **Queene** | But I heare no, they say my sonne of Yorke |
| | Ha's almost overtane him in his growth. |

| | |
|---|---|
| **Yorke** | I Mother, but I would not have it so. |

| | |
|---|---|
| **Dutchesse** | Why my good [4] Cosin, it is good to grow. |

| | |
|---|---|
| **Yorke** | Grandam, one night as we did sit at Supper, |
| | My Unkle [5] Rivers talk'd how I did grow |
| | More then my Brother. |
| |            I, quoth my Unkle Glouster, |
| | Small Herbes have grace, great [6] Weeds do grow apace. |
| | And since, me thinkes I would not grow so fast, |
| | Because sweet Flowres are slow, and Weeds make hast. |

| | |
|---|---|
| **Dutchesse** | Good faith, good faith, the saying did not hold |
| | In him that did object the same to thee. |

5

10

15

---

L 185 - b : 2. 4. 1 - 17

P/N [1]
    Ff suggest this character is the Archbishop of Yorke, Qq that he is the Cardinall (of Canterbury) who appears in the next scene: some commentators are quick to point out the confusion stems from *Holinshed*, who virtually conflates the two historical characters: others suggest that while Shakespeare was aware of the two men, Qq set them as one to avoid a second costume: readers are guided to *The Arden Shakespeare King Richard III*, op. cit., page 16, and *William Shakespeare: A Textual Companion*, op. cit., page 237, footnote to line 2.4.0.1/1354.1

N [2]
    as most modern texts explain, this is the Dutchesse of Yorke, Richard's mother, grandmother to both Edward and Clarence's children

LS [3]
    some texts set Ff as is, some set Qq, whose alternative text reverses the order of the journey, viz.
    'Last night I heare they lay at Northampton.
    At Stonistratford will they be to night,'
for further details, especially as to which might be correct, see the concise explanation offered on page 18 of *The Arden Shakespeare King Richard III*, op. cit.

W [4]
  Ff/most modern texts = 'good', Qq/one modern text = 'young'

W [5]
  Q2-6/Ff/most modern texts = 'Unkle', Q1 = 'Nnckle' which one modern text sets as 'Nunckle'

W [6]
  Qq/Ff/most modern texts = 'great', modern glosses = 'gross' and 'ill'

|  |  |  |
|---|---|---|
| | 20 | He was the wretched'st thing when he was yong, <br> So long a growing, and so leysurely, <br> That if his rule were true, he should be gracious. |
| **{Yorke}** [1] | | And [2] so no doubt he is, my gracious Madam. |
| **Dutchesse** | | I hope he is, but yet let Mothers doubt. |
| **Yorke** | 25 | Now by my troth, if I had beene remembred, <br> I could have given my Unkles Grace, a flout, <br> To touch his growth, neerer then he toucht mine. |
| **Dutchesse** | | How my yong Yorke,→ [3] <br> I *prythee let me heare it. |
| **Yorke** | 30 | Marry (they say) my Unkle grew so fast, <br> That he could gnaw a crust at two houres old, <br> 'Twas full two yeares ere I could get a tooth. <br><br> Grandam, this would have beene a byting Jest. |
| **Dutchesse** | | I *prythee pretty Yorke, who told thee this? |
| **Yorke** | | Grandam, his Nursse. |
| **Dutchesse** | 35 | His Nurse? why she was dead, ere ÿ [4] wast borne. |
| **Yorke** | | If 'twere not she,†[5] I cannot tell who told me. |
| **Queene** | | A parlous Boy: go too, you are too shrew'd. |
| **Dutchesse** | | Good Madam, be not angry with the Childe. |
| **Queene** | | Pitchers have eares. |

**ENTER A MESSENGER** [6]

---

P[1]   Qq set the prefix for the Cardinall, Ff set the prefix used for the young Duke of Yorke, viz. 'Yor.': most modern texts follow Qq and assign the speech to the adult Archbishop/Cardinall

W[2]   Ff/most modern texts = 'And', Qq = 'Why Madame'

SP/WS[3]   arguing white space, most modern texts follow Qq and set these two short Ff lines (4/7 syllables) as one: if the Ff setting were to stand, it might suggest the Dutchesse settling herself and/or setting up the child for an enjoyable moment of back-biting gossip

AB[4]   F1 - F2 = 'ÿ', (printed as such because of lack of column width), F3/most modern texts = 'thou'

COMP/W[5]   the opening old fashioned 's' on the combined type-face of 'sh' is badly twisted, and the word set appears to be 'the': Qq/F2/most modern texts clearly set 'she'

P/LS[6]   some modern texts follow Qq which assign the entry not to a messenger but to Dorset, the Queene's son, and alter the dialogue and prefixes accordingly, viz.

| | |
|---|---|
| Cardinall | Here comes your sonne, Lo: M. Dorset, <br> What newes Lo: Marques? |
| Dorset | Such newes my Lo: as grieves me to unfolde. |

| 40 | **Archbishop** | Heere comes a Messenger: What Newes? |
| | **Messenger** | Such newes my Lord, as greeves me to report. |
| | **Queene** | How doth the Prince? |
| | **Messenger** | Well Madam, and in health. |
| | **Dutchesse** | What is thy Newes? [1] |

| 45 | **Messenger** | Lord Rivers, and Lord Grey,<br>Are sent to Pomfret,° and with them,<br>Sir Thomas Vaughan, Prisoners. ° [2] |

| | **Dutchesse** | Who hath committed them? |
| | **Messenger** | The mighty Dukes,° Glouster and Buckingham. |
| 50 | **Archbishop** | For what offence? ° [3] |

L 185 - b

| | **Messenger** | The summe of all I can, I have disclos'd:<br>Why, or for what, the Nobles were committed,<br>Is all unknowne to me, my gracious Lord. |

| | **Queene** | Aye me! |
| 55 | | I see the ruine of my [4] House:<br>The Tyger now hath seiz'd the gentle Hinde,<br>Insulting Tiranny beginnes to Jutt<br>Upon the innocent and awelesse Throne:<br>Welcome Destruction, Blood, and Massacre, |
| 60 | | I see (as in a Map) the end of all. |

| | **Dutchesse** | Accursed, and unquiet wrangling dayes,<br>How many of you have mine eyes beheld? |
| | | My Husband lost his life, to get the Crowne,<br>And often up and downe my sonnes were tost |
| 65 | | For me to joy, and weepe, their gaine and losse. |
| | | And being seated, and Domesticke broyles<br>Cleane over-blowne, themselves the Conquerors,<br>Make warre upon themselves, [5] Brother to Brother; |

---

L 185 - b / R 185 - b : 2. 4. 38 - 62

[W] [1] Qq/one modern text add 'then': Ff/most modern texts omit the word

[LS] [2] even though Ff set three irregular lines (6/8/7 syllables), possibly suggesting either a breathless reply, or care in the delivery of the news, few modern texts follow the more metrically correct Qq which sets 11/10) as shown

[LS] [3] though Qq/Ff continue the (shocked?) pauses surrounding the news and the reaction to it, by setting an irregular passage of three lines (6/10/4 syllables), most modern texts set two pentameter lines as shown

[W] [4] Ff/most modern texts = 'my', Qq/one modern text = 'our', (a sensible reading if Dorset takes the place of the Messenger - see footnote #6, page 57)

[W] [5] most modern texts set the following Ff only phrase

|    |             |                                                                    |
|----|-------------|--------------------------------------------------------------------|
| 70 |             | Blood to blood, selfe against selfe :   O prepostorous             |
|    |             | And franticke outrage, end thy damned spleene,                     |
|    |             | Or let me dye, to looke on earth [1] no more.                      |
|    | **Queene**  | Come, come my Boy, we will to Sanctuary.                            |
|    |             | [2] Madam, farwell.                                                 |
|    | **Dutchesse** | Stay, I will go with you.                                         |
| 75 | **Queene**  | You have no cause.                                                  |
|    | **Archbishop** | My gracious Lady go,                                             |
|    |             | And thether beare your Treasure and your Goodes,                   |
|    |             | For my part, Ile resigne unto your Grace                           |
|    |             | The Seale I keepe, and so betide to me,                            |
| 80 |             | As well I tender you, and all of yours.                            |
|    |             | Go, Ile conduct you to the Sanctuary.                              |

**[Exeunt]**

---

[1] Ff/most modern texts = 'earth', Qq/one modern text = 'death'

[2] most modern texts set this Ff only line

# Actus Tertius. Scœna Prima

**THE TRUMPETS SOUND.**
**ENTER YONG PRINCE, THE DUKES OF GLOCESTER, AND BUCKINGHAM,**
**LORD CARDINALL, WITH OTHERS** [1]

| | | |
|---|---|---|
| **Buckingham** | Welcome sweete Prince to London,→ [2] | |
| | To your Chamber. | |
| **Richard** | Welcome deere Cosin, my thoughts Soveraign | |
| | The wearie way hath made you Melancholly. | |
| 5 **Prince** | No Unkle, but our crosses on the way, | |
| | Have made it tedious, wearisome, and heavie. | |
| | I want more Unkles heere to welcome me. | |
| **Richard** | Sweet Prince, the untainted vertue of your yeers | |
| | Hath not yet div'd into the Worlds deceit: | |
| 10 | No [3] more can you distinguish of a man, | |
| | Then of his outward shew, which God he knowes, | |
| | Seldome or never jumpeth with the heart. | |
| | Those Unkles which you want, were dangerous: | |
| | Your Grace attended to their Sugred words, | |
| 15 | But look'd not on the poyson of their hearts: | |
| | God keepe you from them, and from such false Friends. | |
| **Prince** | God keepe me from false Friends,→ [4] | |
| | But they were none. | |
| **Richard** | My Lord, the Maior of London comes to greet | |
| 20 | you. | |

**ENTER LORD MAIOR** [5]

---

SD [1] most modern texts include Catesby among the 'Others', while some also add the Derby/Stanley character

SP [2] arguing lack of column width in F1 caused this Ff opening to be set as two short lines (7/4 syllables), most modern texts follow Qq and join the two lines as one: if the Ff setting were to stand, it might well reflect the young Prince's palpable dislike?/fear? of the place, thus occasioning the second line

W [3] Qq/most modern texts = 'Nor', Ff = 'No'

SP [4] arguing lack of column width in F1 caused this Ff speech to be set as two short lines (6/4 syllables), most modern texts follow Qq and join the two lines as one: if the Ff setting were to stand, it allows quite a loaded silence before the Prince continues his second line, and after, before Richard brings in the Maior (however, see the following footnote)

SD [5] though Qq/Ff set the Maior's entry after Richard's line, as if he were being announced, most modern texts advance the entry to before the speech: this resetting also has the effect of all those on-stage being rescued from an awkward silence by the accident of the Maior's arrival, rather than by Richard's deliberate action (see the previous footnote)

| | |
|---|---|
| **Lord.Maior** | God blesse your Grace, with health and<br>happie dayes. |
| **Prince** | I thanke you, good my Lord, and thank you all : |

| | |
|---|---|
| | I thought my Mother, and my Brother Yorke, |
| 25 | Would long, ere this, have met us on the way. |
| | Fie, what a Slug is Hastings, that he comes [1] not<br>To tell us, whether they will come, or no. |

**ENTER LORD HASTINGS**

| | |
|---|---|
| **Buckingham** | And in good time, heere comes the sweating<br>Lord. |
| 30  **Prince** | Welcome, my Lord :  what, will our Mother<br>come? |
| **Hastings** | On what occasion God he knowes, not I ;<br>The Queene your Mother, and your Brother Yorke,<br>Have taken Sanctuarie :  The tender Prince |
| 35 | Would faine have come with me, to meet your Grace,<br>But by his Mother was perforce with-held. |
| **Buckingham** | Fie, what an indirect and peevish course<br>Is this of hers?<br>                         Lord Cardinall, will your Grace |
| 40 | Perswade the Queene, to send the Duke of Yorke<br>Unto his Princely Brother presently?<br>If she denie, Lord Hastings goe with him,<br>And from her jealous Armes pluck him perforce. |
| **Cardinall** | My Lord of Buckingham, if my weake Oratorie |
| 45 | Can from his Mother winne the Duke of Yorke,<br>Anon expect him here :  but if she be obdurate<br>To milde entreaties, God [2] forbid<br>We should infringe the holy Priviledge<br>Of blessed Sanctuarie :  not for all this Land, |
| 50 | Would I be guiltie of so great [3] a sinne. |
| **Buckingham** | You are too sencelesse obstinate, my Lord,<br>Too ceremonious, and traditionall. |

[1] though Qq/Ff /most modern texts set 'comes', both editions of *The Oxford Shakespeare*, ops. cit., offer 'hastes' so as to avoid repetition of 'comes/come' three times in four lines, and to set up a pun on Hasting's name

[2] most modern texts add Qq's 'in heaven' (maintaining a ten or eleven syllable line) which Ff omit

[3] Q1-2/most modern texts = 'deepe', Q3-6/Ff = 'great'

|    |            |                                                           |
|----|------------|-----------------------------------------------------------|
| 55 |            | Weigh it but with the grossenesse of this Age,<br>You breake not Sanctuarie, in seizing him:<br>The benefit thereof is always granted<br>To those, whose dealings have deserv'd the place,<br>And those who have the wit to clayme the place:<br>This Prince hath neyther claym'd it, nor deserv'd it,<br>And therefore, in mine opinion, cannot have it. |
| 60 |            | Then taking him from thence, that is not there,<br>You breake no Priviledge, nor Charter there:<br>Oft have I heard of Sanctuarie men,<br>But Sanctuarie children, ne're till now. |
|    | **Cardinall** | My Lord, you shall o're-rule my mind for once. |
| 65 |            | Come on, Lord Hastings, will you goe with me? |
|    | **Hastings** | I goe, my Lord. |

**[Exit Cardinall and Hastings]** [1]

|    |            |                                                           |
|----|------------|-----------------------------------------------------------|
|    | **Prince** | Good Lords, make all the speedie hast you may. |
|    |            | Say, Unckle Glocester, if our Brother come,<br>Where shall we sojourne, till our Coronation? |
| 70 | **Glocester** | Where it think'st [2] best unto your Royall selfe. |
|    |            | If I may counsaile you, some day or two<br>Your Highnesse shall repose you at the Tower:<br>Then where you please, and shall be thought most fit<br>For your best health, and recreation. |
| 75 | **Prince** | I doe not like the Tower, of any place:<br>Did Julius Cæsar build that place, my Lord? |
|    | **Buckingham** | He did, my gracious Lord, begin that place,<br>Which since, succeeding Ages have re-edify'd. |
|    | **Prince** | Is it upon record?  or else reported |
| 80 |            | Successively from age to age, he built it? |
|    | **Buckingham** | Upon record, my gracious Lord. |
|    | **Prince** | But say, my Lord, it were not registred,<br>Me thinkes the truth should live from age to age,<br>As 'twere retayl'd to all posteritie, |
| 85 |            | Even to the generall ending [3] day. |

L 186 - a :  3. 1. 46 - 78

---

SD [1] most modern texts set the Ff only exit after the next line, thus suggesting it is said to the men as they leave rather than, as Ff suggest, being called off after them

W [2] Q1-2/most modern texts = 'seemes', Q3-6/Ff = 'think'st'

W [3] Qq/most modern texts = 'all-ending', Ff = 'ending'

| | | |
|---|---|---|
| **Glocester** | [1] So wise, so young, they say doe never live long. | |
| **Prince** | What say you, Unckle? | L 186 - a |
| **Glocester** | I say, without Characters, Fame lives long,<br>[2] Thus, like the formall Vice, Iniquitie,<br>I moralize two meanings in one word. | |
| 90 | | |
| **Prince** | That Julius Cæsar was a famous man,<br>With what his Valour did enrich his Wit,<br>His Wit set downe, to make his Valour live:<br>Death makes [3] no Conquest of his [4] Conqueror,<br>For [5] now he lives in Fame, though not in Life. | |
| 95 | | |
| | Ile tell you what, my Cousin Buckingham. | |
| **Buckingham** | What, my gracious [6] Lord? | |
| **Prince** | And if I live untill I be a man,<br>Ile win our ancient Right in France againe,<br>Or dye a Souldier, as I liv'd a King. | |
| 100 | | |
| **Glocester** | Short Summers lightly have a forward Spring. | |

**ENTER YOUNG YORKE, HASTINGS, AND CARDINALL**

| | | |
|---|---|---|
| **Buckingham** | Now in good time, heere comes the Duke of Yorke. | |
| **Prince** | Richard of Yorke, how fares our Noble [7] Brother? | |
| 105 | | |
| **Yorke** | Well, my deare [8] Lord, so must I call you now. | |
| **Prince** | I, Brother, to our griefe, as it is yours:<br>Too late he dy'd, that might have kept that Title,<br>Which by his death hath lost much Majestie. | |
| 110 **Glocester** | How fares our Cousin, Noble Lord of Yorke? | |

---

L 186 - a / R 186 - a :  3. 1. 79 - 101

[A 1] most modern texts suggest this is spoken as an aside

[A/SD 2] most modern texts set the very rare F2 direction that the speech is an aside

[W 3] Qq/Ff /most modern texts = 'makes', one modern text accepts the commonly suggested modern gloss 'made'

[W 4] Q1/most modern texts = 'this', Q2-6/Ff = 'his'

[W 5] Qq/Ff /most modern texts = 'For', one modern text accepts the gloss 'Yet'

[W 6] Qq/Ff = variations of 'gratious/gracious', one modern text accepts the gloss 'good'

[W 7] Q1-2/most modern texts = 'loving', Q3-6/Ff = 'Noble'

[W 8] Q1-2/most modern texts = 'dread', Q3-6/Ff = 'deare'

| | | |
|---|---|---|
| | **Yorke** | I thanke you, gentle Unckle. |
| | | O my Lord, |
| | | You said, that idle Weeds are fast in growth : |
| | | The Prince, my Brother, hath out-growne me farre. |
| 115 | **Glocester** | He hath, my Lord. |
| | **Yorke** | And therefore is he idle? ) |
| | **Glocester** | Oh my faire Cousin, I must not say so. |
| | **Yorke** | Then he is more beholding to you, then I. |
| | **Glocester** | He may command me as my Soveraigne, |
| 120 | | But you have power in me, as in a Kinsman. |
| | **Yorke** | I pray you, Unckle, give me this Dagger. |
| | **Glocester** | My Dagger, little Cousin? with all my heart. |
| | **Prince** | A Begger, Brother? |
| | **Yorke** | Of my kind Unckle, that I know will give, |
| 125 | | And being but a Toy, which is no griefe to give. |
| | **Glocester** | A greater gift then that, Ile give my Cousin. |
| | **Yorke** | A greater gift? |
| | | O, that's the Sword to it. |
| | **Glocester** | I, gentle Cousin, were it light enough. |
| 130 | **Yorke** | O then I see, you will part but with light gifts, |
| | | In weightier things you'le say a Begger nay. |
| | **Glocester** | It is too weightie [1] for your Grace to weare. |
| | **Yorke** | I weigh it lightly, were it heavier. |
| | **Glocester** | What, would you have my Weapon, little Lord? |
| 135 | **Yorke** | I would that I might thanke you, as, as, [2] you |
| | | call me. |
| | **Glocester** | How? |
| | **Yorke** | Little. |
| | **Prince** | My Lord of Yorke will still be crosse in talke : |
| 140 | | Unckle, your Grace knowes how to beare with him. |

[1] Q1/most modern texts = 'heavy', Q2-6/Ff = 'weightie'

[2] Q3/F1 are the only texts that seem to set a stutter with 'as, as,': Q1-2/Q5-6/F2/most modern texts = 'as'

| | |
|---|---|
| **Yorke** | You meane to beare me, not to beare with me: |
| | Unckle, my Brother mockes both you and me, |
| | Because that I am little, like an Ape, |
| | He thinkes that you should beare me on your shoulders. |
| 145    **Buckingham** | With what a sharpe provided wit he reasons: |
| | To mittigate the scorne he gives his Unckle, |
| | He prettily and aptly taunts himselfe: |
| | So cunning, and so young, is wonderfull. |
| **Glocester** | My Lord, wilt please you passe along? |
| 150 | My selfe, and my good Cousin Buckingham, |
| | Will to your Mother, to entreat of her |
| | To meet you at the Tower, and welcome you.      R 186 - a |
| **Yorke** | What, will you goe unto the Tower, my Lord? |
| **Prince** | My Lord Protector [1] will have it so. |
| 155    **Yorke** | I shall not sleepe in quiet at the Tower. |
| **Glocester** | Why, what should you feare? |
| **Yorke** | Marry, my Unckle Clarence angry Ghost: |
| | My Grandam told me he was murther'd there. |
| **Prince** | I feare no Unckles dead. |
| 160    **Glocester** | Nor none that live, I hope. |
| **Prince** | And if they live, I hope I need not feare. |
| | But come my Lord: and [2] with a heavie heart, |
| | Thinking on them, goe I unto the Tower. |

**A SENET. EXEUNT PRINCE, YORKE, HASTINGS, AND DORSET**

**MANET RICHARD, BUCKINGHAM, AND CATESBY**

| | |
|---|---|
| **Buckingham** | Thinke you, my Lord, this little prating Yorke |
| 165 | Was not incensed by his subtile Mother, |
| | To taunt and scorne you thus opprobriously? |
| **Glocester** | No doubt, no doubt: Oh 'tis a perilous [3] Boy, |
| | Bold, quicke, ingenious, forward, capable: |
| | Hee is all the Mothers, from the top to toe. |

---

[1] Q1/most modern texts = 'needes', setting a ten syllable line; Q2-5/Ff omit the word

[2] Ff/one modern text = 'and with', Qq/most modern texts = 'with'

[3] Qq/Ff set a variant of 'perilous', most modern texts = 'parlous'

| 170 | **Buckingham** | Well, let them rest : Come hither Catesby, |
| | | Thou art sworne as deepely to effect what we intend, |
| | | As closely to conceale what we impart : |
| | | Thou know'st our reasons urg'd upon the way. |
| | | |
| 175 | | What think'st thou? is it not an easie matter, |
| | | To make William Lord Hastings [1] of our minde, |
| | | For the installment of this Noble Duke |
| | | In the Seat Royall of this famous Ile? |
| | | |
| | **Catesby** | He for his fathers sake so loves the Prince, |
| | | That he will not be wonne to ought against him. |
| | | |
| 180 | **Buckingham** | What think'st thou then of Stanley? |
| | |                          Will |
| | | not hee? |
| | | |
| | **Catesby** | Hee will doe all in all as Hastings doth. |

| | **Buckingham** | [2] Well then, no more but this : |
| 185 | | Goe gentle Catesby,° and as it were farre off, |
| | | Sound thou Lord Hastings,° |

| | | How he doth stand affected to our purpose, |
| | | [3] And summon him to morrow to the Tower, |
| | | To sit about the Coronation. |
| | | |
| 190 | | If thou do'st finde him tractable to us, |
| | | Encourage him, and tell him all our reasons : |
| | | If he be leaden, ycie, cold, unwilling, |
| | | Be thou so too, and so breake off the [4] talke, |
| | | And give us notice of his inclination : |
| 195 | | For we to morrow hold divided Councels, |
| | | Wherein thy selfe shalt highly be employ'd. |
| | | |
| | **Richard** | Commend me to Lord William : tell him Catesby, |
| | | His ancient Knot of dangerous Adversaries |
| | | To morrow are let blood at Pomfret Castle, |
| 200 | | And bid my Lord, for joy of this good newes, |
| | | Give Mistresse Shore one gentle Kisse the more. |
| | | |
| | **Buckingham** | Good Catesby, goe effect this businesse soundly. |

---

L 187 - a : 3. 1. 157 - 186

w [1] though Qq/Ff agree on the word order, some commentators/one modern text = 'Lord William'

LS [2] as Richard begins to deal with the potential threat of Hastings, Ff set a three line irregular passage (6/11/5 syllables) suggesting a wonderful contrast of short pauses sandwiching a sudden burst of clarity : most modern texts set two slightly onrushed eleven syllable lines as shown (Qq set the same opening as Ff but a somewhat varied ending, partially matching the revision of the modern texts)

LS [3] most modern texts set the next two Ff only lines

w [4] Ff/most modern texts = 'the', Qq/one modern text = 'your'

| | | |
|---|---|---|
| | **Catesby** | My good Lords both, with all the heed I can. |
| | **Richard** | Shall we heare from you, Catesby, ere we sleepe? |
| 205 | **Catesby** | You shall, my Lord. |
| | **Richard** | At Crosby House,[1] there shall you find us both. |

**[Exit Catesby]**

| | | |
|---|---|---|
| | **Buckingham** | Now, my Lord,→ [2] |
| | | What shall wee doe, if wee perceive |
| | | Lord Hastings will not yeeld to our Complots? |
| 210 | **Richard** | Chop off his Head : → |
| | | Something wee will determine : [3] |
| | | And looke when I am King, clayme thou of me |
| | | The Earledome of Hereford, and all the moveables |
| | | Whereof the King, my Brother, was possest. |
| 215 | **Buckingham** | Ile clayme that promise at your Graces hand. |
| | **Richard** | And looke to have it yeelded with all kindnesse. |
| | | Come, let us suppe betimes, that afterwards |
| | | Wee may digest our complots in some forme. |

L 187 - a

**[Exeunt]**

---

L 187 - a / R 187 - a :  3. 1. 187 - 200

w [1]  Ff/some modern texts = 'House', Qq/some modern texts = 'place': see footnote #3, page 15

sp [2]  as Buckingham opens the tricky topic of what to do if Hastings will not join them, Ff set two short lines (3/8 syllables), perhaps suggesting a careful opening: similarly, as Richard replies the same careful two Ff short lines are set (4/7 syllables): most modern texts follow Qq (which set a slightly different text) and join each pair of lines together, with metrically minded modern texts omitting the Qq/Ff 'Now' in Buckingham's opening, thus creating pentameter

w [3]  Qq/most modern texts = 'somewhat we will doe', Ff = 'Something wee will determine'

# Scena Secunda

**ENTER A MESSENGER TO THE DOORE OF HASTINGS** [1]

| | |
|---|---|
| **Messenger** | My Lord, my Lord. |
| **Hastings** | Who knockes? |
| **Messenger** | One from the [2] Lord Stanley. |
| **Hastings** | What is't a Clocke? |
| 5    **Messenger** | Upon the stroke of foure. |

**ENTER LORD HASTINGS**

| | |
|---|---|
| **Hastings** | Cannot my Lord Stanley sleepe these tedious Nights? |
| **Messenger** | So it appeares, by that I have to say: First, he commends him to your Noble selfe. |
| 10    **Hastings** | What then? |
| **Messenger** | Then certifies your Lordship, that this Night He dreamt, the Bore had rased off his Helme: Besides, he sayes there are two Councels kept; And that may be determin'd at the one, Which may make you and him to rue at th'other. |

> Therefore he sends to know your Lordships pleasure,
> If you will presently take Horse with him,
> And with all speed post with him toward the North,
> To shun the danger that his Soule divines.

| | |
|---|---|
| 20    **Hastings** | Goe fellow, goe, returne unto thy Lord, Bid him not feare the seperated Councell: [3] His Honor and my selfe are at the one, And at the other, is my good friend Catesby; |

---

SD 1   from the ensuing dialogue and stage direction, most modern texts suggest the Messenger is knocking at the door, and that Hastings speaks from within

W/SD 2   Ff/most modern texts = 'One from the', Qq/at least one modern text = 'A messenger from the', with some commentators suggesting the dropping of 'the': also most modern texts follow Qq and advance Hasting's entry to after this line

W 3   Ff/most modern texts = variations of 'Councell', Q2-6 = 'councels', Q1/one modern text = 'counsels'

|    |    |    |
|----|----|----|
| 25 |    | Where nothing can proceede, that toucheth us,<br>Whereof I shall not have intelligence:<br>Tell him his Feares are shallow, without instance. |

And for his Dreames, I wonder hee's so simple,[1]
To trust the mock'ry of unquiet slumbers.

30  To flye the Bore, before the Bore pursues,
Were to incense the Bore to follow us,
And make pursuit, where he did meane no chase.

Goe, bid thy Master rise, and come to me,
And we will both together to the Tower,
Where he shall see the Bore will use us kindly.

35  **Messenger**   Ile goe, my Lord, and tell him what you say.

**[Exit]**
**ENTER CATESBY**

**Catesby**   Many good morrowes to my Noble Lord.

**Hastings**   Good morrow Catesby, you are early stirring:
What newes, what newes, in this our tott'ring State?

**Catesby**   It is a reeling World indeed, my Lord:
40  And I beleeve will never stand upright,
Till Richard weare the Garland of the Realme.

| **Hastings** | How weare the Garland? → |
|---|---|
|  | Doest thou meane the Crowne? |
| **Catesby** | I, my good Lord.[2] |

45  **Hastings**   Ile have this Crown of mine cut frõ[3] my shoulders,
Before Ile see the Crowne so foule mis-plac'd:
But canst thou guesse, that he doth ayme at it?          --- R 187 - a

**Catesby**   I, on my life, and hopes to find you forward,
Upon his partie, for the gaine thereof:
50  And thereupon he sends you this good newes,
That this same very day your enemies,
The Kindred of the Queene, must dye at Pomfret.

---

R 187 - a / L 188 - a :  3. 2. 23 - 50

[1] Ff/most modern texts = 'hee's so simple', Qq = 'he is so fond'

[2] the actor has choice as to which two of these three short lines may be joined as one line of split verse:  most modern texts follow Qq and set Hasting's reply (two short lines in Ff, 5/5/ syllables) as a single line of verse :  the Ff setting allows careful hesitations for both as the subject is broached, the Qq hesitations only kick in after Hastings asks for clarification

[3] F1-2 = 'frõ', F3/most modern texts = 'from'

| | |
|---|---|
| **Hastings** | Indeed I am no mourner for that newes, |
| | Because they have beene still my adversaries : |
| 55 | But, that Ile give my voice on Richards side, |
| | To barre my Masters Heires in true Descent, |
| | God knowes I will not doe it, to the death. |
| | |
| **Catesby** | God keepe your Lordship in that gracious |
| | minde. |
| | |
| 60 **Hastings** | But I shall laugh at this a twelve-month hence, |
| | That they which brought me in my Masters hate, |
| | I live to looke upon their Tragedie. |
| | |
| | Well Catesby, ere a fort-night make me older, |
| | Ile send some packing, that yet thinke not *on't. [1] |
| | |
| 65 **Catesby** | 'Tis a vile thing to dye, my gracious Lord, |
| | When men are unprepar'd, and looke not for it. |
| | |
| **Hastings** | O monstrous, monstrous! and so falls it out |
| | With Rivers, Vaughan, Grey : and so 'twill doe |
| | With some men else, that thinke themselves as safe |
| 70 | As thou and I, who (as thou know'st) are deare |
| | To Princely Richard, and to Buckingham. |
| | |
| **Catesby** | The Princes both make high account of you, |
| | [2] For they account his Head upon the Bridge. |
| | |
| **Hastings** | I know they doe, and I have well deserv'd it. |

### ENTER LORD STANLEY

| | |
|---|---|
| 75 | Come on, come on, where is your Bore-speare man? |
| | Feare you the Bore, and goe so unprovided? |
| | |
| **Stanley** | My Lord good morrow, good morrow Catesby : |
| | You may jeast on, but by the holy Rood, |
| | I doe not like these severall Councels, I. |
| | |
| 80 **Hastings** | My Lord, I hold my Life as deare as yours,[3] |
| | And never in my dayes, I doe protest, |
| | Was it so precious to me, as *'tis now : |
| | Thinke you, but that I know our state secure, |
| | I would be so triumphant as I am? |

---

[1] Ff/most modern texts = 'on't', Qq/one modern text = 'on it': for the remainder of the play, there is a spate of such contrasting expansions and contractions between Ff and Qq based modern texts: for the rest of this script each instance will be asterisked without further footnote

[2] most modern texts indicate this line is spoken as an aside

[3] Ff = 'as deare as yours', Qq = 'as you doe yours', some modern texts 'as dear as you': also some modern texts set 'My Lord' as a two syllable separate line

| | | |
|---|---|---|
| 85 | **Stanley** | The Lords at Pomfret, whé [1] they rode from London, |
| | | Were jocund, and suppos'd their states were sure, |
| | | And they indeed had no cause to mistrust: |
| | | But yet you see, how soone the Day o're-cast. |
| | | This sudden stab of Rancour I misdoubt: |
| 90 | | Pray God (I say) I prove a needlesse Coward. |
| | | What, shall we toward the Tower? [2] the day is spent. |
| | **Hastings** | Come, come, have with you: → |
| | | Wot you what, my Lord,[3] |
| | | To day the Lords you talke of, are beheaded. |
| 95 | **Stanley** | They, for their truth, might better wear their Heads, |
| | | Then some that have accus'd them, weare their Hats. |
| | | But come, my Lord, *let's away. |

### ENTER A PURSUIVANT [4]

| | | |
|---|---|---|
| | **Hastings** | [5] Goe on before, Ile talke with this good fellow. |

### [Exit Lord Stanley, and Catesby]

| | | |
|---|---|---|
| | | How now, Sirrha? how goes the World with thee? |
| 100 | **Pursuivant** | The better, that your Lordship please to aske. |
| | **Hastings** | I tell thee man, 'tis better with me now, |
| | | Then when thou met'st me [6] last, where now we meet: |
| | | Then was I going Prisoner to the Tower, |
| | | By the suggestion of the Queenes Allyes. |
| 105 | | But now I tell thee (keepe it to thy selfe) |
| | | This day those enemies are put to death, |
| | | And I in better state then *ere I was. |
| | **Pursuivant** | God hold it, to your Honors good content. |

L 188 - a

---

[AB] [1] F1 = 'whé', F2/most modern texts = 'when'

[LS] [2] most modern texts set the following Ff only phrase

[W/SP] [3] Qq set the alternative single line 'I go: but stay, heare you not the newes,': most modern texts set the Ff text, (altering 'talke' to 'talk'd' in the following line), but join the two lines together: the Ff setting (5/5 syllables) might suggest the momentary pause allows the two men to withdraw a little further away from Catesby

[N/P] [4] Qq set a partial name for the Pursuivant 'Hastin.' which seems to suggest he shares the same name as Hastings: Ff drop the name: some modern texts tentatively draw attention to the similarity: for a possible though convoluted explanation of the similarity, see *The Arden Shakespeare King Richard III*, op. cit., page 338, note to iii.ii.92 S.D.

[ALT] [5] some modern texts set Qq's alternative text
Go you before, Ile follow presently.
Well met, how goes the world with thee?

[W] [6] Qq/most modern texts = 'I met thee', Ff = 'thou met'st me'

| | | |
|---|---|---|
| **Hastings** | | Gramercie fellow: [1] there, drinke that for me. |

**THROWES HIM HIS PURSE**

110 **Pursuivant**   I thanke your Honor. [2]

**[Exit Pursuivant]**
**ENTER A PRIEST**

**Priest**   [3] Well met, my Lord, I am glad to see your Honor.

**Hastings**   I thanke thee, good Sir John, with all my heart.

I am in your debt, for your last Exercise:
115   Come the next Sabboth, and I will content you. [4]

**Priest**   Ile wait upon your Lordship. [5]

**ENTER BUCKINGHAM**

**Buckingham**   What, talking with a Priest, Lord Chamberlaine?

Your friends at Pomfret, they doe need the Priest,
Your Honor hath no shriving worke in hand.

120 **Hastings**   Good faith, and when I met this holy man,
The men you talke of, came into my minde.

What, goe you toward the Tower?

**Buckingham**   I doe, my Lord, but long I cannot stay there:
I shall returne before your Lordship, thence.

125 **Hastings**   Nay like enough, for I stay Dinner there.

**Buckingham**   [6] And Supper too, although thou *know'st it not.
Come, will you goe?

**Hastings**   Ile wait upon your Lordship. [7]

**[Exeunt]**

---

W [1]  Ff based modern texts = 'fellow', Qq based modern texts = 'Hastings'

W [2]  Ff/some modern texts = 'I thanke your Honor.', Qq/one modern text = 'God save your Lordship.'

LS [3]  most modern texts set this Ff only line

SD [4]  most modern texts set Qq's stage direction omitted by Ff, 'He whispers in his eare': (presumably Hastings is doing the whispering)

LS/SD [5]  Ff set the same line twice, here for the Priest, and at the end of the scene for Hastings: Qq do not set the line either time: some modern texts omit this first setting: also though most modern texts suggest the Priest now leaves, Qq/Ff give no such indication: should he stay on-stage, Buckingham's comments might be seen as a little more barbed

A [6]  most modern texts indicate this is spoken as an aside

LS/W [7]  see footnote #5 above

**72**

# Scena Tertia

ENTER SIR RICHARD RATCLIFFE, WITH HALBERDS, CARRYING
THE NOBLES [1] TO DEATH AT POMFRET

∞ [2]

| | |
|---|---|
| **Rivers** | Sir Richard Ratcliffe, let me tell thee this, |
| | To day shalt thou behold a Subject die, |
| | For Truth, for Dutie, and for Loyaltie. |
| **Grey** | God blesse the Prince from all the Pack of you, |
| | A Knot you are, of damned Blood-suckers. |
| **Vaughn** | [3] You live, that shall cry woe for this heere- |
| | after. |
| **Ratcliffe** | Dispatch, the limit of your Lives is out. |
| **Rivers** | O Pomfret, Pomfret! |
| | O thou bloody Prison! |
| | Fatall and ominous to Noble Peeres: |
| | Within the guiltie Closure of thy Walls, |
| | Richard the Second here was hackt to death: |
| | And for more slander to thy dismall Seat, |
| | Wee give to thee our guiltlesse blood to drinke. |
| **Grey** | Now Margarets Curse is falne upon our Heads, |
| | [4] When shee exclaim'd on Hastings, you, and I, |
| | For standing by, when Richard stab'd her Sonne. |
| **Rivers** | Then curs'd shee Richard, → [5] |
| | Then curs'd shee Buckingham, |
| | Then curs'd shee Hastings. |
| | Oh remember God, |

5

10

15

20

---

N/SD [1]
    most modern texts add from Qq the names of the Nobles, viz. 'Rivers, Gray, and Vaughan', and maintain Ff's '
    to death at Pomfret', though this is not set in Qq
ADD [2]
    some, but not all, modern texts add the Qq line spoken by Ratcliffe, 'Come bring foorth the prisoners.'
LS [3]
    most modern texts set this and the following Ff only speech
LS [4]
    some modern texts set this Ff only line
SP [5]
    most modern texts follow Qq and set these two short Ff lines (5/6 syllables) as one, presumably arguing there
    wasn't enough column width in F1 to follow suit: if the Ff setting were to stand it might suggest River's
    realisation of the power and enormity of Margaret's all-encompassing curse forces him to pause: also some texts
    follow Qq and reverse the setting of 'Richard' and 'Hastings'

To heare her prayer for them, as now for us :
And for my Sister, and her Princely Sonnes,
25          Be satisfy'd, deare God, with our true blood,
Which, as thou know'st, unjustly must be spilt.

**Ratcliffe**          Make haste, the houre of death is expiate.

**Rivers**          Come Grey, come Vaughan, let us here embrace.
Farewell, untill we meet againe in Heaven.

**[Exeunt]**

R 188 - a

# Scœna Quarta

**ENTER BUCKINGHAM DARBY, HASTINGS, BISHOP OF ELY,
NORFOLKE, RATCLIFFE, LOVELL, WITH OTHERS,
AT A TABLE** [1]

| | |
|---|---|
| **Hastings** | Now Noble Peeres, the cause why we are met, |
| | Is to determine of the Coronation : |
| | In Gods Name speake, when is the Royall day? |
| **Buckingham** | Is all things ready for the Royall [2] time? |
| Derby as | |
| 5    **Darby** | It is, and wants but nomination. |
| **Ely** | To morrow then I judge a happie day. |
| **Buckingham** | Who knowes the Lord Protectors mind herein? |
| | Who is most inward with the Noble Duke? |
| **Ely** | Your Grace, we thinke, [3] should soonest know his |
| 10 | minde. |
| **Buckingham** | We know each others Faces : for our Hearts, [4] |
| | He knowes no more of mine, then I of yours, |
| | Or I of his, my Lord, then you of mine : |
| | Lord Hastings, you and he are neere in love. |
| 15    **Hastings** | I thanke his Grace, I know he loves me well : |
| | But for his purpose in the Coronation, |
| | I have not sounded him, nor he deliver'd |
| | His gracious pleasure any way therein : |
| | But you, my Honorable Lords, may name the time, |
| 20 | And in the Dukes behalfe Ile give my Voice, |
| | Which I presume *hee'le take in gentle part. |

**ENTER GLOUCESTER**

---

SD / ALT / N / PCT [1]                                        L 189 - a :  3. 4. 1 - 20

      most modern texts add a comma to separate the names of Buckingham and Darby:  also, some of the modern texts basing their editions on Qq note that, in Qq, Catesby is assigned the later Ff stage direction and subsequent dialogue for Ratcliffe and Lovell, lines 94-5 and 102, page 78, and so set his name in place of theirs at the entry:  for further details, see *The Arden Shakespeare King Richard III*, op. cit., page 231, footnote to S.D., and pages 16 - 17 which is somewhat counter-balanced by *William Shakespeare: A Textual Companion*, op. cit., pages 240 - 1, footnote to line 3.4.0.3/1765.2

w [2]

to avoid word repetition from the previous line, one modern text alters Qq/Ff's 'the Royall' to 'that solemn'

w [3]

Ff/most modern texts = 'we thinke', Qq/one modern text = 'me thinke'

w [4]

Qq/Ff/most modern texts = 'Hearts', one recent gloss suggests 'minds'

| | |
|---|---|
| **Ely** | In happie time, here comes the Duke himselfe. |
| **Richard** | My Noble Lords, and Cousins all, good morrow:<br>I have beene long a sleeper: but I trust, |
| 25 | My absence doth neglect no great designe,<br>Which by my presence might have beene concluded. |
| **Buckingham** | Had you not [1] come upon your Q my Lord,<br>William, Lord Hastings, had pronounc'd your part;<br>I meane your Voice, for Crowning of the King. |
| 30  **Richard** | Then my Lord Hastings, no man might be bolder,<br>His Lordship knowes me well, and loves me well. |
| | My Lord of Ely, when I was last in Holborne,<br>I saw good Strawberries in your Garden there,<br>I doe beseech you, send for some of them. |
| 35  **Ely** | Mary and will, my Lord, with all my heart. |

**[Exit Bishop]**

| | |
|---|---|
| **Richard** | Cousin of Buckingham, a word with you. |
| | Catesby hath sounded Hastings in our businesse,<br>And findes the testie Gentleman so hot,<br>That he will lose his Head, ere give consent |
| 40 | His Masters Child, as worshipfully [2] he tearmes it,<br>Shall lose the Royaltie of Englands Throne. |
| **Buckingham** | Withdraw your selfe a while, Ile goe with you. |

**[Exeunt]** [3]

| | |
|---|---|
| **Darby** | We have not yet set downe this day of Triumph:<br>To morrow, in my judgement, is too sudden, |
| 45 | For I my selfe am not so well provided,<br>As else I would be, were the day prolong'd. |

**ENTER THE BISHOP OF ELY**

| | |
|---|---|
| **Ely** | Where is my Lord, the Duke of Gloster?<br>I have sent for these Strawberries. |
| **Hastings** | His Grace looks chearfully & smooth this morning, [4]    L 189 - a |
| 50 | There's some conceit or other likes him well,<br>When that he bids good morrow with such spirit. |

---

W [1] Ff = 'you not', Qq = 'not you'

W [2] Ff/most modern texts = 'worshipfully', Qq/one modern text = 'worshipful'

SD [3] most modern texts indicate the 'Exeunt' is just for Richard and Buckingham

W [4] Qq/most modern texts = 'to day', Ff = 'this morning'

I thinke *there's never a man in Christendome
Can lesser hide his love, or hate, then hee,
For by his Face straight shall you know his Heart.

55  **Darby**      What of his Heart perceive you in his Face,
By any livelyhood [1] he shew'd to day?

**Hastings**    Mary, that with no man here he is [2] offended :
For were he, he had shewne it in his Lookes.
                                ∞ [3]

### ENTER RICHARD, AND BUCKINGHAM

**Richard**     I pray you all, tell me what they deserve,
60              That doe conspire my death with divellish Plots
Of damned Witchcraft, and that have prevail'd
Upon my Body with their Hellish Charmes.

**Hastings**    The tender love I beare your Grace, my Lord,
Makes me most forward, in this princely presence,
65              To doome *th'Offendors, whosoe're [4] they be :
I say, my Lord, they have deserved death.

**Richard**     Then be your eyes the witnesse of their evill. [5]

Looke how I am bewitch'd : behold, mine Arme
Is like a blasted Sapling, wither'd up :
70              And this is Edwards Wife, that monstrous Witch,
Consorted with that Harlot, Strumpet Shore,
That by their Witchcraft thus have marked me.

**Hastings**    If they have done this deed, my Noble Lord.

**Richard**     If? thou Protector of this damned Strumpet,
75              Talk'st thou to me of Ifs : thou art a Traytor,
        ┌──────────────────────────────────────────────────────┐
        │ [6] Off with his Head ;  now by Saint Paul I sweare,  │
        │ I will not dine, untill I see the same.               │
        │                                                       │
        │ Lovell and Ratcliffe, looke that it be done :         │
        └──────────────────────────────────────────────────────┘

---

▼ [1]  Ff/most modern texts = 'livelyhood', Qq/one modern text = 'likelihood'

▼ [2]  Qq/Ff /most modern texts = 'he is', one recent gloss suggests 'is he'

ADD [3]  most modern texts add an extra Qq line for Stanley/Darby, viz. 'I pray God he be not, say I', sometimes omitting the last two words

▼ [4]  Qq = 'whatsoever', which some modern texts set as 'whatso'ere': Ff = 'whoso'ere'

SD [5]  some modern texts suggest Richard displays his crippled hand

LS [6]  Ff based modern texts set the passage as shown; Qq based modern texts set a variant of the following

Off with his Head; now by Saint Paule,
I will not dine I sweare,
Untill I see the same, some see it done.

77

[Exeunt] [1]

The rest that love me, rise, and follow me.

### MANET LOVELL AND RATCLIFFE, [2] WITH THE LORD HASTINGS

| | | |
|---|---|---|
| 80 | **Hastings** | Woe, woe for England, not a whit for me, |
| | | For I, too fond, might have prevented this: |
| | | Stanley did dreame, the Bore did rowse our Helmes,[3] |
| | | And [4] I did scorne it, and disdaine to flye: |
| | | Three times to day my Foot-Cloth-Horse did stumble, |
| 85 | | And started, when he look'd upon the Tower, |
| | | As loth to beare me to the slaughter-house. |

O now I need the Priest, that spake to me:
I now repent I told the Pursuiuant,
As too triumphing, how mine Enemies
To day at Pomfret bloodily were butcher'd,
And I my selfe secure, in grace and favour.

Oh Margaret, Margaret, now thy heavie Curse
Is lighted on poore Hastings wretched Head.

**Ratcliffe**   Come, come, dispatch, the Duke would be at dinner:
Make a short Shrift, he longs to see your Head.

**Hastings**   O momentarie grace of mortall men,
Which we more hunt for, then the grace of God!

Who builds his hope in ayre [5] of your good Lookes,
Lives like a drunken Sayler on a Mast,
Readie with every Nod to tumble downe,
Into the fatall Bowels of the Deepe.

**Lovell**   [6] Come, come, dispatch, 'tis bootlesse to exclaime.

**Hastings**   O bloody Richard: miserable England,
I prophecie the fearefull'st time to thee,
That ever wretched Age hath look'd upon.

SD 1
   most modern texts set the Ff only direction after Richard's next line: Ff's setting would allow Richard the
   dramatic option to call out the last line as he leaves the stage without even checking to see who follows: (Qq
   set a different direction)

SD / N / ALT 2
   Qq replace Lovell and Ratcliffe with Catesby in the stage direction and subsequent line assignments: see
   footnote #1, page 75

W 3
   Qq/most modern texts = 'race his helme', replacing 'race' with 'raze', Ff/one modern text = 'rowse our Helmes'

W 4
   Ff/most modern texts = 'And', Qq/one modern text = 'But'

W 5
   Qq/Ff/most modern texts set variations of 'ayre': one modern text quotes the little referred to Q7 and sets 'th'air'

LS / P 6
   most modern texts set the following Ff only lines; Qq based texts assign Lovell's line to Catesby

Come, lead me to the Block, beare him my Head,
They smile at me, who shortly shall be dead.

[Exeunt]                                         R 189 - a

ENTER RICHARD, AND BUCKINGHAM, IN ROTTEN ARMOUR,
MARVELLOUS ILL-FAVOURED
[Most modern texts create a new scene here, Act Three Scene 5]

**Richard**        Come Cousin,→ [1]
                   Canst thou quake, and change thy colour,
110                Murther thy breath in middle of a word,
                   And then againe begin, and stop againe,
                   As if thou were [2] distraught, and mad with terror?

**Buckingham**     Tut, I can counterfeit the deepe Tragedian,
                   Speake, and looke backe, and prie on every side,
115          [3]   Tremble and start at wagging of a Straw :
                   Intending deepe suspition, gastly Lookes
                   Are at my service, like enforced Smiles ;
                   And both are readie in their Offices,
             [4]   At any time to grace my Stratagemes.

120                But what, is Catesby gone?

**Richard**  [5]   He is, and see he brings the Maior along.

ENTER THE MAIOR, AND CATESBY [6]

**Buckingham**     Lord Maior.

---

R 189 - a / L 190 - a :  3. 4. 106 - 3. 5. 13

SP [1]  Ff set two short lines (2 or 3/8 syllables), perhaps suggesting they need the pause to finish their preparations for the Maior:  most modern texts follow Qq and set the two lines as one, presumably arguing lack of column width precluded F1 from following suit

W [2]  Ff/most modern texts = 'were', Qq/one modern text = 'wert'

LS [3]  most modern texts set this Ff only line, at least one text placing it as the second line of the speech

LS [4]  some, though not all modern texts, set the following Ff only three words and the following Ff only line

LS [5]  Ff based modern texts set the next nine speeches as shown: Qq based texts set (variations of) the following alternative sequence of essentially the same Ff dialogue

| Gloster | Here comes the Maior. |
| Buckingham | Let me alone to entertaine him. |
| | Lo: Maior. |
| Gloster | Looke to the drawbridge there. |
| Buckingham | The reason we have sent. |
| Gloster | Catesby, overlooke the wals. |
| Buckingham | Harke, I heare a drumme. |
| Gloster | Looke backe, defend thee, here are enemies. |
| Buckingham | God and our innocencie defend us. |
| Gloster | O, O, be quiet, it is Catesby. |

SD / ALT / N [6]  Qq based modern texts suggest the Maior enters alone, and that later it is Catesby (not Lovell and Ratcliffe) who brings in Hasting's head and speaks to Richard

79

| | Richard | Looke to the Draw-Bridge there. |
|---|---|---|
| | Buckingham | Hearke, a Drumme. |
| 125 | Richard | Catesby, o're-looke the Walls. |
| | Buckingham | Lord Maior, the reason we have sent. |
| | Richard | Looke back, defend thee, here are Enemies. |
| | Buckingham | God and our Innocencie defend, and guard us. |

**ENTER LOVELL AND RATCLIFFE, WITH HASTINGS HEAD** [1]

| | Richard | Be patient, they are friends: Ratcliffe, and Lovell. |
|---|---|---|
| 130 | Lovell | Here is the Head of that ignoble Traytor, |
| | | The dangerous and unsuspected Hastings. |
| | Richard | So deare I lov'd the man, that I must weepe: |
| | | I tooke him for the plainest harmelesse Creature, |
| | | That breath'd upon the Earth, a Christian. |
| 135 | | Made him my Booke, wherein my Soule recorded |
| | | The Historie of all her secret thoughts. |
| | | So smooth he dawb'd his Vice with shew of Vertue, |
| | | That his apparant open Guilt omitted, |
| | | I meane, his Conversation with Shores Wife, |
| 140 | | He liv'd from all attainder of suspects. [2] |
| | Buckingham | Well, well, he was the covertst sheltred Traytor |
| | | That ever liv'd. [3] |
| | | Would you imagine, or almost beleeve, |
| | | Wert not, that by great preservation |
| 145 | | We live to tell it, that the subtill Traytor |
| | | This day had plotted, in the Councell-House, |
| | | To murther me, and my good Lord of Gloster. |
| | Maior | Had he done so? |
| | Richard | What? thinke you we are Turkes, or Infidels? |
| 150 | | Or that we would, against the forme of Law, |
| | | Proceed thus rashly in the Villaines death, |
| | | But that the extreme perill of the case, |
| | | The Peace of England, and our Persons safetie, |
| | | Enforc'd us to this Execution. |

---

[SD 1] Qq/most modern texts advance the entry two lines, thus giving a visible cause for Richard's 'defend thee' outburst

[W 2] Ff/most modern texts = 'suspects', Qq = 'suspect'

[OM 3] most modern texts omit this Ff only half line

| 155 | **Maior** | Now faire befall you, he deserv'd his death, |
| | | And your good Graces both have well proceeded, |
| | | To warne false Traytors from the like Attempts. |
| | | |
| | **Buckingham** | [1] I never look'd for better at his hands, |
| | | After he once fell in with Mistresse Shore : |
| 160 | | Yet had we not [2] determin'd he should dye, |
| | | Untill your Lordship came to see his end, |
| | | Which now the loving haste of these our friends, |
| | | Something against our meanings, have prevented ; |
| | | Because, my Lord, I would have had you heard [3] |
| 165 | | The Traytor speake, and timorously confesse |
| | | The manner and the purpose of his Treasons : [4] |
| | | That you might well have signify'd the same |
| | | Unto the Citizens, who haply may |
| | | Misconster us in him, and wayle his death. |
| | | |
| 170 | **Maior** | But, my good Lord, your Graces words [5] shal serve, |
| | | As well as I had seene, and heard him speake : |
| | | And doe not doubt, right Noble Princes both, |
| | | But Ile acquaint our dutious Citizens |
| | | With all your just proceedings in this case. [6] |
| | | |
| 175 | **Richard** | And to that end we wish'd your Lordship here, |
| | | * T'avoid the Censures of the carping World. |
| | | |
| | **Buckingham** | Which since you come too late of our intent, |
| | | Yet witnesse what you heare we did intend : |
| | | [7] And so, my good Lord Maior, we bid farwell. |

L 190 - a

**[Exit Maior]**

| 180 | **Richard** | Goe after, after, Cousin Buckingham. |
| | | The Maior towards Guild-Hall hyes him in all poste : |

---

L 190 - a / R 190 - a :  3. 5. 47 - 73

P/ALT [1]
  commentators have detailed the inaccurate prefix problems created by Q1, sometimes considered clarified by
Q4: see *The Arden Shakespeare King Richard III*, op. cit., page 241, footnote to line 51: the general consensus
has been to follow Ff: however, in direct contrast, one modern text establishes the theatrically very satisfying
solution of assigning these first two lines to the end of the Maior's speech, and the remainder of the speech to
Richard, not to Buckingham as in Ff: for further details see *William Shakespeare: A Textual Companion*, op. cit.,
page 242, footnote to line 3.5.50/1922

W [2]
  Ff/most modern texts = 'we not', Qq/one modern text = 'not we'

W [3]
  Ff/Qq/most modern texts = 'heard', one modern text adopts the gloss = 'hear'

W [4]
  Ff/most modern texts = 'Treasons', Qq/one modern text = 'treason'

W [5]
  Ff/most modern texts = 'words', Qq/one modern text = 'word'

W [6]
  Q1-5/most modern texts = 'cause', Ff = 'case'

LS [7]
  most modern texts set this Ff only line

There, at your meetest vantage [1] of the time,
Inferre the Bastardie of Edwards Children:
Tell them, how Edward put to death a Citizen,
185   Onely for saying, he would make his Sonne
Heire to the Crowne, meaning indeed his House,
Which, by the Signe thereof, was tearmed so.

Moreover, urge his hatefull Luxurie,
And beastiall appetite in change of Lust,
190   Which stretcht unto their Servants, Daughters, Wives,
Even where his raging eye, or savage heart,
Without controll, lusted [2] to make a prey.

Nay, for a need, thus farre come neere my Person:
Tell them, when that my Mother went with Child
195   Of that insatiate Edward;   Noble Yorke,
My Princely Father, then had Warres in France,
And by true computation of the time,
Found, that the Issue was not his begot:
Which well appeared in his Lineaments,
200   Being nothing like the Noble Duke, my Father:
Yet touch this sparingly, as *'twere farre off,
Because, my Lord, you know my Mother lives.

**Buckingham**   Doubt not, my Lord, Ile play the Orator,
As if the Golden Fee, for which I plead,
205   Were for my selfe:   and so, my Lord, adue.

**Richard**   If you thrive wel, bring them to Baynards Castle,
Where you shall finde me well accompanied
With reverend Fathers, and well-learned Bishops.

**Buckingham**   I goe, and towards three or foure a Clocke
210   Looke for the Newes that the Guild-Hall affoords.

**[Exit Buckingham]**

**Richard**   [3] Goe Lovell with all speed to Doctor Shaw,[4]
Goe thou to Fryer Peuker, bid them both
Meet me within this houre at Baynards Castle.

**[Exit]**

---

R 190 - a : 3. 5. 74 - 105

W 1   Qq/most modern texts = 'meetst advantage', Ff = 'meetest vantage'

W 2   Ff/most modern texts = 'lusted', Qq/one modern text = 'listed'

LS/WHO 3   nearly all modern texts set these three Ff only lines, indicating that the second line is spoken to Ratcliffe

N 4   in this Ff only passage, Ff set 'Shaw', which some modern texts set as the historically posited 'Shaa' (see *The Arden Shakespeare Richard III*, op. cit., page 243, footnote to line 102), while, in the following line, most modern texts set 'Penker' for F1-2's 'Peuker' and F3 - 4's 'Beuker'

Now will I goe [1] to take some privie order,
215  To draw the Brats of Clarence out of sight,
And to give order, that no manner person
Have any time recourse unto the Princes.

**[Exeunt]**
**ENTER A SCRIVENER** [2]
**[Most modern texts create a new scene here, Act Three Scene 6]**

Scrivener     Here is the Indictment of the good Lord Hastings,
Which in a set Hand fairely is engross'd,
220  That it may be to day read *o're in Paules.

And marke how well the sequell hangs together:
Eleven houres I have spent to write it over,
For yester-night by Catesby was it sent me,
The Precedent was full as long a doing,
225  And yet within these five houres Hastings liv'd,
Untainted, unexamin'd, free, at libertie.

Here's a good World the while.
Who is so grosse,° that cannot see this palpable device?  °[3]  R 190 - a
Yet who [4] so bold, but sayes he sees it not?
230  Bad is the World, and all will come to nought,[5]
When such ill dealing must be seene in thought.

**[Exit]**
**ENTER RICHARD AND BUCKINGHAM AT SEVERALL DOORES**
**[Most modern texts create a new scene here, Act Three Scene 7]**

Richard       How now, how now, what say the Citizens?

Buckingham    Now by the holy Mother of our Lord,
The Citizens are mum, say not a word.

235  Richard       Toucht you the Bastardie of Edwards Children?

Buckingham    I did, with [6] his Contract with Lady Lucy,
And his Contract by Deputie in France,

---

R 190 - a / L 191 - a  :  3. 5. 106 - 3. 7. 6

W [1]  Ff/most modern texts = 'goe', Qq/one modern text = 'in'

SD [2]  modern texts add a description from Qq, 'with a paper in his hand'

LS [3]  Ff set two irregular lines (6/14 syllables) suggesting the Scrivener takes a moment before his outburst:  most
    modern texts follow Qq and set two pentameter lines as shown

W [4]  Q1-2/most modern texts = 'who's', Q3-6/Ff = 'who'

W [5]  Qq/most modern texts = 'naught', Ff = 'nought'

LS [6]  most modern texts set the remainder of this and all the following Ff only line

|       |            | * Th'unsatiate greedinesse of his desire, |
|-------|------------|-------------------------------------------|
|       |            | ¹ And his enforcement of the Citie Wives, |
| 240   |            | His Tyrannie for Trifles, his owne Bastardie, |
|       |            | As being got, your Father then in France, |
|       |            | And his resemblance, being not like the Duke. |

Withall, I did inferre your Lineaments,
Being the right Idea of your Father,
245     Both in your forme,² and Noblenesse of Minde :
Layd open all your Victories in Scotland,
Your Discipline in Warre, Wisdome in Peace,
Your Bountie, Vertue, faire Humilitie :
Indeed, left nothing fitting for your purpose,
250     Untoucht, or sleightly handled in discourse.

And when my Oratorie drew toward end,³
I bid them that did love their Countries good,
Cry, God save Richard, Englands Royall King.

**Richard**     And did they so?

255 **Buckingham**     No, so God helpe me, ⁴ they spake not a word,
But like dumbe Statues, or breathing Stones,
Star'd each on other, and look'd deadly pale :
Which when I saw, I reprehended them,
And ask'd the Maior, what meant this wilfull silence?

260     His answer was, the people were not used
To be spoke to, but by the Recorder.

Then he was urg'd to tell my Tale againe :
⁵ Thus sayth the Duke, thus hath the Duke inferr'd,
But nothing spoke,⁶ in warrant from himselfe.

265     When he had done, some followers of mine owne,
At lower end of the Hall, hurld up their Caps,
And some tenne voyces cry'd, God save King Richard :
⁷ And thus I tooke the vantage of those few.

Thankes gentle Citizens, and friends, quoth I,

---

LS ₁   most modern texts set this and the final line of the sentence both of which are not set in Qq

W ₂   Qq/Ff/most modern texts = 'forme', one modern text suggests 'face'

W ₃   most modern texts set a variety of Ff/Qq alternatives: if all the Qq offerings were set, the line would read as 'And when my oratory grew to an ende'

W ₄   most modern texts set the following Ff only phrase

PCT ₅   most modern texts place quotation marks round the line

W ₆   Q1-5/most modern texts = 'spake', Ff = 'spoke'

LS ₇   most modern texts set this Ff only line

270    This generall applause, and chearefull showt,
       Argues your wisdome, and your love to Richard:
       And even here brake off, and came away.

**Richard**    What tongue-lesse Blockes were they,→ [1]
               Would they not speake?

275    [2]    Will not the Maior then, and his Brethren, come?

**Buckingham**    The Maior is here at hand: intend some feare,
                  Be not you spoke with, but by mightie suit:
                  And looke you get a Prayer-Booke in your hand,
                  And stand betweene two Church-men, good my Lord,
280               For on that ground Ile make [3] a holy Descant:
                  And be not easily wonne to our requests, [4]
                  Play the Maids part, still answer nay, and take it.

**Richard**    I goe: and if you plead as well for them,
               As I can say nay to thee for my selfe,
285            No doubt we bring it to a happie issue.

**Buckingham**    Go, go up to the Leads, the Lord Maior knocks.

### ENTER THE MAIOR, AND CITIZENS [5]

                  Welcome, my Lord, I dance attendance here,
                  I thinke the Duke will not be spoke withall.

                                                              L 191 - a

### ENTER CATESBY [6]

**Buckingham**    Now Catesby, what sayes your Lord to my
290               request?

**Catesby**    He doth entreat your Grace, my Noble Lord,
               To visit him to morrow, or next day:
               He is within, with two right reverend Fathers,
               Divinely bent to Meditation,
295            And in no Wordly suites would he be mov'd,
               To draw him from his holy Exercise.

---

L 191 - a / R 191 - a : 3. 7. 39 - 64

SP [1]  most modern texts follow Qq and set these two short Ff lines (6/4 syllables) as one, suggesting lack of column
width prevented F1 from so doing: if the Ff settings were to stand, it might suggest Richard for once is struck
dumb, however momentarily

LS/ALT [2]  Qq/one modern text replace the Ff line with one for Buckingham: 'No by my troth my Lo:'

W [3]  Qq/most modern texts = 'build', Ff = 'make'

W [4]  Ff/most modern texts = 'requests', Qq/one modern text = 'request'

SD [5]  most modern texts suggest Richard exits before the Maior and Citizens arrive

SD [6]  since Richard finally enters 'aloft', some modern texts suggest Catesby does so now

| | | |
|---|---|---|
| | **Buckingham** | Returne, good Catesby, to the gracious Duke, |
| | | Tell him, my selfe, the Maior and Aldermen, |
| | | In deep designes, in matter of great moment, |
| 300 | | No lesse importing then our generall good, |
| | | Are come to have some conference with his Grace. |

**Catesby**  Ile signifie so much unto him straight.

**[Exit]**

**Buckingham**  Ah ha, my Lord, this Prince is not an Edward,
He is not lulling on a lewd Love-Bed,[1]
305  But on his Knees, at Meditation:
Not dallying with a Brace of Curtizans,
But meditating with two deepe Divines:
Not sleeping, to engrosse his idle Body,
But praying, to enrich his watchfull Soule.

310  Happie were England, would this vertuous Prince
Take on his Grace the Soveraigntie thereof.

But sure I feare we shall not winne him to it.

**Maior**  Marry God defend his Grace should say us
nay.

315  **Buckingham**  I feare he will:  here Catesby comes againe.

**ENTER CATESBY**

Now Catesby, what sayes his Grace?

**Catesby**  He wonders to what end you have assembled
Such troopes of Citizens, to come to him,
His Grace not being warn'd thereof before:
320  He feares, my Lord, you meane no good to him.

**Buckingham**  Sorry I am, my Noble Cousin should
Suspect me, that I meane no good to him:
By Heaven, we come to him in perfit[2] love,
And so once more returne, and tell his Grace.

**[Exit]**

325  When holy and devout Religious men
Are at their Beades, 'tis much to draw them thence,
So sweet is zealous Contemplation.

---

R 191 - a :  3. 7. 65 - 94

▼ 1  Qq offer the verb 'lolling' and the place as a 'day bed'

▼ 2  Qq/F3/most modern texts = 'perfect', F1-2 = 'perfit'

## ENTER RICHARD ALOFT, BETWEENE TWO BISHOPS [1]

|  | | |
|---|---|---|
| **Maior** | | See where his Grace stands, tweene two Clergie men. |
| 330 | **Buckingham** | Two Props of Vertue,for a Christian Prince, To stay him from the fall of Vanitie: |
| | | [2] And see a Booke of Prayer in his hand, True Ornaments to know a holy man. |
| 335 | | Famous Plantagenet, most gracious Prince, Lend favourable eare to our requests,[3] And pardon us the interruption Of thy Devotion, and right Christian Zeale. |
| 340 | **Richard** | My Lord, there needes no such Apologie: I doe beseech your Grace to pardon me, Who earnest in the service of my God, Deferr'd the visitation of my friends. |
| | | But leaving this, what is your Graces pleasure? |
| | **Buckingham** | Even that (I hope) which pleaseth God above, And all good men, of this ungovern'd Ile. |
| 345 | **Richard** | I do suspect I have done some offence, That seemes disgracious in the Cities eye, And that you come to reprehend my ignorance. |
| | **Buckingham** | You have, my Lord :  →[4] Would it might please your Grace, |
| 350 | | On our entreaties, to amend your fault. |
| | **Richard** | Else wherefore breathe I in a Christian Land. |
| | **Buckingham** | Know then, it is your fault, that you resigne The Supreme Seat, the Throne Majesticall, The Sceptred Office of your Ancestors, |
| 355 | | [5] Your State of Fortune, and your Deaw of Birth, The Lineall Glory of your Royall House, |

R 191 - a

---

R 191 - a / L 192 - a  :  3. 7. 95 - 121

SD [1] most modern texts suggest Catesby re-enter with Richard and the Bishops; some suggest 'aloft', some keep him at stage level with everyone else

LS [2] most modern texts set the last Ff only two lines of the sentence

W [3] Ff/most modern texts = 'our requests', Q1/one modern text = 'our request', Q2-6 = 'my request'

SP [4] most modern texts follow Qq and set Ff's two short lines (4/6 syllables) as one line, arguing lack of column width prevented F1 from so doing: if the Ff setting were to stand it might suggest taking a 'pause for effect' before beginning his ploy

LS [5] most modern texts set this Ff only line

To the corruption of a blemisht Stock;
Whiles in the mildnesse of your sleepie thoughts,
Which here we waken to our Countries good,
360  The Noble Ile doth want his [1] proper Limmes:
His Face defac'd with skarres of Infamie,
His Royall Stock grafft with ignoble Plants,
And almost shouldred in the swallowing Gulfe
Of darke Forgetfulnesse, and deepe Oblivion.

365  Which to recure, we heartily solicite
Your gracious selfe to take on you the charge
And Kingly Government of this your Land:
Not as Protector, Steward, Substitute,
Or lowly Factor, for anothers gaine;
370  But as successively, from Blood to Blood,
Your Right of Birth, your Empyrie, your owne.

For this, consorted with the Citizens,
Your very Worshipfull and loving friends,
And by their vehement instigation,
375  In this just Cause come I to move your Grace.

**Richard**    I cannot tell, if to depart in silence,
Or bitterly to speake in your reproofe,
Best fitteth my Degree, or your Condition.

[2]  If not to answer, you might haply thinke,
380  Tongue-ty'd Ambition, not replying, yeelded
To beare the Golden Yoake of Soveraigntie,
Which fondly you would here impose on me.

If to reprove you for this suit of yours,
So season'd with your faithfull love to me,
385  Then on the other side I check'd my friends.

Therefore to speake, and to avoid the first,
And then in speaking, not to incurre the last,
Definitively thus I answer you.

Your love deserves my thankes, but my desert
390  Unmeritable, shunnes your high request.

First, if all Obstacles were cut away,
And that my Path were even to the Crowne,
As the ripe Revenue, and due of Birth:
Yet so much is my povertie of spirit,

L 192 - a  :  3. 7. 122 - 159

[W] [1]
both here and for the opening of the next line a combination of Q1-2 or Qq or modern gloss/most modern texts
= 'her/Her', Ff = 'his/His'
[LS/OM] [2]
some, not all, modern texts set this and the following Ff only sentences

395      So mightie, and so manie my defects,
         That I would rather hide me from my Greatnesse,
         Being a Barke to brooke no mightie Sea;
         Then in my Greatnesse covet to be hid,
         And in the vapour of my Glory smother'd.

400      But God be thank'd, there is no need of me,
         And much I need to helpe you, were there need:
         The Royall Tree hath left us Royall Fruit,
         Which mellow'd by the stealing howres of time,
         Will well become the Seat of Majestie,
405      And make (no doubt) us happy by his Reigne.

         On him I lay that, you would lay on me,
         The Right and Fortune of his happie Starres,
         Which God defend that I should wring from him.

**Buckingham**    My Lord, this argues Conscience in your Grace,
410      But the respects thereof are nice, and triviall,
         All circumstances well considered.

         You say, that Edward is your Brothers Sonne,
         So say we too, but not by Edwards Wife:        L 192 - a
         For first was he contract to Lady Lucie,
415      Your Mother lives a Witnesse to his Vow;
         And afterward by substitute betroth'd
         To Bona, Sister to the King of France.

         These both put off, a poore Petitioner,
         A Care-cras'd Mother to a many Sonnes,
420      A Beautie-waining, and distressed Widow,
         Even in the after-noone of her best dayes,
         Made prize and purchase of his wanton Eye,
         Seduc'd the pitch, and height of his degree,
         To base declension, and loath'd Bigamie.

425      By her, in his unlawfull Bed, he got
         This Edward, whom our Manners call the Prince.

         More bitterly could I expostulate,
         Save that for reverence to some alive,
         I give a sparing limit to my Tongue.

430      Then good, my Lord, take to your Royall selfe
         This proffer'd benefit of Dignitie:
         If not to blesse us and the Land withall,
         Yet to draw forth your Noble Ancestrie
         From the corruption of abusing times,
435      Unto a Lineall true derived course.

| Maior | Do good my Lord, your Citizens entreat you. |
| Buckingham | Refuse not, mightie Lord, this proffer'd love. |
| Catesby | [1] O make them joyfull, grant their lawfull suit. |
| Richard | Alas, why would you heape this Care on me? |

440                            I am unfit for State, and Majestie :
                                     I doe beseech you take it not amisse,
                                     I cannot, nor I will not yeeld to you.

| Buckingham | If you refuse it, as in love and zeale, |

                                     Loth to depose the Child, your Brothers Sonne,

445                            As well we know your tendernesse of heart,
                                     And gentle, kinde, effeminate remorse,
                                     Which we have noted in you to your Kindred,
                                     And egally indeede to all Estates :
                                     Yet know, where [2] you accept our suit, or no,

450                            Your Brothers Sonne shall never reigne our King,
                                     But we will plant some other in the Throne,
                                     To the disgrace and downe-fall of your House :
                                     And in this resolution here we leave you.
                                     Come Citizens, we will [3] entreat no more.

**[Exeunt]**

| 455 | Catesby | Call him againe, sweet Prince, accept their suit : |
| | | [4] If you denie them, all the Land will rue it. |
| | Richard | Will you enforce me to a world of Cares. |

                                     Call them againe,[5] I am not made of Stones,[6]
                                     But penetrable to your kinde entreaties,[7]

460                           Albeit against my Conscience and my Soule.

**ENTER BUCKINGHAM, AND THE REST**

---

R 192 - a : 3. 7. 201 - 226

LS [1] most modern texts set this Ff only speech

W [2] Ff = 'where', which most modern texts set as 'whe'er', Qq/one modern text = 'whether': the same setting occurs for Richard in 15 lines time

O/ADD [3] Ff = 'we will entreat no more': most modern texts set Qq's oath 'zounds ile intreat no more', and before the general 'Exeunt' add an extra line for Richard, viz. 'O do not sweare my Lord of Buckingham'

P [4] Qq assign this line to 'Ano.', (probably for 'Another'): commentators are diametrically opposed as to whether this is an authorial setting or not, *The Arden Shakespeare King Richard III*, op. cit., definitely argues against (page 256, footnote to line 221), while *William Shakespeare: A Textual Companion*, op. cit., argues that it is, page 243, footnote to line 3.7.212/2202

SD [5] most modern texts suggest that at least one person exits to do Richard's bidding

W [6] Qq/Ff/most modern texts = 'Stones', one modern text = 'stone'

W [7] Ff/most modern texts = 'entreaties', Qq/one modern text = 'intreates'

Cousin of Buckingham, and sage grave men,
Since you will buckle fortune on my back,
To beare her burthen, where [1] I will or no.

465     I must have patience to endure the Load :
But if black Scandall, or foule-fac'd Reproach,
Attend the sequell of your Imposition,
Your meere enforcement shall acquittance me
From all the impure blots and staynes thereof ;
For God doth know, and you may partly see,
470     How farre I am from the desire of this.

**Maior**        God blesse your Grace, wee see it, and will
say it.

**Richard**      In saying so, you shall but say the truth.

**Buckingham**     Then I salute you with this Royall Title,
475     Long live King [2] Richard, Englands worthie King.

**All**          Amen.

**Buckingham**     To morrow may it please you to be Crown'd.

**Richard**      Even when you please, for you will have it so.       R 192 - a

**Buckingham**     To morrow then we will attend your Grace,
480     [3] And so most joyfully we take our leave.

**Richard**      Come, let us to our holy Worke againe.
Farewell my Cousins,[4] farewell gentle friends.

**[Exeunt]**

---

R 192 - a / L 193 - a :   3. 7. 227 - 247

W [1]
   see footnote #2, previous page
W [2]
   Q3-6/Ff = 'King', some texts follow Q1-2 and omit the word, setting a nine syllable line: one modern text
   offers 'kind'
LS [3]
   most modern texts set this Ff only line
W [4]
   Qq/most modern texts = 'coosine', Ff = 'Cousins'

# Actus Quartus.  Scena Prima

**ENTER THE QUEENE, ANNE DUCHESSE OF GLOUCESTER, THE DUCHESSE OF YORKE, AND MARQUESSE DORSET** [1]

| | |
|---|---|
| **Duchesse Yorke** | Who meetes us heere?  → [2] |
| | My Neece Plantagenet, |
| | [3] Led in the hand of her kind Aunt of Gloster? |
| | Now, for my Life, shee's wandring to the Tower, |
5 | | On pure hearts love, to greet the tender Prince. |
| | Daughter, well met. |
| **Anne** | God give your Graces both ° a happie |
| | And a joyfull time of day. ° [4] |

| | |
|---|---|
| **Queene** | As much to you, good Sister :   whither away? |
10 **Anne** | No farther then the Tower, and as I guesse, |
| | Upon the like devotion as your selves, |
| | To gratulate the gentle Princes there. |
| **Queene** | Kind Sister thankes, wee'le enter all together : |

**ENTER THE LIEUTENANT** [5]

| | |
|---|---|
| | And in good time, here the Lieutenant comes. |
15 | | Master Lieutenant, pray you, by your leave, |
| | How doth the Prince, and my young Sonne of Yorke? |
| **Lieutenant** | Right well, deare Madame :   by your patience, |
| | I may not suffer you to visit them, |
| | The King hath strictly charg'd the contrary. |

---

L 193 - a :  4. 1. 1 - 17

SD [1] most modern texts follow Qq and have the Duchesse of Gloucester enter from one door, and the remaining characters from the other: from the opening dialogue, most add that Clarence's daughter accompanies the Duchesse of Gloucester

SP [2] most modern texts follow Qq and set Ff's two short line opening (4/6 syllables) as one, suggesting that lack of column width prevented F1 from so doing: if the Ff setting were to stand, it starts out quite awkwardly, fore-shadowing what soon becomes a very painful scene

LS [3] most modern texts set the following Ff only lines:  Qq simply set one line for the Queene, 'Sister well met, whether awaie so fast'

SP [4] Ff set three lines (4/9/7 syllables) furthering the opening awkwardness:  most modern texts set two lines of pentameter as shown

P [5] though Qq/Ff describe the entering character as, and set the prefixes for, the 'Lieutenant', most modern texts set 'Brakenbury' throughout

| | | |
|---|---|---|
| 20 | **Queene** | The King? who's that? |
| | **Lieutenant** | I meane, the Lord Protector. ⁾ |
| | **Queene** | The Lord protect him from that Kingly Title. |
| | | Hath he set bounds betweene their love, and me? |
| | | I am their Mother, who shall barre me from them? |
| 25 | **Duchesse Yorke** | I am their Fathers Mother, I will see |
| | | them. |
| | **Anne** | Their Aunt I am in law, in love their Mother : |
| | | Then bring me to their sights,¹ Ile beare thy blame, |
| | | And take thy Office from thee, on my perill. |
| 30 | **Lieutenant** | No, Madame, no ; I may not leave it so : |
| | | I am bound by Oath, and therefore pardon me. |

**[Exit Lieutenant]**
**ENTER STANLEY**

| | | |
|---|---|---|
| | Derby as <br> •**Stanley**• | Let me but meet you Ladies one howre hence, |
| | | And Ile salute your Grace of Yorke as Mother, |
| | | And reverend ² looker on of two faire Queenes, |
| 35 | | ³ Come Madame, you must straight to Westminster, |
| | | There to be crowned Richards Royall Queene. |

| | | |
|---|---|---|
| | **Queene** | Ah, cut my Lace asunder, |
| | | That my pent heart ° may have some scope to beat, |
| | | Or else I swoone ° with this dead-killing newes. ° ⁴ |
| 40 | **Anne** | ⁵ Despightfull tidings, O unpleasing newes. |
| | **Dorset** | Be of good cheare : Mother, how fares your |
| | | Grace? |
| | **Queene** | O Dorset, speake not to me, get thee gone, |
| | | Death and Destruction dogges thee at thy heeles, |
| 45 | | Thy Mothers Name is ominous to Children. L 193 - a |
| | | If thou wilt out-strip Death, goe crosse the Seas, |
| | | And live with Richmond, from the reach of Hell. |

L 193 - a / R 193 - a : 4. 1. 18 - 42

W ₁ Ff/most modern texts = 'bring me to their sights', Qq = 'feare not thou'

W ₂ Ff/most modern texts = 'reverend', Qq/one modern text = 'reverent'

WHO ₃ most modern texts indicate this is spoken to Anne

LS ₄ some modern texts follow the slightly irregular Ff setting (three lines of 7/10/10 syllables) which suggests a dumb-struck moment before the Queene realises the news' implication: others follow Qq and set the gap at the end of the speech (11/10/6)

LS ₅ most modern texts set this Ff only speech

|   | | |
|---|---|---|
| | | Goe hye thee, hye thee from this slaughter-house, |
| | | Lest thou encrease the number of the dead, |
| 50 | | And make me dye the thrall of Margarets Curse, |
| | | Nor Mother, Wife, nor Englands counted [1] Queene. |

**Stanley**    Full of wise care, is this your counsaile, Madame:
[2] Take all the swift advantage of the howres:
You shall have Letters from me to my Sonne,
55      In your behalfe, to meet you on the way:
Be not ta'ne tardie by unwise delay.

**Duchesse Yorke**    O ill dispersing Winde of Miserie,
O my accursed Wombe, the Bed of Death:
A Cockatrice hast thou hatcht to the World,
60      Whose unavoided Eye is murtherous.

**Stanley**    [3] Come, Madame, come, I in all haste was sent.

**Anne**    And I with [4] all unwillingnesse will goe.
O would to God, that the inclusive Verge
Of Golden Mettall, that must round my Brow,
65      Were red hot Steele, to seare me to the Braines,
Anoynted let me be with deadly Venome,
And dye ere men can say, God save the Queene.

**Queene**    Goe, goe, poore soule, I envie not thy glory,
To feed my humor, wish thy selfe no harme.

70   **Anne**    No:  why? [5]
When he that is my Husband now,
Came to me, as I follow'd Henries Corse, [6]
When scarce the blood was well washt from his hands,
Which issued from my other Angell Husband,
75      And that deare Saint, which then I weeping follow'd:
O, when I say I look'd on Richards Face,
This was my Wish:  Be thou (quoth I) accurst,
For making me, so young, so old a Widow:
And when thou wed'st, let sorrow haunt thy Bed;
80      And be thy Wife, if any be so mad,
More miserable, [7] by the Life of thee,

R 193 - a :  4. 1. 43 - 75

---

[W1] Qq/Ff = 'Englands' (i.e. 'England's') counted Queene', one modern text = 'counted England's'

[WHO2] most modern texts suggest this is spoken to Dorset

[WHO3] most modern texts indicate this is spoken to Anne

[W4] Ff/most modern texts = 'with', Qq/one modern text = 'in'

[W5] most modern texts set 'why', even though it does not appear in Qq

[W6] Ff/most modern texts = 'Corse', Qq/one modern text = 'course'

[W7] Ff/most modern texts = 'More miserable', Qq = 'As miserable', one modern gloss = 'Made more mis'rable'

Then thou hast made me, by my deare Lords death.

Loe, ere I can repeat this Curse againe,
Within [1] so small a time, my Womans heart
85         Grossely grew captive to his honey words,
And prov'd the subject of mine owne Soules Curse,
Which hitherto hath held mine [2] eyes from rest:
For never yet one howre in his Bed
Did I enjoy the golden deaw of sleepe,
90         But with his timorous Dreames was still awak'd.

Besides, he hates me for my Father Warwicke,
And will (no doubt) shortly be rid of me.

**Queene**      Poore heart adieu, I pittie thy complaining.

**Anne**        No more, then with my soule I mourne for
95         yours.

**Dorset**      Farewell, thou wofull welcommer of glory.

**Anne**        Adieu, poore soule, that tak'st thy leave
of it.

**Duchesse Yorke** [3] Go thou to Richmond, & good fortune guide thee,
100       Go thou to Richard, and good Angels tend thee,
Go thou to Sanctuarie, and good thoughts possesse thee,
I to my Grave, where peace and rest lye with mee.

Eightie odde yeeres of sorrow have I seene,
And each howres joy wrackt with a weeke of teene.

105  **Queene** [4] Stay, yet looke backe with me unto the Tower.

Pitty, you ancient Stones, those tender Babes,
Whom Envie hath immur'd within your Walls,
Rough Cradle for such little prettie ones,
Rude ragged Nurse, old sullen Play-fellow,
110       For tender Princes: use my Babies well;
So foolish Sorrowes [5] bids your Stones farewell.

**[Exeunt]**

---

W [1]  Ff/most modern texts = 'Within', Qq/one modern text 'Even in'

W [2]  Q1-5/most modern texts = 'my', Q6/Ff/one modern text = 'mine'

WHO / SD [3]  most modern texts indicate the first line is said to Dorset, the second to Anne and the third to the Queene, and that each character addressed exits after the line spoken to them, (Stanley and Clarence's daughter leaving with the Queene)

LS [4]  some, but not all, modern texts set the following Ff only speech

W [5]  Ff/most modern texts = 'Sorrowes', one modern gloss = 'sorrow'

# Scena Secunda

SOUND A SENNET. ENTER RICHARD IN POMPE, BUC-
KINGHAM, CATESBY, RATCLIFFE, LOVEL [1]

| | |
|---|---|
| **Richard** | Stand all apart. |
| | Cousin of Buckingham. |
| **Buckingham** | [2] My gracious Soveraigne. |
| **Richard** | Give me thy hand. |

**[Sound]** [3]

5
> Thus high, by thy advice,° and thy assistance,
> Is King Richard seated: ° [4]

But shall we weare these Glories for a day?

Or shall they last, and we rejoyce in them?

| | |
|---|---|
| **Buckingham** | Still live they, and for ever let them last. |
| 10   **Richard** | Ah Buckingham, now doe I play the Touch, |
| | To trie if thou be currant Gold indeed : |
| | Young Edward lives, thinke now what I would speake. |
| **Buckingham** | Say on my loving Lord. |
| **Richard** | Why Buckingham, I say I would be King. |
| 15   **Buckingham** | Why so you are, my thrice-renowned Lord. [5] |
| **Richard** | Ha? am I King? 'tis so: but Edward lives. |
| **Buckingham** | True, Noble Prince. |
| **Richard** | O bitter consequence! |
| | That Edward still should live true Noble Prince. |

---

SD 1
   most modern texts add from Qq that Richard is 'crowned' and that the group is augmented by 'other Nobles':
also, because of ensuing dialogue some modern texts add a 'Page'

LS 2
   most modern texts set this Ff only response

ADD 3
   most modern texts add from Qq 'Here he ascendeth the throne', setting it before Ff's music cue 'Sound'

LS 4
   Ff set the pause (11/6 syllables) just after he makes his first remarks as King, a wonderful underlining of his,
literally, crowning glory: Qq/most modern texts set the pause before (6/11), presumably just after he sits

W 5
   Ff/most modern texts = 'Lord', Qq = 'liege'

| | | |
|---|---|---|
| 20 | | Cousin, thou wast not wont to be so dull. |
| | | Shall I be plaine? |
| | | I wish the Bastards dead, |
| | | And I would have it suddenly [1] perform'd. |
| | | What say'st thou now? speake suddenly, be briefe. |
| 25 | **Buckingham** | Your Grace may doe your pleasure. |
| | **Richard** | Tut, tut, thou art all Ice, thy kindnesse freezes : |
| | | Say, have I thy consent, that they shall dye? |
| | **Buckingham** | Give me some litle breath, some pawse, deare Lord, |
| | | Before I positively speake in this : |
| 30 | | I will resolve you herein presently. |

**[Exit Buck.{ingham}]**

| | | |
|---|---|---|
| | **Catesby** | [2] The King is angry, see he gnawes his Lippe. |
| | **Richard** | [3] I will converse with Iron-witted Fooles, |
| | | And unrespective Boyes : none are for me, |
| | | That looke into me with considerate eyes, |
| 35 | | High-reaching Buckingham growes circumspect. |
| | | [4] Boy. |
| | **Page** | My Lord. |
| | **Richard** | Know'st thou not any, whom corrupting Gold |
| | | Will tempt unto a close exploit of Death? |
| 40 | **Page** | I know a discontented Gentleman, |
| | | Whose humble meanes match not his haughtie spirit : |
| | | Gold were as good as twentie Orators, |
| | | And will (no doubt) tempt him to any thing. |
| | **Richard** | What is his Name? |
| 45 | **Page** | His Name, my Lord, is Tirrell. [} ] |
| | **Richard** | [5] I partly know the man : goe call him hither, |
| | | Boy. |

---

L 194 - a :  4. 2. 17 - 41

[w][1] Qq/Ff /most modern texts = 'suddenly'; to avoid repetition with the following line, one modern text sets 'immediately'

[A][2] one modern text suggests this is spoken as an aside to an unspecified (number of) person(s)

[A][3] most modern texts indicate this is spoken as an aside

[LS][4] most modern texts set this Ff only one word sentence

[LS/A][5] most modern texts set the Ff only opening phrase, as well as the Ff only final phrase before Stanley's entry: they also suggest that after this opening line the rest of the speech until Stanley's entry is spoken as an aside

**[Exit]**

The deepe revolving wittie Buckingham,
No more shall be the neighbor to my counsailes.

50    Hath he so long held out with me, untyr'd,
And stops he now for breath?

Well, be it so.

**ENTER STANLEY**

How now, Lord Stanley, what's the newes?

| Stanley | Know my loving Lord,° the Marquesse Dorset |
|---|---|
| 55 | As I heare, is fled ° to Richmond, |
| | In the parts where he abides. ° ¹ |

Richard    Come hither Catesby, rumor it abroad,
That Anne my Wife is very grievous sicke,          L 194 - a
I will take order for her keeping close.

60    Inquire me out some meane poore ² Gentleman,
Whom I will marry straight to Clarence Daughter :
The Boy is foolish, and I feare not him.

Looke how thou dream'st :  I say againe, give out,
That Anne, my Queene, is sicke, and like to dye.

65    About it, for it stands me much upon
To stop all hopes, whose growth may dammage me. ³

I must be marryed to my Brothers Daughter,
Or else my Kingdome stands on brittle Glasse :
Murther her Brothers, and then marry her,

70    Uncertaine way of gaine
But I am in
So farre in blood, that sinne will pluck on sinne,
Teare-falling Pittie dwells not in this Eye.

**ENTER TYRREL**

Is thy Name Tyrrel?

---

LS ₁
  Ff's irregular setting (10/8/7 syllables) suggests Stanley hesitating as he reaches the crux of his bad news:  those texts setting the Ff text restructure as shown (5/10/10) , reversing Stanley's process, allowing him a hesitant start and a more confident finish: one modern text follows Qq and sets
            My Lord, I heare the Marques Dorset
                Is fled to Richmond, in those partes beyond the seas where he abides.
W ₂
  Ff/most modern texts = 'poore', Qq/one modern text = 'borne'
SD/A ₃
      most modern texts suggest Catesby now exits, and that the remainder of Richard's speech is spoken as an aside

| | | |
|---|---|---|
| 75 | **Tyrell** | James Tyrel, and your most obedient subject. |
| | **Richard** | Art thou indeed? |
| | **Tyrell** | Prove me, my gracious Lord. <sup>}</sup> |
| | **Richard** | Dar'st thou resolve to kill a friend of mine? |
| | **Tyrell** | Please you : → [1] |
| 80 | | But I had rather kill two enemies. |
| | **Richard** | Why then [2] thou hast it : two deepe enemies, |
| | | Foes to my Rest, and my sweet sleepes disturbers, |
| | | Are they that I would have thee deale upon : |
| | | Tyrrel, I meane those Bastards in the Tower. |
| 85 | **Tyrell** | Let me have open meanes to come to them, |
| | | And soone Ile rid you from the feare of them. |
| | **Richard** | Thou sing'st sweet Musique : → [3] |
| | | Hearke, come hither Tyrel, |
| | | Goe by this token : rise, and lend thine Eare, [4] |

**[Whispers]**

| | | |
|---|---|---|
| 90 | | There is [5] no more but so : say it is done, |
| | | And I will love thee, and preferre thee for it. |
| | **Tyrell** | I will dispatch it straight. ∞ [6] |

**[Exit]**
**ENTER BUCKINGHAM**

| | | |
|---|---|---|
| | **Buckingham** | My Lord, I have consider'd in my minde, |
| | | The late request that you did sound me in. |
| 95 | **Richard** | Well, let that rest : Dorset is fled to Richmond. |

---

LS [1] Ff 's two lines (2/10 syllables) suggest Tyrel takes care in making his countering gambit: most modern texts join the lines together, following Qq's layout of a somewhat different text

W [2] Ff/most modern texts = 'then', Qq/one modern text = 'there'

SP [3] most modern texts follow Qq and set Ff's two short lines (5/6 syllables) as one (Qq omitting Ff's 'Hearke'), presumably arguing lack of column width prevented F1 from following suit: if the Ff setting were to stand, it might suggest Richard takes a moment to ensure no-one sees or hears the following exchange

PCT [4] Qq/Ff set a comma, suggesting the whisper is part of the continuous action: most modern texts set a period

W [5] Ff/most modern texts = 'There is', Qq/one modern text = ' 'Tis'

ADD [6] at least one modern text adds the following Qq passage
| King | Shal we heare from thee Tirrel ere we sleep? |
|---|---|
| Tirrel | Ye shall my lord. |

| | | |
|---|---|---|
| | **Buckingham** | I heare the newes, my Lord. |
| | **Richard** | Stanley, hee is your Wives Sonne: well, looke unto [1] it. |
| 100 | **Buckingham** | My Lord, I clayme the gift, my due by promise, For which your Honor and your Faith is pawn'd, * Th'Earledome of Hertford,[2] and the moveables, Which you have promised I shall possesse. |
| | **Richard** | Stanley looke to your Wife: if she convey Letters to Richmond, you shall answer it. |
| 105 | **Buckingham** | What sayes your Highnesse to my just request? [3] |
| | **Richard** | I doe remember me, Henry the Sixt Did prophecie, that Richmond should be King, When Richmond was a little peevish Boy, A King perhaps. [4] |

∞ [5]

| | | |
|---|---|---|
| 110 | **Buckingham** | May it please you to resolve me in my suit. |
| | **Richard** | Thou troublest me, I am not in the vaine. |

**[Exit]** [6]

| | | |
|---|---|---|
| | **Buckingham** | And is it thus? repayes he my deepe service With such contempt? made I him King for this? O let me thinke on Hastings, and be gone To Brecnock, while my fearefull Head is on. |
| 115 | | |

**[Exit]**
**ENTER TYRREL** [7]
**[Most modern texts create a new scene here, Act Four Scene 3]**

---

R 194 - a / 4. 2. 86 - 122
this includes 18 lines of the so-called 'clock sequence' as set in Q1:
see footnote #5, and Appendix B

W 1 Ff/most modern texts = 'unto', Qq/one modern text = 'to'

N 2 F1= 'Hertford', Q1-3/F2/most modern texts set the more recogniseable 'Hereford'

W 3 Ff = 'request', Qq/most modern texts set the much more potent 'demand'

W 4 most modern texts follow Qq and set 'perhaps, perhaps' (sometimes adding an extra 'perhaps'): Ff set a single 'perhaps', and Qq's line for Buckingham, 'My lord'

ADD 5 most modern texts add the famous 'clock' sequence set by Qq: (see Appendix I at the end of this text), and replace Buckingham's next line with, 'Whie then resolve me whether you wil or no?'

SD 6 most modern texts suggest that everyone follow Richard save Buckingham

N 7 Q1 sets the interesting addendum to the direction, naming Tyrrel as 'Sir Francis Tyrrel', suggesting he is not of the usual murderer's stamp (a middle-man perhaps): however, this should be approached cautiously, since Q1 has set the wrong given name, Francis, (Tyrrel earlier called himself 'James')

| | |
|---|---|
| **Tyrell** | The tyrannous and bloodie Act is done,[1] |
| | The most arch deed of pittious massacre |
| | That ever yet this Land was guilty of: |
| | Dighton and Forrest, who [2] I did suborne |
| 120 | To do this peece†[3] of ruthfull [4] Butchery, |
| | Albeit they were flesht Villaines, bloody Dogges, |
| | Melted with tendernesse, and milde compassion, |
| | Wept like to [5] Children, in their deaths sad Story. |

R 194 - a

O thus (quoth Dighton) lay the gentle Babes:
125 Thus, thus (quoth Forrest) girdling one another
Within their Alablaster innocent Armes:
Their lips were foure red Roses on a stalke,
And in their Summer Beauty kist each other.

A Booke of Prayers on their pillow lay,
130 Which one [6] (quoth Forrest) almost chang'd my minde:
But oh the Divell, there the Villaine stopt:
When Dighton thus told on, we smothered
The most replenished sweet worke of Nature,
That from the prime Creation *ere she framed.

135 Hence both are gone with Conscience and Remorse,
They could not speake, and so I left them both,
To beare this tydings to the bloody King.

**ENTER RICHARD**

And heere he comes.
All health my Soveraigne Lord.

| | |
|---|---|
| 140 | **Richard** | Kinde Tirrell, am I happy in thy Newes. |
| | **Tyrell** | If to have done the thing you gave in charge, |
| | | Beget your happinesse, be happy then, |
| | | For it is done. |
| | **Richard** | But did'st thou see them dead. |
| 145 | **Tyrell** | I did my Lord. |
| | **Richard** | And buried gentle Tirrell. |

---

w[1] Qq reverse the setting of 'Act' and 'deed' (next line) , which some commentators support for the alliteration
w[2] Ff/some modern texts = 'who', Qq/one modern text = 'whom'
w[3] F1 = 'p eece', F2/most modern texts = 'peece'
w[4] Q1-2 = 'ruthles peece of', Ff = 'peece of ruthfull'
w[5] Qq/most modern texts set the rather literal 'two', Ff set the more evocative 'to'
w[6] Qq/F4/most modern texts = 'once', F1-3 = 'one'

| | |
|---|---|
| **Tyrell** | The Chaplaine of the Tower hath buried them,<br>But where (to say the truth) I do not know. |
| **Richard**<br>150 | Come to me Tirrel soone, and after Supper,[1]<br>When thou shalt tell the processe of their death. |
| | Meane time, but thinke how I may do the [2] good,<br>And be inheritor of thy desire. |
| | Farewell till then. |
| **Tyrell** | [3] I humbly take my leave. |
| 155 **Richard** | The Sonne of Clarence have I pent up close,<br>His daughter meanly have I matcht in marriage,<br>The Sonnes of Edward sleepe in Abrahams bosome,<br>And Anne my wife hath bid this world good night. |
| 160 | Now for I know the Britaine [4] Richmond aymes<br>At yong Elizabeth my brothers daughter,<br>And by that knot lookes proudly on [5] the Crowne,<br>To her go I, a jolly thriving wooer. |

### ENTER RATCLIFFE [6]

| | |
|---|---|
| **Ratcliffe** | My Lord. |
| **Richard**<br>165 | Good or bad newes, [7] that thou com'st in so<br>bluntly? |
| **Ratcliffe** | Bad news my Lord, Mourton [8] is fled to Richmond,<br>And Buckingham backt with the hardy Welshmen<br>Is in the field, and still his power encreaseth. |

---

[1] Qq/most modern texts = 'soone at after supper', Ff = 'soone, and after Supper'

[2] F1 = 'the', Qq/F2/most modern texts = 'thee'

[LS/SD] most modern texts set this Ff only farewell, and add Qq's earlier stage direction 'Exit Tirrel'

[N/W 4] as most commentators point out, Qq/Ff's 'Britaine' was the current rendition of what today would be shown as
'Breton' or 'Brittany': most modern texts set one or the other accordingly: this is the only time such changes will be noted

[5] Ff/most modern texts = 'on', Qq/one modern text = 'ore'

[SD 6] Ff /most modern texts set the entry for Ratcliffe, Qq for Catesby

[W/PCT -] Ff /most modern texts = 'Good or bad newes,', Qq/one modern text = 'Good newes or bad' with no punctuation

[F/N 8] historically, the fleeing character was known by two names, 'Mourton', the Ff setting (or 'Morton' as the name is spelled by most modern texts) and the Bishop of Ely, the Qq setting: Ff also referred to him as Ely in the so-called 'strawberry' scene, pages 76-7

| | |
|---|---|
| **Richard** | Ely with Richmond troubles me more neere, |
| 170 | Then Buckingham and his rash[†1] levied Strength. |

Come, I have learn'd, that fearfull commenting
Is leaden servitor to dull delay.

Delay leds [2] impotent and Snaile-pac'd Beggery:
Then fierie expedition be my wing,

175 Joves Mercury, and [3] Herald for a King:
Go muster men: My counsaile is my Sheeld,
We must be breefe, when Traitors brave the Field.

**[Exeunt]**

L 195 - b

---

L 195 - b : 4. 3. 49 - 57

COMP [1] once again, the 's' of the F1 type face suggests a 'th' rather than 'sh': thus while F1 appears to set 'rath', Qq/F2 and most modern texts clearly set 'rash'

w [2] Qq/F2/most modern texts = 'leades', Ff = 'leds'

w [3] Qq/Ff/most modern texts = 'and', one modern text = 'an'

# Scena Tertia

### [Most modern texts number this scene, Act Four Scene 4]

#### ENTER OLD QUEENE MARGARET

| | |
|---|---|
| **Margaret** | So now prosperity begins to mellow, |
| | And drop into the rotten mouth of death : |
| | Heere in these Confines slily have I lurkt, |
| | To watch the waining of mine enemies. |
| 5 | A dire induction, am I witnesse to, |
| | And will to France, hoping the consequence |
| | Will prove as bitter, blacke, and Tragicall. |
| | Withdraw thee wretched Margaret, who comes heere? |

#### ENTER DUTCHESSE AND QUEENE [1]

| | |
|---|---|
| **Queene** | Ah my poore Princes! ah my tender Babes : |
| 10 | My unblowed [2] Flowres, new appearing sweets : |
| | If yet your gentle soules flye in the Ayre, |
| | And be not fixt in doome perpetuall, |
| | Hover about me with your ayery wings, |
| | And heare your mothers Lamentation. |
| 15 | **Margaret** [3] Hover about her, say that right for right |
| | Hath dim'd your Infant morne, to Aged night. |

| | |
|---|---|
| **Dutchesse** | [4] So many miseries have craz'd my voyce, |
| | That my woe-wearied tongue is still and mute. |
| | Edward Plantagenet, why art thou dead? |
| 20 **Margaret** | Plantagenet doth quit Plantagenet, |
| | Edward for Edward, payes a dying debt. |

| | |
|---|---|
| **Queene** | Wilt thou, O God, flye from such gentle Lambs, |
| | And throw them in the intrailes of the Wolfe? |
| | When didst thou sleepe, when such a deed was done? |
| 25 **Margaret** | When holy Harry dyed, and my sweet Sonne. |

SD 1 most modern texts advance the Qq/Ff entry one line, adding Qq's explanation that the Dutchesse is that of Yorke

W 2 Ff/most modern texts = 'unblowed', Qq/one modern text = 'unblowne'

A 3 most modern texts suggest this and her next two speeches are spoken as asides

Q 4 Qq set this speech later, after line 34 page 105, and omit Margaret's response: most modern texts set Ff as is

| | |
|---|---|
| **Dutchesse** | Dead life, blind sight, poore mortall living ghost, |
| | Woes Scene, Worlds shame, Graves due, by life usurpt, |
| | [1] Breefe abstract and record of tedious dayes, |
| | Rest thy unrest on Englands lawfull earth, |
| 30 | Unlawfully made drunke with innocent [2] blood. |
| | |
| **Queene** | [3] Ah that thou would'st assoone affoord a Grave, |
| | As thou canst yeeld a melancholly seate : |
| | Then would I hide my bones, not rest them heere, |
| | Ah who hath any cause to mourne but wee? |
| | |
| 35    **Margaret** | If ancient sorrow be most reverent, [4] |
| | Give mine the benefit of signeurie, |
| | And let my greefes frowne on the upper hand |
| | If sorrow can admit Society. |

∞ [5]

|    |    |
|---|---|
| | I had an Edward, till a Richard kill'd him : |
| 40 | I had a Husband, till a Richard kill'd him : |
| | Thou had'st an Edward, till a Richard kill'd him : |
| | Thou had'st a Richard, till a Richard kill'd him. |
| | |
| **Dutchesse** | I had a Richard too, and thou did'st kill him ; |
| | I had a Rutland too, thou hop'st [6] to kill him. |
| | |
| 45    **Margaret** | Thou had'st a Clarence too, → [7] |
| | And Richard kill'd him. |
| | From forth the kennell of thy wombe hath crept |
| | A Hell-hound that doth hunt us all to death : |
| | That Dogge, that had his teeth before his eyes, |
| 50 | To worry Lambes, and lap their gentle blood : |

> [8] That foule defacer of Gods handy worke :
> That reignes in gauled eyes of weeping soules :
> That excellent grand Tyrant of the earth,

> Thy wombe let loose to chase us to our graves.

---

LS/SD [1]   most modern texts set this Ff only line, and suggest the Dutchesse sits at the beginning of the next

W [2]   Ff/most modern texts set 'innocent', Qq/one modern text set the plural noun used in apposition, 'innocents'

SD [3]   most modern texts suggest the Queene also sits sometime during this speech

W [4]   Qq/Ff = 'reverent', most modern texts = 'reverend'

ADD [5]   most modern texts add a Qq line to finish her sentence, 'Tell over your woes againe by vewing mine,'

W [6]   Q3-6/F2/most modern texts = 'holp'st', Q1-2/F1 = 'hop'st'

SP [7]   most modern texts follow Qq and set these two Ff short lines (6/5 syllables) as one, presumably arguing there was insufficient width for F1 to follow suit: if the Ff setting were to stand, it might suggest Margaret takes a moment before she begins to intensify her attack

LS/ALT [8]   most modern texts set these three Ff only lines, but often in a different order: some texts follow Ff as shown, some completely reverse the sequence, while one early commentator suggests setting them as #1, followed by #3, followed by #2

| | | |
|---|---|---|
| 55 | | O upright, just, and true-disposing God, |
| | | How do I thanke thee, that this carnall [1] Curre |
| | | Prayes on the issue of his Mothers body, |
| | | And makes her Pue-fellow with others mone. |
| | **Dutchesse** | Oh Harries wife, triumph not in my woes: |
| 60 | | God witnesse with me, I have wept for thine. |
| | **Margaret** | Beare with me: I am hungry for revenge, |
| | | And now I cloy me with beholding it. |
| | | Thy Edward he is dead, that kill'd my Edward, |
| | | The [2] other Edward dead, to quit my Edward: |
| 65 | | Yong Yorke, he is but boote, because both they |
| | | Matcht not the high perfection of my losse. |
| | | Thy Clarence he is dead, that stab'd my Edward, |
| | | And the beholders of this franticke play, |
| | | Th'adulterate Hastings, Rivers, Vaughan, Gray, |
| 70 | | Untimely smother'd in their dusky Graves. |
| | | Richard yet lives, Hels blacke Intelligencer, |
| | | Onely reserv'd their Factor, to buy soules, |
| | | And send them thither: But at hand, at hand |
| | | Insues his pittious and unpittied end. |
| 75 | | Earth gapes, Hell burnes, Fiends roare, Saints pray, |
| | | To have him sodainly convey'd from hence: |
| | | Cancell his bond of life, deere God I pray, |
| | | That I may live and say, The Dogge is dead. |
| | **Queene** | O thou did'st prophesie, the time would come, |
| 80 | | That I should wish for thee to helpe me curse |
| | | That bottel'd Spider, that foule bunch-back'd [3] Toad. |
| | **Margaret** | I call'd thee then, vaine flourish of my fortune: |
| | | I call'd thee then, poore Shadow, painted Queen, |
| | | The presentation of but what I was; |
| 85 | | The flattering Index of a direfull Pageant; |
| | | One heav'd a high, to be hurl'd downe below: |
| | | A Mother onely mockt with two faire Babes; |
| | | A dreame of what thou wast, a garish Flagge |
| | | To be the ayme of every dangerous Shot; |
| 90 | | A signe of Dignity, a Breath, a Bubble; |
| | | A Queene in jest, onely to fill the Scene. |

R 195 - b

---

R 195 - b / L 196 - b : 4. 4. 56 - 91

[1] Qq/Ff = 'carnall', one modern text sets 'charnel'

[2] Qq/most modern texts = 'Thy', Ff = 'The'

[3] Q1/Ff = 'bunch-back'd', Q2 - 6 = 'hunch-backt'

Where is thy Husband now?
                              Where be thy Brothers?
Where be [1] thy two Sonnes?
95                              Wherein dost thou Joy?
Who sues, and kneeles, and sayes, God save the Queene?
Where be the bending Peeres that flattered thee?
Where be the thronging Troopes that followed thee?
Decline all this, and see what now thou art.

100          For happy Wife, a most distressed Widdow:
             For joyfull Mother, one that wailes the name:

> [2] For one being sued too, one that humbly sues:
> For Queene, a very Caytiffe, crown'd with care:
> For she that scorn'd at me, now scorn'd of me:
105 For she being feared of all, now fearing one:
> For she commanding all, obey'd of none.

Thus hath the course of Justice whirl'd about,
And left thee but a very prey to time,
Having no more but Thought of what thou wast. [3]

110          To torture thee the more, being what thou art,
Thou didst usurpe my place, and dost [4] thou not
Usurpe the just proportion of my Sorrow?

Now thy proud Necke, beares halfe my burthen'd yoke,
From which, even heere I slip my wearied [5] head,
115          And leave the burthen of it all, on thee.

Farwell Yorkes wife, and Queene of sad mischance,
These English woes, shall make me smile in France.

**Queene**          O thou well skill'd in Curses, stay a-while,
And teach me how to curse mine enemies.

120  **Margaret**    Forbeare to sleepe the night, and fast the day: [6]
Compare dead happinesse, with living woe:
Thinke that thy Babes were sweeter then they were,
And he that slew them fowler then he is:

---

[W1] Q1-2/most modern texts = 'are', Q3-6/Ff = 'be'

[Q/LS2] most modern texts follow the Ff five line sequence as shown: Qq omit the fourth line, and set the sequence as #2, #1, #5, #3; one modern text shows the sequence as #2, #1,# 3, #4, #5

[W3] Ff/most modern texts = 'wast', Q1-2/one modern text = 'wert', Q3-6 = 'art'

[W4] Ff/most modern texts = 'dost', Qq/one modern text = 'doest'

[W5] Q1-5/most modern texts = 'wearie', Q6/Ff = 'wearied'

[W6] Q1-2/most modern texts set the plural 'nights' and 'days', Q3-6/Ff set the singular 'night' and 'day'

|     |           |                                                            |            |
|-----|-----------|------------------------------------------------------------|------------|
|     |           | Bett'ring thy losse, makes the bad causer worse,           | L 196 - b  |
| 125 |           | Revolving this, will teach thee how to Curse.              |            |

| Queene | My words are dull, O quicken them with thine. |

| Margaret | Thy woes will make them sharpe,→ [1] |
|          | And pierce like mine. |

**[Exit Margaret]**

| Dutchesse | Why should calamity be full of words? |

| 130 | Queene | Windy Atturnies to their Clients [2] Woes, |
|     |        | Ayery succeeders of intestine [3] joyes, |
|     |        | Poore breathing Orators of miseries, |
|     |        | Let them have scope, though what they will impart, |
|     |        | Helpe nothing els, yet do they ease the hart. |

| 135 | Dutchesse | If so then, be not Tongue-ty'd : go with me, |
|     |           | And in the breath of bitter words, let's smother |
|     |           | My damned Son, that thy two sweet Sonnes smother'd. |

The Trumpet sounds, be copious in exclaimes.

**ENTER KING RICHARD, AND HIS TRAINE [4]**

| Richard | Who intercepts me in my Expedition? |

| 140 | Dutchesse | O she, that might have intercepted thee |
|     |           | By strangling thee in her accursed wombe, |
|     |           | From all the slaughters (Wretch) that thou hast done. |

| Queene | Hid'st thou that Forhead with a Golden Crowne |
|        | Where't [5] should be branded, if that right were right? [6] |
| 145 |        | The slaughter of the Prince that ow'd that Crowne, |
|     |        | And the dyre death of my poore Sonnes, and Brothers. |

Tell me thou Villaine-slave, where are my Children?

---

L 196 - b / R 196 - b : 4. 4. 122 - 144

SP [1]
most modern texts follow Qq and join Ff's two short lines (6/4 syllables), presumably arguing lack of F1 column width prevented it from following suit: if the Ff setting were to stand the minute pauses would serve to emphasise both Margaret's weariness and her exit

W [2]
Ff/some modern texts = 'their Clients', Q1-3/one modern text = 'your Clients'

W [3]
Qq = 'intestate', Ff = 'intestine': also, while Qq/Ff = 'succeeders', one modern text sets 'recorders'

SD [4]
since Catesby is needed much later in the scene, most modern texts add him to this entry, (even though he could come on either with Ratcliffe, post line 457, page 119, or when actually called for, line 466, page 119): also, most texts add from Qq that Richard and his party is 'marching with Drummes and Trumpets'

W [5]
Qq/most modern texts = 'Where', Ff = 'Where't'

PCT [6]
most modern texts replace Ff's question mark with Qq's comma: however, in contemporary type setting it can function simply as an exclamation point, a perfectly understandable piece of punctuation given the circumstances

| | | |
|---|---|---|
| 150 | **Dutchesse** | Thou Toad, thou Toade,→ [1]<br>Where is thy Brother Clarence?<br>And little Ned Plantagenet his Sonne? |
| | **Queene** | Where is the gentle Rivers, Vaughan, Gray? |
| | **Dutchesse** | [2] Where is kinde Hastings? |
| 155 | **Richard** | A flourish Trumpets, strike Alarum Drummes:<br>Let not the Heavens heare these Tell-tale women<br>Raile on the Lords Annointed. |

Strike I say.

FLOURISH.     ALARUMS

| | | |
|---|---|---|
| | | Either be patient, and intreat me fayre,<br>Or with the clamorous report of Warre,<br>Thus will I drowne your exclamations. |
| 160 | **Dutchesse** | Art thou my Sonne? |
| | **Richard** | I, I thanke God, my Father, and your selfe. |
| | **Dutchesse** | Then patiently heare my impatience. |
| | **Richard** | Madam, I have a touch of your condition,<br>That cannot brooke the accent of reproofe. |
| 165 | **Dutchesse** | O let me speake. |
| | **Richard** | Do then, but Ile not heare.) |
| | **Dutchesse** | I will be milde, and gentle in my words. |
| | **Richard** | And breefe (good Mother) for I am in hast. |
| 170 | **Dutchesse** | Art thou so hasty?<br>          I have staid for thee<br>(God knowes) in torment, and in agony. |
| | **Richard** | And came I not at last to comfort you? |
| | **Dutchesse** | No by the holy Rood, thou know'st it well,<br>Thou cam'st on earth, to make the earth my Hell. |
| 175 | | A greevous burthen was thy Birth to me,<br>Tetchy and wayward was thy Infancie. |

R 196 - b :  4. 4. 145 - 173

SP [1] most modern texts follow Qq and set these two short Ff lines (4/7 syllables) as one, presumably arguing insufficient column width prevented F1 from following suit

LS [2] most modern texts set this Ff only line

Thy School-daies frightfull, desp'rate, wilde, and furious,
Thy prime of Manhood, daring, bold, and venturous:
Thy Age confirm'd, proud, subtle, slye, and bloody,
180 More milde, but yet more harmfull; Kinde in hatred:
What comfortable houre canst thou name,
That ever grac'd me with [1] thy company?

**Richard** Faith none, but Humfrey Hower,[2]
That call'd your Grace
185 To Breakefast once, forth of my company.

If I be so disgracious in your eye,
Let me march on, and not offend you Madam.

[3] Strike up the Drumme.

**Dutchesse** I prythee heare me speake. ) R 196 - b

190 **Richard** You speake too bitterly.

**Dutchesse** Heare me a word: )
For I shall never speake to thee againe.

**Richard** [4] So.

**Dutchesse** Either thou wilt dye, by Gods just ordinance
195 Ere from this warre thou turne a Conqueror:
Or I with greefe and extreame Age shall perish,
And never more behold [5] thy face againe.

Therefore take with thee my most greevous [6] Curse,
Which in the day of Battell tyre thee more
200 Then all the compleat Armour that thou wear'st.

My Prayers on the adverse party fight,
And there the little soules of Edwards Children,
Whisper the Spirits of thine Enemies,
And promise them Successe and Victory:
205 Bloody thou art, bloody will be thy end:
Shame serves thy life, and doth thy death attend.

**[Exit]**

---

W [1]
Ff/most modern texts = 'with', Qq/one modern text = 'in'

W [2]
the term 'Humfrey Hower' has been the subject of much discussion and possible emendation, see *William
Shakespeare: A Textual Companion,* op. cit., page 245, footnote to line 4.4.176/2681, and *The Arden Shakespeare
King Richard III,* op. cit., page 283 -4, footnote to line 176

LS [3]
most modern texts set this Ff only sequence

LS [4]
most modern texts set this Ff only one word speech

W [5]
Qq/Ff = 'never more' which some modern texts set as 'nevermore'

W [6]
Ff/most modern texts = 'greevous', Qq/one modern text = 'heavy'

| | Queene | Though far more cause, yet much lesse spirit to curse |
| | | Abides in me, I say Amen to her. [1] |
| | Richard | Stay Madam, I must talke a word with you. |
| 210 | Queene | I have no more sonnes of the Royall Blood |
| | | For thee to slaughter. |
| | | For [2] my Daughters (Richard) |
| | | They shall be praying Nunnes, not weeping Queenes : |
| | | And therefore levell not to hit their lives. |
| 215 | Richard | You have a daughter call'd Elizabeth, |
| | | Vertuous and Faire, Royall and Gracious? |
| | Queene | And must she dye for this? |
| | | O let her live, |
| | | And Ile corrupt her Manners, staine her Beauty, |
| 220 | | Slander my Selfe, as false to Edwards bed : |
| | | Throw over her the vaile of Infamy, |
| | | So she may live unscarr'd of bleeding slaughter, |
| | | I will confesse she was not Edwards daughter. |
| | Richard | Wrong not her Byrth, she is a Royall Princesse. |
| 225 | Queene | To save her life, Ile say she is not so. |
| | Richard | Her life is safest onely in her byrth. |
| | Queene | And onely in that safety, dyed her Brothers. |
| | Richard | Loe at their Birth,[3] good starres were opposite. |
| | Queene | No, to their lives, ill friends were contrary. |
| 230 | Richard | All unavoyded is the doome of Destiny. |
| | Queene | True :   when avoyded grace makes Destiny. |
| | | My Babes were destin'd to a fairer death, |
| | | If grace had blest thee with a fairer life. |
| | Richard | [4] You speake as if that I had slaine my Cosins? |
| 235 | Queene | Cosins indeed, and by their Unckle couzend, |
| | | Of Comfort, Kingdome, Kindred, Freedome, Life, |

L 197 - b   :   4. 4. 197 - 224

W 1
Ff/most modern texts = 'her', Qq/one modern text = 'all'

PCT 2
Ff/most modern texts set two different sentences, viz. 'to slaughter.  For my Daughters . . .' : Qq/one modern
text set a continuous sentence (with a different first word), viz. 'to murther for my daughters . . .

W 3
Ff/most modern texts = 'Birth', Qq/one modern text = 'births'

LS 4
some, but not all, modern texts set this and the following Ff only speech

Whose hand soever lanch'd [1] their tender hearts,
Thy head (all indirectly) gave direction.

No doubt the murd'rous Knife was dull[†2] and blunt,
240    Till it was whetted on thy stone-hard heart,
To revell in the Intrailes of my Lambes.

But that still use of greefe, makes wilde greefe tame,
My tongue should to thy eares not name my Boyes,
Till that my Nayles were anchor'd in thine eyes:
245    And I in such a desp'rate Bay of death,
Like a poore Barke, of sailes and tackling reft,
Rush all to peeces on thy Rocky bosome.

**Richard**    Madam, so thrive I in my enterprize
And dangerous successe of bloody warres,
250    As I intend more good to you and yours,
Then ever you and [3] yours by me were harm'd.

**Queene**    What good is cover'd with the face of heaven,
To be discovered, that can do me good.

**Richard**    * Th'advancement of your children, gentle Lady

255    **Queene**    Up to some Scaffold, there to lose their heads.

**Richard**    Unto the dignity and height of Fortune,
The high Imperiall Type of this earths glory.    L 197 - b

**Queene**    Flatter my sorrow with report of it:
Tell me, what State, what Dignity, what Honor,
260    Canst thou demise to any childe of mine.

**Richard**    Even all I have; I, and my selfe and all,
Will I withall indow a childe of thine:
So in the Lethe of thy angry soule,
Thou drowne the sad remembrance of those wrongs,
265    Which thou supposest I have done to thee.

**Queene**    Be breefe, least that the processe of thy kindnesse
Last longer telling then thy kindnesse date.

**Richard**    Then know,→ [4]
That from my Soule, I love thy Daughter.

---

L 197 - b / R 197 - b  :  4. 4. 225 - 256

[W1] Ff = 'lanch'd', most modern texts set the early gloss 'lanc'd'

[W2] F1 = 'wa sdull', F2/most modern texts = 'was dull'

[W3] Q1-5/most modern texts = 'or', Q6/Ff = 'and'

[SP4] as Richard responds, Ff set two short lines (2/9 syllables) perhaps suggesting even he needs a breath before beginning his monstrous wooing: this is so even though there is enough room to set the two lines as one, as do Qq/most modern texts

| | | |
|---|---|---|
| 270 | **Queene** | My daughters Mother thinkes it with her soule. |
| | **Richard** | What do you thinke? |
| | **Queene** | That thou dost love my daughter from thy soule [1]<br>So from thy Soules love didst thou love her Brothers,<br>And from my hearts love, I do thanke thee for it. |
| 275 | **Richard** | Be not so hasty to confound my meaning :<br>I meane that with my Soule I love thy daughter,<br>And do intend to make her Queene of England. |
| | **Queene** | Well then, who dost ÿ [2] meane shallbe her King. |
| | **Richard** | Even he that makes her Queene : →[3] |
| 280 | | Who else should bee? |
| | **Queene** | What, thou? |
| | **Richard** | Even so : How thinke you of it? |
| | **Queene** | How canst thou woo her? |
| | **Richard** | That I would [4] learne of you, |
| 285 | | As one being best acquainted with her humour. |
| | **Queene** | And wilt thou learne of me? |
| | **Richard** | Madam, with all my heart. |
| | **Queene** | Send to her by the man that slew her Brothers,<br>A paire of bleeding hearts : thereon ingrave |
| 290 | | Edward and Yorke, then haply will she weepe :<br>Therefore present to her, as sometime [5] Margaret<br>Did to thy Father, steept in Rutlands blood,<br>A hand-kercheefe, which say to her did dreyne<br>The purple sappe from her sweet Brothers body, |
| 295 | | And bid her wipe her weeping eyes withall.<br>If this inducement move her not to love,<br>Send her a Letter of thy Noble deeds : |

---

R 197 - b : 4. 4. 257 - 280

PCT [1]
   F1-2 set no punctuation, suggesting the Queene ungrammatically rushes on to the next stage of her argument: Qq/F3 set a comma, most modern texts a colon

AB [2]
   F1= 'ÿ', (printed as such because of lack of column width), F2/most modern texts = 'thou', also F3 expands F1-2's 'shallbe' to 'shall be'

SP [3]
   most modern texts follow Qq and set these two short Ff lines (6 or 7/4 syllables) as one, presumably arguing lack of column width prevented F1 from following suit: if the Ff setting were to stand it might suggest Richard taking care (to maintain civility?) in framing his reply

W [4]
   Q1-2/most modern texts = 'would I', Q3-6/Ff = 'I would'

W [5]
   Q1-2 = 'sometimes', Q3-6/Ff = 'sometime'

|     |         |                                                                    |
|-----|---------|--------------------------------------------------------------------|
|     |         | Tell her, thou mad'st [1] away her Unckle Clarence,                |
|     |         | Her Unckle Rivers, I (and for her sake)                            |
| 300 |         | Mad'st quicke conveyance with her good Aunt Anne.                  |
|     | **Richard** | You mocke me Madam, this [2] not the way                       |
|     |         | To win your daughter.                                              |
|     | **Queene** | There is no other way,                                          |
|     |         | Unlesse thou could'st put on some other shape,                    |
| 305 |         | And not be Richard, that hath done all this.                      |
|     | **Richard** | [3] Say that I did all this for love of her.                  |
|     | **Queene** | Nay then indeed she cannot choose but hate thee               |
|     |         | Having bought love, with such a bloody spoyle.                    |
|     | **Richard** | Looke what is done, cannot be now amended:                    |
| 310 |         | Men shall deale unadvisedly sometimes,                            |
|     |         | Which after-houres gives leysure to repent.                       |

If I did take the Kingdome from your Sonnes,
To make amends, Ile give it to your daughter:
If I have kill'd the issue of your wombe,
To quicken your encrease, I will beget
Mine [4] yssue of your blood, upon your Daughter:
A Grandams name is little lesse in love,
Then is the doting Title of a Mother;
They are as Children but one steppe below,
Even of your mettall, of your very blood:
Of all one paine, save for a night of groanes
Endur'd of her, for whom you bid like sorrow.

Your Children were vexation to your youth,                                        R 197 - b
But mine shall be a comfort to your Age,
The losse you have, is but a Sonne being King,
And by that losse, your Daughter is made Queene.

I cannot make you what amends I would,
Therefore accept such kindnesse as I can.

Dorset your Sonne, that with a fearfull soule
Leads discontented steppes in Forraine soyle,
This faire Alliance, quickly shall call home
To high Promotions, and great Dignity.

---

W 1  even though Qq/Ff set variations of 'madst/mad'st' in an already long line, at least one modern text expands the word to 'madest'

W 2  Qq/F2 /most modern texts = 'is', F1 omits the word

LS/OM 3  some, but not all, modern texts set this and the subsequent three Ff only speeches, some fifty-five lines in all

W 4  Ff = 'Mine', one modern gloss = 'More'

The King that calles your beauteous Daughter Wife,
Familiarly shall call thy Dorset, Brother:
335      Againe shall you be Mother to a King:
And all the Ruines of distresseful Times,
Repayr'd with double Riches of Content.

What? we have many goodly dayes to see:
The liquid drops of Teares that you have shed,
340      Shall come againe, transform'd to Orient Pearle,
Advantaging their Love, with interest
Often-times [1] double gaine of happinesse.

Go then (my Mother) to thy Daughter go,
Make bold her bashfull yeares, with your experience,
345      Prepare her eares to heare a Woers Tale.

Put in her tender heart, th'aspiring Flame
Of Golden Soveraignty: Acquaint the Princesse
With the sweet silent houres of Marriage joyes:
And when this Arme of mine hath chastised
350      The petty Rebell, dull-brain'd Buckingham,
Bound with Triumphant Garlands will I come,
And leade thy daughter to a Conquerors bed:
To whom I will retaile my Conquest wonne,
And she shalbe [2] sole Victoresse, Caesars Caesar.

| | |
|---|---|
| 355   **Queene** [3] | What were I best to say, her Fathers Brother<br>Would be her Lord?<br>              Or shall I say her Unkle?<br>Or he that slew her Brothers, and her Unkles?<br>Under what Title shall I woo for thee,<br>360   That God, the Law, my Honor, and her Love,<br>Can make seeme pleasing to her tender yeares? |

**Richard**        Inferre faire Englands peace by this Alliance.

**Queene**        Which she shall purchase with stil lasting warre.

**Richard**        Tell her, the King that may command, intreats.

365   **Queene**        That at her hands, which the kings King forbids.

**Richard**        Say she shall be a High and Mighty Queene.

**Queene**        To vaile the Title, as her Mother doth.

---

[w 1] Ff = 'Often-times', most modern texts set the early gloss 'Of ten times'

[w 2] in this Ff only passage, F1-2 = 'shalbe', F3/most modern texts = 'shall be'

[RST 3] this speech can be set as anywhere between one and four sentences

| | | |
|---|---|---|
| | Richard | Say I will love her everlastingly. |
| | Queene | But how long shall that title ever ¹ last? |
| 370 | Richard | Sweetly in force, unto her faire lives end. |
| | Queene | But how long fairely shall her sweet life last? |
| | Richard | As long as Heaven and Nature lengthens it. |
| | Queene | As long as Hell and Richard likes of it. |
| | Richard | Say, I her Soveraigne, am her Subject low. |
| 375 | Queene | But she your Subject, lothes such Soveraignty. |
| | Richard | Be eloquent in my behalfe to her. |
| | Queene | An honest tale speeds best, being plainly told. |
| | Richard | Then plainly to her, tell my loving tale. |
| | Queene | Plaine and not honest, is too harsh a style. |
| 380 | Richard | Your Reasons are too shallow, and to quicke. |
| | Queene | O no, my Reasons are too deepe and dead, |
| | | Too deepe and dead (poore Infants) in their graves, |
| | | ² Harpe on it still shall I, till heart-strings breake. |
| | Richard | Harpe not on that string Madam, that is past. |
| 385 | | Now by my George, my Garter, and my Crowne. |
| | Queene | Prophan'd, dishonor'd, and the third usurpt. |
| | Richard | I sweare. ³ |
| | Queene | By nothing, for this is no Oath: ⁾ |
| | | Thy George prophan'd, hath lost his Lordly ⁴ Honor; |
| 390 | | Thy Garter blemish'd, pawn'd his Knightly Vertue; |
| | | Thy Crowne usurp'd, disgrac'd his Kingly Glory: |
| | | If something thou would'st sweare to be beleev'd, |
| | | Sweare then by something, that thou hast not wrong'd. |

L 198 - b

---

PCT ₁ most modern texts set the word 'ever' in quotation marks

LS ₂ most modern texts sensibly follow Q1 and set this line after the first line of Richard's next sentence, (Q2-6 omit the line)

PCT ₃ F1 shows a mark half-way up the word which F2/most modern texts set as a period: if F1 is not setting a period,

w it emphasises the dialogue, highlighting the fact the Queene interrupts him

w ₄ Qq/most modern texts = 'holie', Ff set 'Lordly', which one modern text transfers to the next line, replacing 'Knightly'

| | Richard | [1] Then by my Selfe. |
|---|---|---|
| 395 | Queene | Thy Selfe, is selfe-misus'd. } |
| | Richard | Now by the World. |
| | Queene | 'Tis full of thy foule wrongs. } |
| | Richard | My Fathers death. |
| | Queene | Thy life hath it dishonor'd. } |
| 400 | Richard | Why then, by Heaven. |

**Queene**
Heavens [2] wrong is most of all : }
If thou didd'st feare to breake an Oath with him,
The unity the King my husband made,
Thou had'st not broken, nor my Brothers died.

405
If thou had'st fear'd to breake an oath by him,
Th'Imperiall mettall, circling now thy head,[3]
Had grac'd the tender temples of my Child,
And both the Princes had bene breathing heere,
Which now two tender Bed-fellowes for dust,
410
Thy broken Faith hath made the prey for Wormes.

What can'st thou sweare by now. [4]
                                        }

**Richard**
The time to come.

**Queene**
That thou hast wronged in the time ore-past :
For I my selfe have many teares to wash
415
Heereafter time, for time past, wrong'd by thee.

The Children live, whose Fathers thou hast slaughter'd,
Ungovern'd youth, to waile it with [5] their age :
The Parents live, whose Children thou hast butcher'd,
Old barren Plants, to waile it with their Age.

420
Sweare not by time to come, for that thou hast
Misus'd ere us'd, by times ill-us'd repast. [6]

---

W [1]
Qq/most modern texts set the two lines about 'my Selfe' after the exchanges over 'the world' and 'My Fathers
death': one modern text sets Ff as is
O [2]
Qq/most modern texts set the image 'God/Gods', Ff = 'Heaven/Heavens'
W [3]
Ff/most modern texts = 'head, Qq = 'brow'
PCT [4]
in this Ff only line, F1 sets a period, suggesting the Queene is making a dismissive statement rather than asking
a question: F2/most modern texts set a question mark
W [5]
Qq/most modern texts = 'in', Ff = 'with'
W [6]
Qq = 'orepast', which most modern texts set as 'o'erpast': Ff = 'repast'

| Richard | As I entend to prosper, and repent: |
| | So thrive I in my dangerous Affayres |
| | Of hostile Armes: My selfe, my selfe confound: |
425 | | [1] Heaven, and Fortune barre me happy houres: |
| | Day, yeeld me not thy light; nor Night, thy rest. |
| | |
| | Be opposite all Planets of good lucke |
| | To my proceeding, if with deere hearts love, |
| | Immaculate devotion, holy thoughts, |
430 | | I tender not thy beautious Princely daughter. |
| | |
| | In her, consists my Happinesse, and thine: |
| | Without her, followes to my selfe, and thee; |
| | Her selfe, the Land, and many a Christian soule, |
| | Death, Desolation, Ruine, and Decay: |
435 | | It cannot be avoyded, but by this: |
| | It will not be avoyded,†[2] but by this. |
| | |
| | Therefore deare Mother [3] (I must call you so) |
| | Be the Atturney of my love to her: |
| | Pleade what I will be, not what I have beene; |
440 | | Not my deserts, but what I will deserve: |
| | Urge the Necessity and state of times, |
| | And be not peevish found,[4] in great Designes. |
| | |
| Queene | Shall I be tempted of the Divel thus? |
| | |
| Richard | I, if the Divell tempt you to do good. |
| | |
445 | Queene | Shall I forget my selfe, to be my selfe. |
| | |
| Richard | I, if your selfes remembrance wrong your selfe. |
| | |
| Queene | Yet thou didst kil my Children. |
| | |
| Richard | But in your daughters wombe I bury [5] them. |
| | |
| | Where in that Nest of Spicery they will breed |
450 | | Selves of themselves, to your recomforture. [6] |
| | |
| Queene | Shall I go win my daughter to thy will? |
| | |
| Richard | And be a happy Mother by the deed. |

---

LS/O [1]
  most modern texts set this Ff only line, usually altering 'Heaven' to 'God'

W [2]
  F1 = 'avo yded', F2/most modern texts = 'avoyded'

W [3]
  Ff/most modern texts = 'deare Mother', one text sets Qq's 'good mother', explaining that the phrase in
  contemporary parlance meant 'mother-in -law'

W [4]
  Ff/most modern texts = 'peevish found', Qq/one modern text = 'peevish, fond'

W [5]
  Q3/Ff/most modern texts = 'I bury', Q1-2 = 'I buried', Q3 = 'Ile burie'

W [6]
  Ff/most modern texts = 'recomforture': one modern text sets Qq's 'recomfiture' even though admitting the
  words mean the same

| | | |
|---|---|---|
| **Queene** | I go, write to me very shortly, | |
| | ¹ And you shal understand from me her mind. | |

### [Exit Q.{ueene}] ²

| | | |
|---|---|---|
| 455 | **Richard** | Beare her my true loves kisse, and so farewell. |
| | | Relenting Foole, and shallow-changing Woman. |
| | | ³ How now, what newes? |

R 198 - b

### ENTER RATCLIFFE

| | | |
|---|---|---|
| | **Ratcliffe** | Most mightie Soveraigne, on the Westerne Coast |
| | | Rideth a puissant Navie : to our Shores |
| 460 | | Throng many doubtfull hollow-hearted friends, |
| | | Unarm'd, and unresolv'd to beat them backe. |
| | | 'Tis thought, that Richmond is their Admirall : |
| | | And there they hull, expecting but the aide |
| | | Of Buckingham, to welcome them ashore. |
| 465 | **Richard** | Some light-foot friend post to ÿ ⁴ Duke of Norfolk : |
| | | Ratcliffe thy selfe, or Catesby, where is hee? |
| | **Catesby** | Here, my good Lord. |
| | **Richard** | Catesby, flye to the Duke. |
| | **Catesby** | ⁵ I will, my Lord, with all convenient haste. |
| 470 | **Richard** | Catesby come hither, poste to Salisbury : |
| | | When thou com'st thither : ⁶ Dull unmindfull Villaine, |
| | | Why stay'st thou here, and go'st not to the Duke? |
| | **Catesby** | First, mighty Liege, tell me your Highnesse pleasure, |
| | | What from your Grace I shall deliver to him. |
| 475 | **Richard** | O true, good Catesby, bid him levie straight |
| | | The greatest strength and power that he can make, |
| | | And meet me suddenly at Salisbury. |

---

R 198 - b / L 199 - a : 4. 4. 428 - 451

LS ₁ most modern texts set this Ff only line

SD ₂ naturally most modern texts follow Qq and set her exit after Richard's next line, also suggesting he kisses her before she leaves, though he could quite easily call the repulsive idea off after her without touching her

LS/SD ₃ most modern texts set this Ff only line, and move Ratcliffe's entry to before Richard's question

AB ₄ F1 = 'ÿ', (printed as such because of lack of column width), F2/most modern texts = 'the'

LS ₅ most modern texts set this Ff only speech and the first half of the next Ff only line, usually altering the first word of Richard's speech from 'Catesby' to 'Ratcliffe'

WHO ₆ most modern texts suggest this is spoken to Catesby

| | | |
|---|---|---|
| Catesby | [1] | I goe. |

[Exit]

| | |
|---|---|
| Ratcliffe | What, may it please you, shall I doe at Salis- |
480 | | bury? |

| | |
|---|---|
| Richard | Why, what would'st thou doe there, before I |
| | goe? |

| | |
|---|---|
| Ratcliffe | Your Highnesse told me I should poste before. |

| | |
|---|---|
| Richard | My minde is chang'd: |

**ENTER LORD STANLEY**

485                           Stanley, what newes with you?

| | |
|---|---|
| Stanley | None, good my Liege, to please you with ÿ [2] hearing, |
| | Nor none so bad, but well may be reported. |

| | |
|---|---|
| Richard | Hoyday, a Riddle, neither good nor bad: |
| | What need'st [3] thou runne so many miles [4] about, |
490 | | When thou mayest tell thy Tale the neerest way? |
| | Once more, what newes? |

| | |
|---|---|
| Stanley | Richmond is on the Seas. |

| | |
|---|---|
| Richard | There let him sinke, and be the Seas on him, |
| | White-liver'd Runnagate, what doth he there? |

| | |
|---|---|
| 495   Stanley | I know not, mightie Soveraigne, but by guesse. |

| | |
|---|---|
| Richard | Well, as you guesse. |

| | |
|---|---|
| Stanley | Stirr'd up by Dorset, Buckingham, and Morton, [5] |
| | He makes for England, here to clayme the Crowne. |

| | | |
|---|---|---|
| Richard | [6] | Is the Chayre emptie? is the Sword unsway'd? |
500 | | Is the King dead? the Empire unpossest? |
| | What Heire of Yorke is there alive, but wee? |
| | And who is Englands King, but great Yorkes Heire? |
| | Then tell me, what makes he upon the Seas? |

---

LS [1] most modern texts set this Ff only reply

AB [2] F1 = 'ÿ', (printed as such because of lack of column width), F2/most modern texts = 'the'

▼ [3] Ff/most modern texts = 'What need'st', Qq = 'Why doest', one modern text = 'Why need'st'

▼ [4] Ff/most modern texts = 'miles', Qq/one modern text = 'mile'

▼ [5] Ff/most modern texts = 'Morton', Qq/one modern text = 'Elie': see footnote #8, page 102

PST [6] this speech could be set as anywhere between one and five sentences long

| | | |
|---|---|---|
| | **Stanley** | Unlesse for that, my Liege, I cannot guesse. |
| 505 | **Richard** | Unlesse for that he comes to be your Liege, |
| | | You cannot guesse wherefore the Welchman comes. |
| | | Thou wilt revolt, and flye to him, I feare. |
| | **Stanley** | No, my good Lord, therefore mistrust me not. |
| | **Richard** | Where is thy Power then, to beat him back? |
| 510 | | Where be thy Tenants, and thy followers? |
| | | Are they not now upon the Westerne Shore, |
| | | Safe-conducting the Rebels from their Shippes? |
| | **Stanley** | No, my good Lord, my friends are in the |
| | | North. |
| 515 | **Richard** | Cold friends to me : what do they in the North, |
| | | When they should serve their Soveraigne in the West? L 199 - a |
| | **Stanley** | They have not been commanded, mighty King : |
| | | Pleaseth your Majestie to give me leave, |
| | | Ile muster up my friends, and meet your Grace, |
| 520 | | Where, and what time your Majestie shall please. |
| | **Richard** | I,[1] thou would'st be gone, to joyne with Richmond : |
| | | But Ile not trust thee. |
| | **Stanley** | Most mightie Soveraigne, |
| | | You have no cause to hold my friendship doubtfull, |
| 525 | | I never was, nor never will be false. |
| | **Richard** | Goe then, and muster men : but leave behind |
| | | Your Sonne George Stanley : looke your heart be firme, |
| | | Or else his Heads assurance is but fraile. |
| | **Stanley** | So deale with him, as I prove true to you. |

**[Exit Stanley]**
**ENTER A MESSENGER**

| | | |
|---|---|---|
| 530 | **Messenger** | My gracious Soveraigne, now in Devonshire, |
| | | As I by friends am well advertised, |
| | | Sir Edward Courtney, and the haughtie Prelate, |
| | | Bishop of Exeter, his elder Brother, |
| | | With many moe Confederates, are in Armes. |

**ENTER ANOTHER MESSENGER**

---

L 199 - a / R 199 - a : 4. 4. 474 - 502

[W][1] Qq = 'I, I', most modern texts = 'Ay, ay': Ff set the single 'I'

| 535 | **Messenger** | In Kent, my Liege, the Guilfords are in Armes, |
| | | And every houre more Competitors |
| | | Flocke to the Rebels, and their power growes strong. |

**ENTER ANOTHER MESSENGER**

**Messenger** My Lord, the Armie of great Buckingham.

**Richard** Out on ye,[1] Owles, nothing but Songs of Death,

**[He striketh him]**

540 There, take thou that, till thou bring better newes.

**Messenger** The newes I have to tell your Majestie,
Is, that by sudden Floods, and fall of Waters,[2]
Buckinghams Armie is dispers'd and scatter'd,
And he himselfe wandred away alone,
545 No man knowes whither.

**Richard** I cry thee mercie:
[3] There is my Purse, to cure that Blow of thine.

Hath any well-advised friend proclaym'd
Reward to him that brings the Traytor in?

550 **Messenger** Such Proclamation hath been made, my Lord.

**ENTER ANOTHER MESSENGER**

**Messenger** Sir Thomas Lovell, and Lord Marquesse Dorset,
'Tis said, my Liege, in Yorkshire are in Armes:
But this good comfort bring I to your Highnesse,
The Brittaine Navie is dispers'd by Tempest.

555 Richmond in Dorsetshire sent out a Boat
Unto the shore, to aske those on the Banks,
If they were his Assistants, yea, or no?

Who answer'd him, they came from Buckingham,
Upon his partie: he mistrusting them,
560 Hoys'd[4] sayle, and made his course againe for Brittaine.

**Richard** March on, march on, since we are up in Armes,

[1] Q1-5/most modern texts = 'you', Ff/one modern text = 'ye'

[2] Ff/most modern texts set the plural 'Floods' and 'Waters', Qq/one modern text set the singular 'floud' and 'water'

[3] Ff/most modern texts = 'There is my Purse, to cure that Blow of thine.', Qq/one modern text = 'Ratcliffe reward him, for the blow I gave him'

[4] Ff/most modern texts = 'Hoys'd', Qq/one modern text = 'Hoist'

> If not to fight with forraine Enemies,
> Yet to beat downe these Rebels here at home.

**ENTER CATESBY**

| | |
|---|---|
| **Catesby** | My Liege, the Duke of Buckingham is taken, |
| 565 | That is the best newes : that the Earle of Richmond |
| | Is with a mighty power Landed at Milford, |
| | Is colder Newes,[1] but yet they must be told. |

R 199 - a

| | |
|---|---|
| **Richard** | Away towards Salsbury, while we reason here, |
| | A Royall batteil might be wonne and lost : |
| 570 | Some one take order Buckingham be brought |
| | To Salsbury, the rest march on with me. |

**[Florish. Exeunt]**

---

R 199 - a / L 200 - b : 4. 4. 529 - 538

[1] Q1-5/most modern texts = 'colder tidings, yet', Ff = 'colder Newes, but yet'

# Scena Quarta

**[At least one modern text creates a new scene here, Act Four Scene 5]**

ENTER DERBY, AND SIR CHRISTOPHER [1]

| | |
|---|---|
| *Derby* | Sir Christopher, tell Richmond this from me, |
| | That in the stye of the [2] most deadly Bore, |
| | My Sonne George Stanley is frankt up in hold : |
| | If I revolt, off goes yong Georges head, |
| 5 | The feare of that, holds off my present ayde. |
| | [3] So get thee gone : commend me to thy Lord. |
| | Withall say, that the Queene hath heartily consented |
| | He should espouse Elizabeth hir daughter. |
| | But tell me, where is Princely Richmond now? |
| 10 Christopher | At Penbroke, [4] or at Hertford West [5] in Wales. |
| Derby | What men of Name resort to him. |
| Christopher | Sir Walter Herbert, a renowned Souldier, |
| | Sir Gilbert Talbot, Sir William Stanley, |
| | Oxford, redoubted Pembroke, Sir James Blunt, |
| 15 | And Rice ap Thomas, with a valiant Crew, |
| | And many other of great name and worth : |
| | And towards London do they bend their power, |
| | If by the way they be not fought withall. |
| Derby | Well hye thee to thy Lord : I kisse his hand,[6] |
| 20 | My Letter will resolve him of my minde. |
| | Farewell. |

**[Exeunt]**

---

L 200 - b : 4. 5. 1 - 21

SD / N [1]
    most modern texts explain Sir Christopher is a priest, and some add his surname, 'Urswick'

W [2]
    Ff/most modern texts = 'the', Qq/one modern text = 'this'

LS /OM / ALT [3]
    some, not all, modern texts set this Ff only line: also, as per Qq, at least one modern text moves the next
    two lines to after the first line of Derby's last speech (replacing 'Withall say, that' with 'Tell him')

N [4]
    F1-3 = 'Penbroke': Qq/F4/most modern texts set the correct name, 'Pembroke'

N [5]
    the modern version of this place-name is 'Havorfordwest': with all the variations offered by Qq/Ff and early
    commentators, most modern texts set the metrically acceptable abbreviation, 'Ha'rfordwest'

W [6]
    Ff/most modern texts = 'I kisse his hand': Qq/one modern text = 'commend me to him'

# Actus Quintus.  Scena Prima

ENTER BUCKINGHAM WITH HALBERDS, LED
TO EXECUTION [1]

| | |
|---|---|
| **Buckingham** | Will not King Richard let me speake with him? |
| **Sherife** | No my good Lord, therefore be patient. |
| **Buckingham** | Hastings, and Edwards children, Gray & Rivers, |
| | Holy King Henry, and thy faire Sonne Edward, |

5 Vaughan, and all that have miscarried
By under-hand corrupted foule injustice,
If that your moody discontented soules,
Do through the clowds behold this present houre,
Even for revenge mocke my destruction.

10 This is All-soules day (Fellow) is it not?

| **Sherife** | It is. |
|---|---|
| **Buckingham** | Why then Al-soules day, is my bodies doomsday [2] |

This is the day, which in King Edwards time[t3]
I wish'd might fall on me, when I was found
15 False to his Children, and his Wives Allies.

This is the day, wherein I wisht to fall
By the false Faith of him whom most I trusted.

This, this All-soules day to my fearfull Soule,
Is the determin'd respit of my wrongs :
20 That high All-seer, which I dallied with,                    L 200 - b
Hath turn'd my fained Prayer on my head,
And given in earnest, what I begg'd in jest.

Thus doth he force the swords of wicked men
To turne their owne points in their Masters bosomes.

25 Thus Margarets curse falles heavy on my necke :
When he (quoth she) shall split thy heart with sorrow,
Remember Margaret was a Prophetesse :
Come leade me Officers to the blocke of shame,
Wrong hath but wrong, and blame the due of blame.

30

[Exeunt Buckingham with Officers]

---

L 200 - b / R 200 - b  :  5. 1. 1 - 29

SD/P₁  Qq/Ff neglect to indicate who is supervising the guard escorting Buckingham:  within the dialogue,in terms of prefix, most modern texts follow Ff and set 'Sher.' for a Sherife, Qq set 'Rat' for 'Ratcliffe'

PCT 2  probably because of lack of column width F1-2 set no punctuation which, if it stood, would suggest Buckingham moving ungrammatically on to his next point:  Q1 sets a colon, F3/most modern texts a period

▼3  F1 = 't ime', F2/most modern texts = 'time'

# Scena Secunda

ENTER RICHMOND, OXFORD, BLUNT, HERBERT, AND
OTHERS, WITH DRUM AND COLOURS

**Richmond**  Fellowes in Armes, and my most loving Frends
Bruis'd underneath the yoake of Tyranny,
Thus farre into the bowels of the Land,
Have we marcht on without impediment;
5  And heere receive we from our Father Stanley
Lines of faire comfort and encouragement:
The wretched, bloody, and usurping Boare,
(That spoyl'd [1] your Summer Fields, and fruitfull Vines)
Swilles your warm blood like wash, & makes his trough
10  In your embowel'd [2] bosomes : This foule Swine
Is [3] now even in the Centry [4] of this Isle,
Ne're [5] to the Towne of Leicester, as we learne:
From Tamworth thither, is but one dayes march.

In Gods name cheerely on, couragious Friends,
15  To reape the Harvest of perpetuall peace,
By this one bloody tryall of sharpe Warre.

**Oxford**  Every mans Conscience is a thousand men, [6]
To fight against this guilty Homicide.

**Herbert**  I doubt not but his Friends will turne to us.

20 **Blunt**  He hath no friends, but what are friends for fear,
Which in his deerest neede will flye from him.

**Richmond**  All for our vantage, then in Gods name march,
True Hope is swift, and flyes with Swallowes wings,
Kings it makes Gods, and meaner creatures Kings.

**[Exeunt Omnes]**

---

[1] Qq/Ff/most modern texts = 'spoyl'd', one modern text sets 'spoils'

[2] Ff/most modern texts = 'embowel'd', Q1-5 = 'inboweld'

[3] Ff/most modern texts = 'Is', Qq/one modern text = 'Lies'

[4] Qq/most modern texts = 'center', Ff/one modern text = 'Centry'

[5] Q1-5 /F3/most modern texts = 'Neare', F1-2 = 'Ne're'

[6] Ff/most modern texts = 'men', Qq/one modern text = 'swordes'

126

**ENTER KING RICHARD IN ARMES, WITH NORFOLKE, RATCLIFFE,
AND THE EARLE OF SURREY** [1]
**[Most modern texts create a new scene here, Act Five Scene 3]**

| | | |
|---|---|---|
| 25 | **Richard** | Here pitch our Tent, even here in Bosworth field, My Lord of Surrey, why looke you so sad? |
| | **Surrey** | My heart is ten times lighter then my lookes. |

| | | |
|---|---|---|
| | **Richard** | My Lord of Norfolke. |
| | **Norfolke** | [2] Heere most gracious Liege. ⟩ |
| 30 | **Richard** | Norfolke, we must have knockes : → Ha, must we not? |

| | | |
|---|---|---|
| | **Norfolke** | We must both give and take my loving Lord. |
| | **Richard** | Up with my Tent, heere wil I lye to night, But where to morrow? |
| 35 | | Well, *all's one for that. Who hath descried the number of the Traitors? |
| | **Norfolke** | Six or seven thousand is their utmost power. |
| | **Richard** | Why our Battalia trebbles that account : Besides, the Kings name is a Tower of strength, |
| 40 | | Which they upon the adverse Faction want. |
| | | Up with the Tent : Come Noble Gentlemen, Let us survey the vantage of the ground. |
| | | Call for some men of sound direction :        R 200 - b Let's lacke no Discipline, make no delay, |
| 45 | | For Lords, to morrow is a busie day. |

**[Exeunt]** [3]
**ENTER RICHMOND, SIR WILLIAM BRANDON, OX-
FORD, AND DORSET** [4]
**[At least one modern text creates a new scene here, Act Five Scene 4]**

---

P/SD [1]
    Ff/most modern texts name the character the Earle of Surrey; Qq/one modern text replace him with Catesby, altering the opening of Richard's second line to 'Whie, how now Catesbie,': also, most modern texts suggest Richard's tent is erected (to one side of the stage) as he commands

LS/SP [2]
    most modern texts set this and the following Ff only speech, joining Richard's two short lines (6/4 syllables) together, presumably arguing lack of column width prevented F1 from following suit: if the Ff setting were to stand it might suggest Norfolke is as gloomy as Surrey, and the pause indicating his initial non-response pushes Richard to his second reply-demanding line

SD [3]
    some modern texts suggest Richard and his party (the tent having been erected) exit through one door, and Richmond and his party enter through the other, and begin to erect Richmond's tent on the other side of the stage

ALT/N [4]
    since Dorset does not participate in the scene, and since both Blunt and Sir Walter Herbert are referred to and/or speak in the scene, most modern texts drop Dorset and add Blunt and Herbert to the entry, though one modern text omits the latter character (cutting the textual reference to him) and keeps Dorset in the scene

| | |
|---|---|
| **Richmond** | The weary Sunne, [1] hath made a Golden set, |
| | And by the bright Tract [2] of his fiery Carre, |
| | Gives token of a goodly day to morrow. |
| | Sir William Brandon, you shall beare my Standard : |
| 50 | [3] Give me some Inke and Paper in my Tent : |
| | Ile draw the Forme and Modell of our Battaile, |
| | Limit each Leader to his severall Charge, |
| | And part in just proportion our small Power. |
| | My Lord of Oxford, you Sir William Brandon, |
| 55 | And your [4] Sir Walter Herbert stay with me : |
| | The Earle of Pembroke keepes his Regiment ; |
| | Good Captaine Blunt, beare my goodnight to him, |
| | And by the second houre in the Morning, |
| | Desire the Earle to see me in my Tent : |
| 60 | Yet one thing more (good Captaine) do for me : |
| | Where is Lord Stanley quarter'd, do you know ? |
| **Blunt** | Unlesse I have mistane his Colours much, |
| | (Which well I am assur'd I have not done) |
| | His Regiment lies halfe a Mile at least |
| 65 | South, from the mighty Power of the King. |
| **Richmond** | If without perill it be possible, |
| | Sweet Blunt, make some good meanes to speak with him |
| | And give him from me, this most needfull Note. |
| **Blunt** | Upon my life, my Lord, Ile undertake it, |
| 70 | [5] And so God give you quiet rest to night. |
| **Richmond** | Good night good Captaine Blunt : → [6] |
| | Come Gentlemen, |
| | Let us consult upon to morrowes Businesse ; |
| | Into my Tent, the Dew is rawe and cold. |

**[They withdraw into the Tent]**

---

[W 1] Q2-6/Ff/most modern texts = 'Sunne', Q1/one modern text = 'sonne'

[W 2] Qq/most modern texts = 'tracke', Ff = 'Tract'

[ALT/LS 3] most modern texts follow Qq and transfer the remainder of Richard's sentence to after his farewell to Blunt, line 71 below: also, some modern texts follow Qq and cut the opening two lines of the following sentence

[W 4] F2/most modern texts set 'you', F1 = 'your'

[LS 5] most modern texts set this Ff only line

[SD/SP 6] most modern texts indicate Blunt now exits, and set Ff's two short lines (6/4 syllables) as one, presumably arguing that lack of column width prevented F1 from following suit (Qq do not set the second line): if the Ff setting were to stand it would allow a silent moment of farewell between the two men before Richmond turns to the remainder of his party

ENTER RICHARD, RATCLIFFE, NORFOLKE, & CATESBY [1]

[at least one modern text creates a new scene here, Act Five Scene 5]

| | | |
|---|---|---|
| 75 | **Richard** | What is't a Clocke? |
| | **Catesby** | It's Supper time my Lord, it's nine a clocke. |
| | Richard as [2] •**King**• | I will not sup to night,→ [3]<br>Give me some Inke and Paper:<br>What, is my Beaver easier then it was? |
| 80 | | And all my Armour laid into my Tent? |
| | **Catesby** | It is my Liege: and all things are in readinesse. |
| | •**Richard**• | Good Norfolke, hye thee to thy charge,<br>Use carefull Watch, choose trusty Centinels, |
| | **Norfolke** | I go my Lord. |
| 85 | **Richard** | Stir[t4] with the Larke to morrow, gentle Norfolk. |
| | **Norfolke** | I warrant you my Lord. |
| | | **[Exit]** |
| | **Richard** | Ratcliffe. [5] |
| | **Ratcliffe** | My Lord. |
| | **Richard** | Send out a }Pursuivant at Armes |
| 90 | | To Stanleys Regiment: bid him bring his power<br>Before Sun-rising, least his Sonne George fall<br>Into the blinde Cave of eternall night. [6] |
| | | Fill me a Bowle of Wine: Give me a Watch,<br>Saddle white Surrey for the Field to morrow: |
| 95 | | Look that my Staves be sound, & not too heavy. |

Ratcliff.

---

[SD1] some modern texts add Soldiers, while at least one suggests a table is brought in

[P2] from now till the end of the play, Richard's prefix keeps shifting from the personal 'Richard' to the royal status 'King': as such it seems to reflect his growing personal confusion - also see footnote #5 below, #2 and #3 next page, and #6, page 137

[SP3] most modern texts follow Qq and set the two short Ff lines (6/7 syllables) as one, presumably arguing that lack of column width prevented F1 from following suit: however, a thirteen syllable line may not be the best reading here, and Ff's minute pauses might suggest surprise that Richard is refusing food

[COMP4] the letter 't' in what Qq/F2/most modern texts set as 'stir' is so twisted in F1 the word appears to be 'scir'

[N/W5] because of Ff's seeming confusion below, where Ratcliffe appears to be called upon to do two things at once, most modern texts follow Qq and replace Ff's Ratcliffe with Catesby until the end of the first sentence of Richard's second speech: however, if kept, the Ff settings might well be a deliberate indication that Richard is in a state of confusion

[SD6] most modern texts suggest whomever they show as participating in this brief exchange (Catesby or Ratcliffe) exits to do Richard's bidding

| | |
|---|---|
| **Ratcliffe** | My Lord. |
| **Richard** | Saw'st [1] the melancholly Lord Northumberland? |
| **Ratcliffe** | Thomas the Earle of Surrey, and himselfe, |
| | Much about Cockshut time, from Troope to Troope |
| | Went through the Army, chearing up the Souldiers. |

100

| | | |
|---|---|---|
| **°King°** | So, I am satisfied: Give me a Bowle of Wine,[2] | |
| | I have not that Alacrity of Spirit, | L 201 - b |
| | Nor cheere of Minde that I was wont to have. | |
| | Set it downe. | |
| | Is Inke and Paper ready? | |

105

| | |
|---|---|
| **Ratcliffe** | It is my Lord. |

> **°Richard°** [3] Bid my Guard watch.
> Leave me.
> Ratcliffe, about the mid of night come to my Tent
> And helpe to arme me.

110

Leave me I say.

**[Exit Ratclif]** [4]
**ENTER DERBY TO RICHMOND IN HIS TENT** [5]

| | |
|---|---|
| **Derby** | Fortune, and Victory sit on thy Helme. |
| **Richmond** | All comfort that the darke night can affoord, |
| | Be to thy Person, Noble Father in Law. |
| | Tell me, how fares our Noble [6] Mother? |

115

---

L 201 - b / R 201 - b : 5. 3. 67 - 82

[W][1] Qq/most modern texts = 'thou', Ff omit the word

[LS][2] one modern text makes an unwarranted assumption both here and in four lines time, that Richard should be metrically at ease (despite all indications in the scene to the contrary): thus here, while Qq/Ff set a twelve syllable line, including the phrase 'a Bowle of Wine', this text sets 'some wine', creating a normal pentameter line: see also the next footnote

[LS/ALT][3] the following is the second attempt by one modern text to set some form of normal delivery, despite Qq/Ff suggesting Richard is metrically ill at ease (see the previous footnote): here, while Ff/Qq set the second and third line as a peculiar outburst followed by a shorter line (4 +6 as a shared line/12/9 syllables)
> Bid my Guard watch. Leave me.
> Ratcliffe, about the mid of night come to my Tent
> And helpe to arme me. Leave me I say.
the modern text reverses the text of the opening line, and sets the last two as almost normal (10/11 syllables), a totally unwarranted interference
> Leave me. Bid my Guard watch.
> About the mid of night come to my Tent
> Ratcliffe, and helpe to arme me. Leave me I say.

[SD][4] those modern texts who added Soldiers to the previous entry now direct them to stand guard over Richard's tent

[SD][5] since most modern texts had Richmond's supporters exit with him to his tent, they suggest these characters are present in this scene, and leave with Derby when he exits

[W][6] Q1-2/most modern texts = 'loving', Q3-6/Ff set a repetition of 'Noble' from the previous line

**Derby**          I by Attourney, blesse thee from thy Mother,
                   Who prayes continually for Richmonds good :
                   So much for that.
120                                      The silent houres steale on,
                   And flakie darknesse breakes within the East.

                   In breefe, for so the season bids us be,
                   Prepare thy Battell early in the Morning,
                   And put thy Fortune to th'Arbitrement
125                Of bloody stroakes, and mortall staring [1] Warre :
                   I, as I may, that which I would, I cannot,
                   With best advantage will deceive the time,[†2]
                   And ayde thee in this doubtfull shocke of Armes.

                   But on thy side I may not be too forward,
130                Least being seene, thy Brother, tender George
                   Be executed in his Fathers sight.

                   Farewell :  the leysure, and the fearfull time
                   Cuts off the ceremonious Vowes of Love,
                   And ample enterchange of sweet Discourse,
135                Which so long sundred Friends should dwell upon :
                   God give us leysure for these rites [3] of Love.

                   Once more Adieu, be valiant, and speed well.

**Richmond**       Good Lords conduct him to his Regiment :
                   Ile strive with troubled noise,[4] to take a Nap,
140                Lest leaden slumber peize me downe to morrow,
                   When I should mount with wings of Victory :
                   Once more, good night kinde Lords and Gentlemen.

                   **[Exeunt.          Manet Richmond]**

               [5]  O thou, whose Captaine I account my selfe,
                   Looke on my Forces with a gracious eye :
145                Put in their hands thy bruising Irons of wrath,
                   That they may crush downe with a heavy fall,
*                  Th'usurping Helmets of our Adversaries :
                   Make us thy ministers of Chasticement,
                   That we may praise thee in thy victory :
150                To thee I do commend my watchfull soule,

---

[1] Qq/Ff /most modern texts = 'staring', one modern text = 'sharing'

[2] F1 appears to set 'zdvantage will deceive thet ime', F2/most modern texts = 'advantage will deceive the time'

[3] Qq/most modern texts = 'rights', Ff = 'rites'

[4] Qq/most modern texts = 'thoughts', Ff = 'noise'

[SD 5] most modern texts suggest Richmond now kneels to pray

Ere I let fall the windowes of mine eyes:
Sleeping, and waking, oh defend me still.

**[Sleeps]**

**ENTER THE GHOST OF PRINCE EDWARD,[1] SONNE TO
HENRY THE SIXT**

**Ghost** [to •Richard•]  Let me sit heavy on thy soule to morrow:
Thinke how thou stab'st me in my prime of youth
155                At Teukesbury: Dispaire therefore, and dye.

**Ghost** [to Richmond]  Be chearefull Richmond,→ [2]
For the wronged Soules
Of butcher'd Princes, fight in thy behalfe:
King Henries issue Richmond comforts thee.

**ENTER THE GHOST OF HENRY THE SIXT**

160    **Ghost**    [3] When I was mortall, my Annointed body
By thee was punched full of[4] holes;
Thinke on the Tower, and me: Dispaire, and dye,
Harry the sixt, bids thee dispaire, and dye.

[to Richmond]  Vertuous and holy be thou Conqueror:
165                Harry that prophesied thou should'st be King,
Doth comfort thee in[5] sleepe: Live, and flourish.[6]    R 201 - b

**ENTER THE GHOST OF CLARENCE**

**Ghost**    Let me sit heavy in thy soule to morrow.

I that was wash'd to death with Fulsome Wine:
Poore Clarence by thy guile betray'd to death:
170                To morrow in the battell thinke on me,
And fall thy edgelesse Sword, dispaire and dye.

---

SD 1  most modern texts set Q1-2's fuller description' 'young Prince Edward': also, one modern text suggests this
and all subsequent apparitions should appear 'above'

SP 2  most modern texts follow Qq and set these two short Ff lines (5/4 or 5 syllables) as one, presumably arguing
that lack of column width prevented F1 from following suit

WHO/W3 most modern texts follow Qq and point out that the first lines of this Ghost (and all subsequent apparitions)
are spoken to Richard, until the switch to Richmond is set as a specific prefix (this is the only time this will be
footnoted): also Q1-4/Ff set 'in thy soule', Q4/one modern text replaces 'in' with 'on'

W 4  Q1/most modern texts = 'deadlie', omitted by Q2-6/Ff

W 5  Qq/most modern texts = 'thy', omitted by Ff: since this creates an eleven syllable line, one metrically minded
modern text maintains 'thy', but replaces 'Doth comfort' with 'Comfort' to maintain pentameter

SD 6  Qq/Ff set no exits for any of the Ghosts, perhaps suggesting they stay on-stage until Richard wakes, post line 221,
page 134: most modern texts have each Ghost, or set of Ghosts, exit when their sequence finishes

[to Richmond] Thou off-spring of the house of Lancaster
The wronged heyres of Yorke do pray for thee,
Good Angels guard thy battell, Live and Flourish.

**ENTER THE GHOSTS OF RIVERS, GRAY, AND VAUGHAN**

**Rivers**   Let me sit heavy in [1] thy soule to morrow,
175              Rivers, that dy'de at Pomfret : dispaire, and dye.

**Grey**    Thinke upon Grey, and let thy soule dispaire.

**Vaughan**  Thinke upon Vaughan, and with guilty feare
              Let fall thy [2] Lance, dispaire and dye.

**All** [to Richmond]  Awake,→ [3]
180              And thinke our wrongs in Richards Bosome,
              Will conquer him.
                          Awake, and win the day.

**ENTER THE GHOST OF LORD HASTINGS** [4]

**Ghost**   Bloody and guilty : guiltily awake,
              And in a bloody Battell end thy dayes.
185              Thinke on Lord Hastings : dispaire, and dye.

**Hastings** [to Richmond]  Quiet untroubled soule,→
              Awake, awake :
              Arme, fight, and conquer, for faire Englands sake.

**ENTER THE GHOSTS OF THE TWO YONG PRINCES**

**Ghosts**   Dreame on thy Cousins→
190              Smothered in the Tower :
              Let us be laid [5] within thy bosome Richard,
              And weigh thee downe to ruine, shame, and death,
              Thy Nephewes soule bids [6] thee dispaire and dye.

---

L 202 - b  :  5. 3. 136 - 158 (149)

W [1]
     again, Q1-4/Ff set 'in thy soule', Q4/one modern text replaces 'in' with 'on'
W [2]
     since Qq/Ff set an eight syllable line, and since in line 171, page 132 above the term 'edgelesse Sword' was used,
     one modern text ingeniously adds 'pointless' to 'lance' to both counterbalance the image and create pentameter
SP [3]
     this is the first of eight pairs of Ff short lines set in the left-hand column of page 202 of the History section:
     unlike many other examples of such paired short lines in this play, in at least six cases there is enough column
     width for them to be set as a single line: most modern texts follow Qq and set all eight examples as single lines,
     arguing white space created the need for such expanded line setting - however, there is only one similar example
     in the adjacent right-hand column of the same page: each of the eight occurs at the very start of a speech either
     damning Richard or blessing Richmond, and, as such, if the Ff setting were to stand, could well suggest each
     opening moment involves a ritual or special preparation demanding a moment of silence from each apparition:
     each subsequent pair of short lines will be marked → without further annotation
ALT [4]
     some modern texts follow Q1-2 and set Hastings' sequence after that for the 'two yong Princes': hence the extra
     (bracketed) line numbers on both this and the next page
W [5]
     Q1/most modern texts = 'lead', Q2-6/Ff = 'laid'
W [6]
     Qq/most modern texts = 'soules bid', Ff = 'soule bids'

| | | |
|---|---|---|
| **Ghosts** [to Richmond] | Sleepe Richmond,→ | |
| 195 | Sleepe in Peace, and wake in Joy, | |
| | Good Angels guard thee from the Boares annoy, | |
| | Live, and beget a happy race of Kings, | |
| | Edwards unhappy Sonnes, do bid thee flourish. | |

**ENTER THE GHOST OF ANNE, HIS WIFE**

|  |  |
|---|---|
| **Ghost** [to Richard] | Richard, thy Wife,→ |
| 200 | That wretched Anne thy Wife, |
| | That never slept a quiet houre with thee, |
| | Now filles thy sleepe with perturbations, |
| | To morrow in the Battaile, thinke on me, |
| | And fall thy edgelesse Sword, dispaire and dye: ¹ |

|  |  |
|---|---|
| 205 **Ghost** [to Richmond] | Thou quiet soule,→ |
| | Sleepe thou a quiet sleepe: |
| | Dreame of Successe, and Happy Victory, |
| | Thy Adversaries Wife doth pray for thee. |

**ENTER THE GHOST OF BUCKINGHAM**

|  |  |
|---|---|
| **Ghost** [to Richard] | The first was I→ |
| 210 | That help'd thee to the Crowne: |
| | That last was I that felt thy Tyranny. |
| | O, in the Battaile think on Buckingham, |
| | And dye in terror of thy guiltinesse. |
| | Dreame on, dreame on, of bloody deeds and death, |
| 215 | Fainting dispaire; dispairing yeeld thy breath. |

|  |  |
|---|---|
| **Ghost** [to Richmond] | I dyed for hope→ |
| | Ere I could lend thee Ayde; |
| | But cheere thy heart, and be thou not dismayde: |
| | God, and good Angels fight on Richmonds side, |
| 220 | And Richard fall ² in height of all his pride |

**[Richard starts out of his dreame]**

|  |  |
|---|---|
| **Richard** | Give me another Horse, bind up my Wounds: |
| | Have mercy Jesu. |
| | Soft, I did but dreame. |
| | O coward Conscience! how dost thou afflict me? |
| 225 | The Lights burne blew. |
| | It is not ³ dead midnight. |

---

PCT ¹ F1 shows a mark above a period which might turn the punctuation into a colon: F2/most modern texts set a period

W ² Qq/most modern texts = 'fals', Ff = 'fall'

W ³ Q1 most modern texts = 'now', Q2-6/Ff = 'not'

Cold fearefull drops stand on my trembling flesh.      L 202 - b
What? do I feare my Selfe?
             There's none else by,
230     Richard loves Richard, that is, I am I. [1]
Is there a Murtherer heere?
            No; Yes, I am:
Then flye; What from my Selfe?
            Great reason: why?
235     Lest I Revenge.
          What? my Selfe upon my Selfe?
Alacke, I love my Selfe.
          Wherefore?
             For any good
240     That I my Selfe, have done unto my Selfe?
O no.
       Alas, I rather hate my Selfe,
For hatefull Deeds committed by my Selfe.
I am a Villaine: yet I Lye, I am not.
245     Foole, of thy Selfe speake well: Foole, do not flatter.
My Conscience hath a thousand severall Tongues,
And every Tongue brings in a severall Tale,
And everie Tale condemnes me for a Villaine;
Perjurie, [2] in the high'st Degree,
250     Murther, sterne murther, in the dyr'st degree,
All severall sinnes, all us'd in each degree,
Throng all *to'th Barre,[†3] crying all, Guilty, Guilty.
I shall dispaire, there is no Creature loves me;
And if I die, no soule shall [4] pittie me.
255     Nay,[5] wherefore should they?
            Since that I my Selfe,
Finde in my Selfe, no pittie to my Selfe.
Me thought, the Soules of all that I had murther'd
Came to my Tent, and every one did threat
260     To morrowes vengeance on the head of Richard.

---

L 202 - b / R 202 - b : 5. 3. 181 - 206

[W]1 Q1/most modern texts = 'I and I', Q2-6/Ff = 'I am I'

[W]2 Q1-2/most modern texts = 'Perjurie, perjurie'; Q3-6/Ff set just one 'Perjurie', thus reducing the line to eight syllables

[PCT]3 F2 = 'to'the'Barre', F1 shows a faint mark where the second apostrophe should be, viz. 'to'th Barre'

[W]4 Q1-2/most modern texts = 'will', Q3-6/Ff = 'shall'

[W]5 Qq/most modern texts = 'And', Ff = 'Nay'

**ENTER RATCLIFFE**

| | |
|---|---|
| **Ratcliffe** | My Lord. |
| **˙King˙** [1] | Who's there? [2] |
| **Ratcliffe** | Ratcliffe [3] my Lord, 'tis I: the early Village Cock<br>Hath twice done salutation to the Morne, |
| 265 | Your Friends are up, and buckle on their Armour. |
| | ∞ [4] |
| **King** | O Ratcliffe I feare, I feare. |
| **Ratcliffe** | Nay good my Lord, be not affraid of Shadows. |
| **King** | By the Apostle Paul, shadowes to night<br>Have stroke more terror to the soule of Richard, |
| 270 | Then can the substance of ten thousand Souldiers<br>Armed in proofe and led by shallow Richmond. |
| | 'Tis not yet neere day.<br>            Come go with me,<br>Under our Tents Ile play the Ease-dropper,[5] |
| 275 | To heare [6] if any meane to shrinke from me. |

**[Exeunt Richard & Ratcliffe]** †[7]
**ENTER THE LORDS TO RICHMOND SITTING**
**IN HIS TENT**

| | |
|---|---|
| **{Richmond}**[8] | Good morrow Richmond. |
| **Richmond** | Cry mercy Lords, and watchfull Gentlemen,<br>That you have tane a tardie sluggard heere? |

---

R 202 - b : 5. 3. 207 - 225

[P][1] quite fascinatingly, Ff show Richard's prefix shifting once more from the personal 'Rich' of his nightmare back to the status conscious 'King' in front of Ratcliffe: his Ff prefix now stays as 'King' to almost, but not quite, the end of the play, see footnote #5, page 142

[O][2] Qq/most modern texts set the oath 'Zoundes, who is there?', Ff = 'Who's there?'

[W][3] one modern text omits Qq/Ff's 'Ratcliffe', so as to create a ten syllable line

[ADD][4] some, not all, modern texts add the following two and a half lines from Qq
  Richard     O Ratcliffe, I have dreamd a fearefull dreame,
              What thinkst thou, will our friendes prove all true?
  Ratcliffe   No doubt my Lord.
some omitting 'O' from Richard's next Ff line, presumably to maintain the shared line as ten syllables

[W][5] F4/most modern texts = 'eavesdropper': F1 = 'Ease-dropper': between them F2 - 3, Q1 - 6 set five different and obscure words

[W][6] Q1-2/most modern texts = 'see', Q3-6/Ff = 'heare'

[W][7] F2/most modern texts set 'Ratcliffe', F1 omits the 'c', setting 'Ratliffe'

[P][8] F1 sets the incorrect 'Richm', implying Richmond greets himself: Q3-6/F2/most modern texts = 'Lords', Q1-2 = 'Lo/Lor.',

| | | |
|---|---|---|
| **Lords** [1] | | How have you slept my Lord? |
| 280 | **Richmond** | The sweetest sleepe,→ |
| | | And fairest boading Dreames, [2] |

That ever entred in a drowsie head,
Have I since your departure had my Lords.
Me thought their Soules, whose bodies Rich. [3] murther'd,

285 Came to my Tent, and cried on Victory:
I promise you my Heart [4] is very jocond,
In the remembrance of so faire a dreame, [5]
How farre into the Morning is it Lords?

**Lord{s}**   Upon the stroke of foure.

290 **Richmond**   Why then 'tis time to Arme, and give direction.

**[His Oration to his Souldiers]**

[6] More then I have said, loving Countrymen,
The leysure and inforcement of the time
Forbids to dwell upon: yet remember this,   R 202 - b
God, and our good cause, fight upon our side,
295 The Prayers of holy Saints and wronged soules,
Like high rear'd Bulwarkes, stand before our Faces,
(Richard except) those whom we fight against,
Had rather have us win, then him they follow.

For, what is he they follow?
300                                    Truly Gentlemen,
A bloudy Tyrant, and a Homicide:
One rais'd in blood, and one in blood establish'd;
One that made meanes to come by what he hath,
And slaughter'd those that were the meanes to help him:
305 A base soule Stone, made precious by the soyle [7]

---

[P][1] F1's prefixes for the Lords are somewhat bizarre: here the prefix 'Lords' seems to suggest a peculiar group question to Richmond, and the next prefix, 'Lor' - (the responses to the time) could be singular or plural: Qq set 'Lo' throughout: most modern texts solve the problem by assigning the next two speeches to a '1. Lord'

[LS][2] the reader has choice as to which two of these three short lines may be joined as one line of split verse: however, most modern texts follow Qq and set Richmond's two short lines (4/6 syllables) as one

[AB][3] because of lack of column width, F1 sets 'Rich': Qq/F2/most modern texts set the full name 'Richard'

[W][4] Qq/most modern texts = 'soule', Ff = 'Heart'

[PCT][5] F1-2 set a comma, the swift move from one topic to another perhaps betraying his underlying nervousness: Qq/F3/most modern texts set a period

[ALT/W][6] one modern text has seen its way to make eight brand new amendments to Qq/Ff in the following speech, some for the sake of meter, some because of source material, some for accuracy of image, only one of which will be set here: for further details, readers are invited to explore *William Shakespeare: A Textual Companion*, op. cit., pages 248 - 9, footnotes to lines 5.5.191/3282 through to 5.5.221/3312 inclusive

[W][7] Q1-2/most modern texts = 'foile', Q3-6/Ff = variations of 'soyle/soile'

137

Of Englands Chaire, where he is falsely set :
One that hath ever beene Gods Enemy.

Then if you fight against Gods Enemy,
310     God will in justice ward you as his Soldiers.

If you do sweare [1] to put a Tyrant downe,
You sleepe in peace, the Tyrant being slaine :
If you do fight against your Countries Foes,
Your Countries Fat shall pay your paines the hyre.
315     If you do fight in safegard of your wives,
Your wives shall welcome home the Conquerors.

If you do free your Children from the Sword,
Your Childrens Children quits it in your Age.

Then in the name of God and all these rights,
320     Advance your Standards, draw your willing Swords.

For me, the ransome of my bold attempt,
Shall be this [2] cold Corpes on the earth's cold face.

But if I thrive, the gaine of my attempt,
The least of you shall share his part thereof.

325     Sound Drummes and Trumpets boldly, and cheerefully,
God, and Saint George, Richmond, and Victory. [3]

**ENTER KING RICHARD, RATCLIFFE, AND CATESBY**
**[At least one modern text creates a new scene here, Act Five Scene 6]**

**King**          What said Northumberland as touching Richmond?

**Ratcliffe**     That he was never trained up in Armes.

**King**          He said the truth : and what said Surrey then?

330  **Ratcliffe**     He smil'd and said, the better for our purpose.

**King**          He was in the right, and so indeed it is.

Tell the clocke there.

**[Clocke strikes]** [4]

Give me a Kalender : ° Who saw the Sunne to day?

---

L 203 - b  :  5. 3. 251 - 277

[w1] Q1-2/most modern texts = 'you doe sweate', Q3-5/Ff = 'you do sweare'

[w2] for clarity, one modern text suggests substituting 'my' from the previous line for 'this' here, and vice versa

[SD3] most modern texts set an exit for Richmond and his supporters and soldiers (one text adding the sound of drums and trumpets), and add Soldiers to Richard's entry immediately following

[SD4] since 'Tell the clocke' means count the chimes, most modern texts advance the sound to before Richard says the line

138

| Ratcliffe | Not I my Lord. °¹ |
|---|---|

335 King      Then he disdaines to shine : For by the Booke
He should have brav'd the East an houre ago,
A blacke day will it be to somebody.
                             Ratcliffe. ²

Ratcliffe      My Lord.

340 King      The Sun will not be seene to day,
The sky doth frowne, and lowre upon our Army.
I would these dewy teares were from the ground.
Not shine to day?
                        Why, what is that to me
345 More then to Richmond?
                           For the selfe-same Heaven
That frownes on me, looks sadly upon him.

### ENTER NORFOLKE

Norfolke      Arme, arme, my Lord : the foe vaunts in the field.

King      Come, bustle, bustle. ³
350                             Caparison my horse,
Call up Lord Stanley, bid him bring his power,
I will leade forth my Soldiers to the plaine,
⁴ And thus my Battell shal be ordred.

My Foreward shall be drawne ⁵ in length,
355 Consisting equally of Horse and Foot :
Our Archers shall be placed in the mid'st ;
John Duke of Norfolke, Thomas Earle of Surrey,
Shall have the leading of the Foot and Horse.

---

LS ₁
   Qq/Ff set three irregular lines (4/12/4 syllables), establishing not only that Richard needs to hear the clocke strike before he can check in the 'kalendar' (subsequently realising that the sun won't be seen:) but that, via the on-rushed line, the lack of (metrical) self-control seen by his men before his nightmare is still present: most modern texts set two pentameter lines as shown

LS ₂
   again Ff (and to a lesser extent Q1, which sets just 'Rat' for Ff's 'Ratcliffe') set an on-rushed line, showing once more Richard's metrical lack of self-control: most modern texts create a normal line followed by a very short one by setting the single word 'Ratcliffe' on a separate line

SD ₃
   most modern texts suggest Richard begins to arm himself, and some add an exit for one of his Soldiers to go to Lord Stanley at the end of the next line

ALT/W ₄
   arguing suspicious repetition within the speech as originally set ('shall be' set three times in four lines; the repetition of 'Horse and Foot' with 'Foot and Horse' just three lines later) one modern text makes five brand new amendments to the remainder of the Qq/Ff speech, ignoring the possibility that such repetition may be deliberately authorial designed to show Richard's growing inability to cope with the situation: none of the new amendments will be shown here, but for further details see *William Shakespeare: A Textual Companion*, op. cit., page 249, footnotes to lines 5.6.25/3340 - 5.6.29/3344

W ₅
   Qq/most modern texts = 'drawn out all', setting a ten syllable line: Ff create a short line by simply setting 'drawne'

| | | |
|---|---|---|
| 360 | They thus directed, we will follow[†][1] | L 203 - b |

They thus directed, we will follow[†][1]
360     In the maine Battell, whose puissance on either side
Shall be well-winged with our cheefest Horse:
This, and Saint George to boote. →[2]

What think'st thou Norfolke.

**Norfolke**     A good direction warlike Soveraigne,
365     This found I[3] on my Tent this Morning.

[4] *Jockey of Norfolke, be not so bold,*
*For Dickon thy maister is bought and sold.*

**King**     A thing devised by the Enemy.

Go Gentlemen, every[5] man to[6] his Charge,
370     Let not our babling Dreames affright our soules:
For Conscience is a word[7] that Cowards use,
Devis'd at first to keepe the strong in awe,
Our strong armes be our Conscience, Swords our Law.

March on, joyne bravely, let us *too't pell mell,
375     If not to heaven, then hand in hand to Hell.

[8] What shall I say more then I have inferr'd?

Remember whom you are to cope withall,
A sort of Vagabonds, Rascals, and Run-awayes,
A scum of Brittaines, and base Lackey Pezants,
380     Whom their o're-cloyed Country vomits forth
To desperate Adventures,[9] and assur'd Destruction.

---

[W][1] F1 = 'fllow', F2/most modern texts = 'follow'

[SP][2] as Richard reaches the end of his seemingly ill-phrased plan (see footnote #4, page 139) Ff set two short lines (6/5 syllables) as if the silence that greets him forces him to demand a response from Norfolke: most modern texts follow Qq and set the two lines as one, presumably arguing that lack of column width prevented F1 from following suit

[W][3] Qq/Ff = 'found I', which one modern text reverses without annotation: since it is a short nine syllable line, at least one other modern text sets 'This paper found I', ignoring the fact that the line may be deliberately short, illustrating Norfolke's ill-ease at bringing the contents of the note to the attention of all those present, especially Richard

[SD][4] most modern texts suggest Richard reads aloud the note: Qq/Ff leave it to Norfolke

[W][5] Qq/Ff = 'every', setting at least an eleven syllable line: one metrically minded text creates pentameter by setting 'each'

[W][6] Qq/most modern texts = 'unto' (implying for the metrically minded that 'every' is spoken as a two syllable word, 'ev/ry'), Ff = 'to' (implying 'every' is spoken as a three syllable word, 'ev/er/y')

[W][7] Qq/most modern texts = 'Conscience is but a word', Ff = 'For Conscience is a word'

[SD][8] most modern texts add a heading from Qq, 'His Oration to his army'

[W][9] Qq/Ff = 'Adventures', one modern gloss/modern text = 'ventures', even though the reduction does not create a line of pentameter

You sleeping safe, they bring you to ¹ unrest:
You having Lands, and blest with beauteous wives,
They would restraine ² the one, distaine the other,
385    And who doth leade them, but a paltry Fellow?
Long kept in Britaine at our Mothers ³ cost,
A Milke-sop, one that never in his life
Felt so much cold, as over shooes in Snow:
Let's whip these straglers o're the Seas againe,
390    Lash hence these over-weening Ragges of France,
These famish'd Beggers, weary of their lives,
Who (but for dreaming on this fond exploit)
For want of meanes (poore Rats) had hang'd themselves.

If⁴ we be conquered, let men conquer us,
395    And not these bastard Britaines, whom our Fathers
Have in their owne Land beaten, bobb'd, and thump'd,
And on ⁵ Record, left them the heires of shame.

Shall these enjoy our Lands? lye with our Wives?

Ravish our daughters? → ⁶

**[Drum afarre off]**

400    Hearke, I hear their Drumme,
Right ⁷ Gentlemen of England, fight boldly ⁸ yeomen,
Draw Archers draw your Arrowes to the head,
Spurre your proud Horses hard, and ride in blood,
Amaze the welkin with your broken staves.

**ENTER A MESSENGER**

405    What sayes Lord Stanley, will he bring his power?

**Messenger**    My ⁹ Lord, he doth deny to come.

---

R 203 - b  :  5. 3. 320 - 343

ᵂ¹ Q1/most modern texts = 'to you', Q2-6/Ff = 'you to'

ᵂ² Qq/Ff/most modern texts = 'restraine', one modern gloss accepted by at least one modern text = 'distrain'

ᵂ³ Qq/Ff/some modern texts = 'Mothers', other modern texts set the historically correct 'brother's': for further
details, see *The Arden Shakespeare King Richard III*, op. cit., page 326, footnote to line 325

ᵂ⁴ F1 = 'I f', F2/most modern texts = 'If'

ᵂ⁵ Q1-2/most modern texts = 'in', Q3-6/Ff = 'on'

ˢᴾ⁶ Ff set two short lines (5/5 syllables) interrupted by the direction for the sound of the (off-stage) enemies' drums
which presumably, creates a momentary silence before Richard continues: Qq do not set the direction, and set
the two lines as one: most modern texts do set the direction and despite the implication of Ff, set the lines as
one, presumably suggesting Richard continues speaking over the sound

ᵂ⁷ Q1-2/most modern texts = 'Fight', Q3-6/Ff = 'Right'

ᵂ⁸ Q1/most modern texts = 'bold', Q2-6/Ff = 'boldly'

ᵂ⁹ Qq/Ff /most modern texts set an eight syllable line, perhaps suggesting a Messenger amazed, or ill-at-ease, or
out-of-breath: one metrically minded modern text adds 'gracious', thus creating pentameter

| | | |
|---|---|---|
| | King | Off with his sonne Georges head. |
| | Norfolke | My Lord, the enemy is past the Marsh: |
| | | After the battaile, let George Stanley dye. |
| 410 | King | A thousand hearts are great within my bosom. |

Advance our Standards, set upon our Foes,
Our Ancient word of Courage, faire S. George
Inspire us with the spleene of fiery Dragons:
Upon them, Victorie sits on our helpes. [1]

**ALARUM, EXCURSIONS. ENTER CATESBY [2]**
**[Most modern texts create a new scene here, Act Five, Scene 4 or 7] [3]**

415    Catesby    Rescue my Lord of Norfolke,→ [4]
Rescue, Rescue:
The King enacts more wonders then a man,
Daring an opposite to every danger:
His horse is slaine, and all on foot he fights,
420    Seeking for Richmond in the throat of death :    R 203 - b
Rescue faire Lord, or else the day is lost.

**ALARUMS.**
**ENTER RICHARD [5]**

‘Richard’    A Horse, a Horse, my Kingdome for a Horse.

Catesby    Withdraw my Lord, Ile helpe you to a Horse

Richard    Slave, I have set my life upon a cast,
425    And I will stand the hazard of the Dye: [6]
I thinke there be sixe Richmonds in the field,
Five have I slaine to day, in stead of him.
A Horse, a Horse, my Kingdome for a Horse.

---

R 203 - b / L 204 - b  :  5. 3. 344 - 5. 4. 13

W/SD [1] Q1-2/Q4/most modern texts = 'helmes', Q3/Q5 - 6/Ff = 'helpes': also, most modern texts add 'Exeunt' from Q1-2

SD [2] most modern texts add that prior to Catesby's entry at one door, Norfolke and his Soldiers have entered at the other, and they also add an exit for Norfolke and his forces at the end of Catesby's speech

ALT [3] see pages 127, 129 and 138 for where some texts create earlier Scenes Four, Five, and Six

SP [4] most modern texts follow Qq and set these two short lines (7/4 syllables) as one, presumably arguing that both white space and lack of column width prevented F1 from following suit: if the Ff setting were to stand, the minute pauses could well suggest breathlessness in the heat of battle

P/SD [5] as defeat grows ever nearer, the Ff prefix for his last two speeches in the play change from the status of 'King' back to the personal 'Rich' (though Q1 maintains 'King'): also, most modern texts add off-stage 'Alarums' before his entry

W [6] Q1-2/most modern texts = 'die', thus emphasising the pun of 'dice' and 'death': Q3/Q5 - 6/Ff = 'Dye', Q4 = 'day'

[1] ALARUM,[†2] ENTER RICHARD AND RICHMOND, THEY FIGHT, RICHARD
IS SLAINE

RETREAT, AND FLOURISH  ENTER RICHMOND, DERBY BEARING THE
CROWNE, WITH DIVERS OTHER LORDS
[Most modern texts create a new scene here, Act Five, Scene 5 or 8] [3]

| | | |
|---|---|---|
| | **Richmond** | God, and your Armes→ [4] |
| 430 | | Be prais'd Victorious Friends; |
| | | The day is ours, the bloudy Dogge is dead. |
| | **Derby** | Couragious Richmond,→ |
| | | Well hast thou acquit thee: Loe, [5] |
| | | Heere these long usurped Royalties, [6] |
| 435 | | From the dead Temples of this bloudy Wretch, |
| | | Have I pluck'd off, to grace thy Browes withall. |
| | | Weare it, [7] and make much of it. |
| | **Richmond** | Great God of Heaven, say Amen to all. |
| | | But tell me, is yong George Stanley living? |
| 440 | **Derby** | He is my Lord, and safe in Leicester Towne, |
| | | Whither (if you please) we may [8] withdraw us. |
| | **Richmond** | What men of name are slaine on either side? |
| | **Derby** | John Duke of Norfolke, Walter Lord Ferris, |
| | | Sir Robert Brokenbury, and Sir William Brandon. [9] |

L 204 - b

---

L 204 - b / R 204 - b  :  5. 5. 1 - 14

SD[1] most modern texts add some or all of the following to the Qq/Ff stage directions
1/ first, that Richard exits, only to come on moments later fighting with Richmond
2/ that after killing Richard, Richmond leaves the stage
3/ Soldiers then remove Richard's body prior to the triumphant re-entry already set
4/ Richmond's Soldiers enter with him

W[2] F1 = 'Alatum', F2 /most modern texts = 'Alarum'

ALT[3] see see footnote #3, page 142

SP[4] most modern texts follow Qq and set the two pairs of short Ff lines (4/6 or 7, and 5/7 syllables) as two longer single lines, presumably arguing that both white space and lack of column width prevented F1 from following suit: if the Ff setting were to stand, the pauses would allow both Richmond and Derby a silent moment to respond to the momentous event

SD[5] most modern texts indicate that somewhere during the speech Derby presents Richmond with the Crown

W[6] Qq/most modern texts transfer 'Loe' from the previous line and (replacing Ff's 'these' and 'Royalties' with the singular): they thus set 'Loe here this long usurped royaltie',

W[7] Q1-2/most modern texts = 'enjoy it', which Q3-6/Ff omit

W[8] Qq/most modern texts = 'Whether if it please you we may now', Ff = 'Whither (if you please) we may'

F[9] as various commentators point out, the list is historically inaccurate: Brokenbury (named Brookenbury in Qq, known in most modern texts as Brakenbury) was not a 'Sir' at this point in time, and Ferris was more often then known as Ferrers

| | | |
|---|---|---|
| 445 | **Richmond** | Interre their Bodies, as become their Births, |
| | | Proclaime a pardon to the Soldiers fled, |
| | | That in submission will returne to us, |
| | | And then as we have tane the Sacrament, |
| | | We will unite the White Rose, and the Red. |
| 450 | | Smile Heaven upon this faire Conjunction, |
| | | That long have frown'd upon their Enmity: |
| | | What Traitor heares me, and sayes not Amen? |
| | | England hath long beene mad, and scarr'd her selfe; |
| | | The Brother blindely shed the Brothers blood; |
| 455 | | The Father, rashly slaughtered his owne Sonne; |
| | | The Sonne compell'd, beene Butcher to the Sire; |
| | | All this divided Yorke and Lancaster, |
| | | Divided,[1] in their dire Division. |
| | | O now, let Richmond and Elizabeth, |
| 460 | | The true Succeeders of each Royall House, |
| | | By Gods faire ordinance, conjoyne together: |
| | | And let thy [2] Heires (God if thy will be so) |
| | | Enrich the time to come, with Smooth-fac'd Peace, |
| | | With smiling Plenty, and faire Prosperous dayes. |
| 465 | | Abate the edge of Traitors, Gracious Lord, |
| | | That would reduce these bloudy dayes againe, |
| | | And make poore England weepe in Streames of Blood; |
| | | Let them not live to taste this Lands increase, |
| | | That would with Treason, wound this faire Lands peace. |
| 470 | | Now Civill wounds are stopp'd, Peace lives agen; |
| | | That she may long live heere, God say, Amen. |

**[Exeunt]**

---

# FINIS

R 204 - b

---

R 204 - b  :  5. 5. 15 - 34

[1] since 'Divided, in their dire division' seems an unnecessary repetition, one modern text substitutes 'United' for Qq/Ff's 'Divided'

[2] Q1-2/most modern texts = 'their', Q3-6/Ff = 'thy'

# APPENDIX A
## THE 'CLOCK' SEQUENCE FROM ACT FOUR, SCENE 2, AS SET IN Q1
## (SEE PAGE 100 OF THIS SCRIPT)

**Buckingham** My Lord.

**King** How chance the prophet could not at that time,
Have told me I being by, that I should kill him

**Buckingham** My Lord, your promise for the Earledome.

**King** Richmond, when last was I at Exeter,
The Maior in curtsie showd me the Castle,
And called it Ruge-mount, at which name I started,
Because a Bard of Ireland told me once
I should not live long after I saw Richmond.

**Buckingham** My Lord.

**King** I, whats a clocke?

**Buckingham** I am thus bold to put your grace in mind
     <sup>1</sup> Of what you promisd me.

**King** Wel, but whats a clocke?

**Buckingham** Upon the stroke of ten.

**King** Well, let it strike.

**Buckingham** Whie let it strike?

**King** Because that like a Jacke thou keepst the stroke
Betwixt thy begging and my meditation,
I am not in the giving vaine to day.

---

<sup>LS</sup>₁ modern texts set the following five short lines in various permutations of split lines

145

# APPENDIX B
## A LACKADAISICAL APPLICATION OF THE 1606 ACTE
## TO RESTRAINE THE ABUSES OF PLAYERS ?

### AN INTERESTING QUESTION INITIALLY POSED BY MY EDITORIAL/PROOFING COLLEAGUE, JULIE M. STOCKTON

For some reason the words 'God' (89 times) and 'Gods' (17) are far more prevalent in *Richard III* than in any other F1 History play.

Explanations could range from sloppy work by the supposed censors through to a dispensing tolerance from a kindly supervising eye, since much of the usage surrounds invocations to the deity for blessing or protection.

As the following tables show, whatever the reason, there is an amazing discrepancy between this and all other History plays. Indeed, apart from *Henry V* ('God' 63 times, 'Gods' 10) the combined usage in *Richard III* is nearly 50% more than the next play, *Henry VI Part II* ('God' 49 times, 'Gods 10), and more than twenty times the usage in *Henry IV Part II* ('God 4 times, 'Gods' 1).

### F1 APPEARANCE OF THE WORDS 'GOD'/'GODS' IN DESCENDING ORDER OF USE

| PLAY | GOD | GODS | % of play [1] |
|------|-----|------|-----------|
| Richard III | 89 | 17 | 3.7443 |
| Henry V | 63 | 10 | 2.8541 |
| Henry VI Part II | 49 | 10 | 2.4130 |
| Henry VI Part III | 29 | 7 | 1.5453 |
| Richard II | 32 | 3 | 1.6048 |
| Henry VIII | 27 | 8 | 1.5005 |
| Henry VI Part I | 20 | 5 | 1.2673 |
| Henry IV Part I | 17 | 3 | 0.8348 |
| King John | 6 | 2 | 0.3924 |
| Henry IV Part II | 4 | 1 | 0.1945 |

---

[1] This is calculated by dividing the number of total occurrences in the play by the total number of words, the latter taken from the data provided in Spevack's mammoth opus, (for citation see page xlv footnote #13 in the Specific Introduction to this play). Thus, for *The Tragedy of Richard III* the total occurrence of 'God' and 'Gods' (106) has been divided by the total number of words (28,309). However, it should be pointed out the data comes from two different sources. 'God'/'Gods' occurrences are taken directly from F1. Spevack's data is taken from a modern text occasionally based on Qq, *The Riverside Shakespeare* (for citation see under Recommended Texts, page li, again in the Specific Introduction to this play).

# APPENDIX C
# THE UNEASY RELATIONSHIP OF FOLIO,
# QUARTOS, AND MODERN TEXTS

Between the years 1590 and 1611, one William Shakespeare, a playwright and actor, delivered to the company of which he was a major shareholder at least thirty-seven plays in handwritten manuscript form. Since the texts belonged to the company upon delivery, he derived no extra income from publishing them. Indeed, as far as scholars can establish, he took no interest in the publication of his plays.

Consequently, without his supervision, yet during his lifetime and shortly after, several different publishers printed eighteen of these plays, each in separate editions. Each of these texts, known as **'Quartos'** because of the page size and method of folding each printed sheet, was about the size of a modern hardback novel. In 1623, seven years after Shakespeare's death, Heminges and Condell, two friends, theatrical colleagues, actors, and fellow shareholders in the company, passed on to the printer, William Jaggard, the handwritten copies of not only these eighteen plays but a further eighteen, of which seventeen had been performed but not yet seen in print.[1] These thirty-six plays were issued in one large volume, each page about the size of a modern legal piece of paper. Anything printed in this larger format was known as 'folio', again because of the page size and the method of sheet folding. Thus the 1623 printing of the collected works is known as **the First Folio,** its 1632 reprint (with more than 1600 unauthorised corrections) the Second Folio, and the next reprint, the 1666 Third Folio, added the one missing play, *Pericles* (which had been set in quarto and performed).

The handwritten manuscript used for the copies of the texts from which both Quartos and the First Folio were printed came from a variety of sources. Closest to Shakespeare were those in his own hand, known as the 'foul papers' because of the natural blottings, crossings out, and corrections. Sometimes he had time to pass the material on to a manuscript copyist who would make a clean copy, known as the 'fair papers'. Whether fair (if there was sufficient time) or foul (if the performance deadline was close), the papers would be passed on to the Playhouse, where a 'Playhouse copy' would be made, from which the 'sides' (individual copies of each part with just a single cue line) would be prepared for each actor. Whether Playhouse copy, fair papers, or foul, the various Elizabethan and Jacobean handwritten manuscripts from which the quartos and Folio came have long since disappeared.

The first printed texts of the Shakespeare plays were products of a speaking-hearing society. They were based on rhetoric, a verbal form of arranging logic and ar-

---

[1]  Though written between 1605–09, *Timon of Athens* was not performed publicly until 1761.

gument in a persuasive, pleasing, and entertaining fashion so as to win personal and public debates, a system which allowed individuals to express at one and the same time the steppingstones in an argument while releasing the underlying emotional feelings that accompanied it.[2] Naturally, when ideas were set on paper they mirrored this same form of progression in argument and the accompanying personal release, allowing both neat and untidy thoughts to be seen at a glance (see the General Introduction, pp. xvi–xxi). Thus what was set on paper was not just a silent debate. It was at the same time a reminder of how the human voice might be heard both logically and passionately in that debate.

Such reminders did not last into the eighteenth century. Three separate but interrelated needs insisted on cleaning up the original printings so that silent and speaking reader alike could more easily appreciate the beauties of one of England's greatest geniuses.

First, by 1700, publishing's main thrust was to provide texts to be read privately by people of taste and learning. Since grammar was now the foundation for all writing, publication, and reading, all the Elizabethan and early Jacobean material still based on rhetoric appeared at best archaic and at worst incomprehensible. All printing followed the new universality of grammatical and syntactical standards, standards which still apply today. Consequently any earlier book printed prior to the establishment of these standards had to be reshaped in order to be understood. And the Folio/Quarto scripts, even the revamped versions which had already begun to appear, presented problems in this regard, especially when dealing in the moments of messy human behaviour. Thus, while the first texts were reshaped according to the grammatical knowledge of the 1700s, much of the shaping of the rhetoric was (inadvertently) removed from the plays.

Secondly, the more Shakespeare came to be recognized as a literary poet rather than as a theatrical genius, the less the plays were likely to be considered as performance texts. Indeed plot lines of several of his plays were altered (or ignored) to satisfy the more refined tastes of the period. And the resultant demands for poetic and literary clarity, as well as those of grammar, altered the first printings even further.

Thirdly, scholars argued a need for revision of both Quarto and Folio texts because of 'interfering hands' (hands other than Shakespeare's) having had undue influence on the texts. No matter whether foul or fair papers or Playhouse copy, so the argument ran, several intermediaries would be involved between Shakespeare's writing of the plays and the printing of them. If the fair papers provided the source text,

---

[2]    For an extraordinarily full analysis of the art of rhetoric, readers are guided to Sister Miriam Joseph, *Shakespeare's Use of the Arts of Language* (New York: Haffner Publishing Co., 1947). For a more theatrical overview, readers are directed to Bertram Joseph, *Acting Shakespeare* (New York: Theatre Arts Books, 1960). For an overview involving aspects of Ff/Qq, readers are immodestly recommended to Neil Freeman, *Shakespeare's First Texts*, op. cit.

a copyist might add some peculiarities, as per the well documented Ralph Crane.[3] If the Playhouse copy was the source text, extra information, mainly stage directions, would have been added by someone other than Shakespeare, turning the play from a somewhat literary document into a performance text. Finally, while more than five different compositors were involved in setting the First Folio, five did the bulk of the printing house work: each would have their individual pattern of typesetting — compositor E being singled out as far weaker than the rest. Thus between Shakespeare and the printed text might lie the hand(s) of as few as one and as many as three other people, even more when more than one compositor set an individual play. Therefore critics argue because there is the chance of so much interference between Shakespearean intent and the first printings of the plays, the plays do not offer a stylistic whole, i.e., while the words themselves are less likely to be interfered with, their shapings, the material consistently altered in the early 1700s, are not that of a single hand, and thus cannot be relied upon.

These well-intentioned grammatical and poetic alterations may have introduced Shakespeare to a wider reading audience, but their unforeseen effect was to remove the Elizabethan flavour of argument and of character development (especially in the areas of stress and the resulting textual irregularities), thus watering down and removing literally thousands of rhetorical and theatrical clues that those first performance scripts contained. And it is from this period that the division between ancient and modern texts begins. As a gross generalisation, the first texts, the First Folio and the quartos, could be dubbed 'Shakespeare for the stage'; the second, revamped early 1700 texts 'Shakespeare for the page'.

And virtually all current editions are based on the page texts of the early 1700s. While the words of each play remain basically the same, what shapes them, their sentences, punctuation, spelling, capitalisation and sometimes even line structure, is often altered, unwittingly destroying much of their practical theatrical value.

It is important to neither condemn the modern editions nor blindly accept the authority of the early stage texts as gospel. This is not a case of 'old texts good, so modern texts bad'. The modern texts are of great help in literary and historical research, especially as to the meanings of obscure words and phrases, and in explaining literary allusions and historical events. They offer guidance to alternative text readings made by reputed editors, plus sound grammatical readings of difficult passages and clarification of errors that appear in the first printings.[4] In short, they can

---

[3]    Though not of the theatre (his principle work was to copy material for lawyers) Crane was involved in the preparation of at least five plays in the Folio, as well as two plays for Thomas Middleton. Scholars characterise his work as demonstrating regular and careful scene and act division, though he is criticised for his heavy use of punctuation and parentheses, apostrophes and hyphens, and 'massed entry' stage directions, i.e. where all the characters with entrances in the scene are listed in a single direction at the top of the scene irrespective of where they are supposed to enter.

give the starting point of the play's journey, an understanding of the story, and the conflict between characters within the story. But they can only go so far.

They cannot give you fully the conflict within each character, the very essence for the fullest understanding of the development and resolution of any Shakespeare play. Thanks to their rhetorical, theatrical base the old texts add this vital extra element. They illustrate with great clarity the 'ever-changing present' (see p. xvi in the General Introduction) in the intellectual and emotional life of each character; their passages of harmony and dysfunction, and transitions between such passages; the moments of their personal costs or rewards; and their sensual verbal dance of debate and release. In short, the old texts clearly demonstrate the essential elements of living, breathing, reacting humanity—especially in times of joyous or painful stress.

By presenting the information contained in the First Folio, together with modern restructurings, both tested against theatrical possibilities, these texts should go far in bridging the gap between the two different points of view.

---

⁴ For example, the peculiar phrase 'a Table of greene fields' assigned to Mistress Quickly in describing the death of Falstaffe, *Henry V* (Act Two, Scene 3), has been superbly diagnosed as a case of poor penmanship being badly transcribed: the modern texts wisely set 'a babbled of green fields' instead.

NEIL FREEMAN trained as an actor at the Bristol Old Vic Theatre School. He has acted and directed in England, Canada, and the USA. Currently he is an Head of Graduate Directing and Senior Acting Professor in the Professional Training Programme of the Department of Theatre, Film, and Creative Writing at the University of British Columbia. He also teaches regularly at the National Theatre School of Canada, Concordia University, Brigham Young University in both Provo and Hawaii, and is on the teaching faculty of professional workshops in Montreal, Toronto and Vancouver. He is associated with Shakespeare & Co. in Lenox; the Will Geer Theatre in Los Angeles; Bard on the Beach in Vancouver; Repercussion Theatre in Montreal; and has worked with the Stratford Festival, Canada, and Shakespeare Santa Cruz.

His ground breaking work in using the first printings of the Shakespeare texts in performance, on the rehearsal floor and in the classroom has lead to lectures at the Shakespeare Association of America and workshops at both the ATHE and VASTA, and grants/fellowships from the National Endowment of the Arts (USA), The Social Science and Humanities Research Council (Canada), and York University in Toronto.

His three collations of Shakespeare and music - *A Midsummer Nights Dream* (for three actors, chorus, and Orchestra); *If This Be Love* (for three actors, mezzo-soprano, and Orchestra); *The Four Seasons of Shakespeare and Vivaldi* (for two actors, violin soloist and Chamber Orchestra) - commissioned and performed by Bard On The Beach and The Vancouver Symphony Orchestra have been received with great public acclaim.

# SHAKESPEARE'S FIRST TEXTS
## by Neil Freeman

"THE ACTOR'S BEST CHAMPION OF THE
FOLIO"                    —Kristin Linklater
            author of *Freeing Shakespeare's Voice*

Neil Freeman provides students, scholars, theatre-
lovers, and, most importantly, actors and directors, with a highly readable, illuminating, and indis-
pensable guide to William Shakespeare's own first
quill-inscribed texts — SHAKESPEARE'S FIRST TEXTS.

  Four hundred years later, most of the grammatical
and typographical information conveyed by this representation in Elizabethan type by the first play compositors has been lost. Or, rather, discarded, in order
to conform to the new standards of usage. Granted,
this permitted more readers access to Shakespeare's
writing, but it also did away with some of
Shakespeare himself.

## ISBN 1-155783-335-4

## APPLAUSE